by *Reverend Robert D. Smith*

The Mark

of

92889

Holiness

The Newman Press • Westminster, Maryland

1961

Nihil obstat: JOHN J. WALSH, S.J.
   Diocesan Censor

Imprimatur: ✠RICHARD CARDINAL CUSHING
   Archbishop of Boston

August 12, 1959

Table of Contents

Introduction

1. *The Holiness of the Church as an Indicative Miracle*

Ever since the beginning of the public life of Jesus Christ, Christians have pointed to miracles and prophecies as motives for belief in the teachings of the Master. Christian indicative[1] miracles and prophecies can be divided into four categories: physical miracles worked by Christ, prophecies either fulfilled in Christ or made by Him, physical miracles and prophecies centering around Christian saints other than Christ, and moral miracles.

An indicative physical miracle[2] can be defined as an effect perceptible to the senses and beyond the physical range of all created nature.[3] Such effects point to the agency of God. They can include the raising of the dead, control over the elements, instantaneous cures of organic diseases, etc.

An indicative prophecy is a certain and determined prediction of a future event not knowable from natural causes. As stated above, for indicative value, a prophecy must be certain, that is, not just given as a guess. It must be determined or specific, and not just a very broad or general statement. And it must be of such a nature that an intelligent guess, based on natural knowledge, is impossible.

An indicative moral miracle is an effect which exceeds the intellectual and moral powers of human nature or its customary modes of acting. Such an effect, considering the constant and uniform manner in which human liberty reacts in given circumstances, is possible only with the intervention of God.[4] An example of a moral miracle would be the absence of all sin, large or small, in a large city for the period of a week.

The indicative value of the physical miracles and of the prophecies relating to Christ Himself has always been ranked very high by Christian writers. As a result, the notions themselves of physical miracle and prophecy have been explained and developed in great detail. This has led indirectly to a more thorough appreciation of those physical miracles and prophecies associated with the Christian saints.

The fourth type of motive of belief, moral miracles, to be sure, has also been set forth frequently. Moral miracles have by no means taken an unimportant place in the array of inducements for belief offered by Christian writers. Nevertheless, the theology of moral miracles has not yet been developed to the extent of the theology of physical miracles and prophecies. The main outline of Catholic teaching on moral miracles has been set down. Many details, however, remain unclarified.

Among the most important of the moral miracles in Christianity, without doubt, are the four "marks" of the Church: apostolicity, unity, catholicity, and holiness. Apostolicity as a mark of the Church signifies that she is the only one among the various churches which claim to be Christian that can trace herself back to the Apostles either in succession of authority or in faith and morals. Unity, catholicity, and holiness pertain not only to her relation with other Christian religions but also to her relation with all religions in the world, both Christian and non-Christian. The mark of unity signifies that she alone of all major religions is one in authority, in teaching, and in worship. That of catholicity signifies that she alone has appealed to and been accepted by human beings of both sexes, of all ages, of all stages of culture and education, and in all places. That of holiness signifies that she is holier than all other religions on earth.

The holiness of the Church can be considered from two points of view: in its indicative sense, as a mark, and in its speculative sense. Speculatively, the holiness of the Church includes not only those aspects of the holiness of the Church which can be measured or seen, but also those aspects which cannot be measured. Speculative or theoretical holiness, then, includes those holy elements in the Church which are not indicative. The holy elements of the Church which are not indicative would be such things as Baptism, Confirmation, and the other sacraments. By definition, the effects of the sacraments cannot be seen or measured in themselves, and thus cannot be used as signs of the divine origin of the Church.

It is only the holiness of the Church in the indicative sense that is included, strictly speaking, in the mark of holiness. It is only holiness in this latter sense that will be treated here.

Of the four marks, holiness is certainly not the least important. It is recognized by all peoples to be the motive of belief *sine qua non* of any religion. And holiness as an inducement to belief is also the motive out of all motives which will first arouse interest in a new religion.

In view of this it is surprising to learn that the theology of holiness of the Church, like that of the other moral miracles, has many points in it which have not been fully developed. In these pages, we shall endeavor to explore these undeveloped aspects of the holiness of the Church.

The premise from which all Christian treatments of this subject begin is that the Catholic Church is holy in her teaching, in her founder, and in her members.

Her teaching is holy. "The moral law which the Catholic

Church inculcates in her children is the highest and holiest standard of perfection ever presented to any people, and furnishes the strongest incentives to virtue."[5]

Her founder is holy. Christ towers over even the wisest and holiest of other men of any nation or of any time, as the perfect exemplar of virtue.

Her members are holy. "No other religion has ever brought about a moral reform even remotely comparable in breadth or depth . . . with the one effected by the Catholic Church."[6] The Church has always embraced an innumerable multitude of the faithful of every age and condition who have possessed sanctity to a common degree, avoiding mortal sin and observing God's precepts. She also can number in her ranks, past and present, a greater proportion of those who have achieved heroic sanctity.

No faithful Catholic questions the indicative value of the holiness of the Church. The Popes have seconded each other in stating that the holiness of the Church together with its spread, unity, and stability even provides an irrefragable testimony of its divine mission.[7] Outlines of this evidence have been given by various Catholic writers. Modern expositions of this subject, however, have been brief. Curiously enough no one, in recent times at least, has given a detailed and extensive treatment of the holiness of the Church in her teaching, founder and members. Usually little more is presented than a definition of terms and a statement of a proposition. Even the longer treatments of the holiness of the Church do little more than sketch out reasons why she can, with truth, call herself holy. Little is said as to precisely on what points and why other religions fall short.

No one as yet has taken a general survey of all the salient points entering into the holiness of the Church in her teaching, founder and members and contrasted them in detail with the teachings, founders, and members of the totality of the major non-Catholic religions.

The subject of the holiness of the Church brings a further question to the minds of many people. When we speak of the holiness of the Church, do we mean that other religions are holy and the Church is simply more holy, or do we mean that the other religions are unholy? Do the other religions of the world differ only on such points as time and frequency of observance of the sabbath,[8] or on the practice of other virtues, or do they differ on more basic issues? And if the difference lies in the latter, i.e., in the very definition of virtue, how do we know whose definition is correct?

This brings up still another, and perhaps the most important question. If the difference between the Catholic Church and non-Catholic churches lies in the definition of virtue itself, and even if we were able to prove that non-Catholic definitions of virtue are false, how culpable are non-Catholics in accepting such false definitions? The members of non-Catholic religions who follow false ideals of virtue would be theoretically unholy, but to what extent would they be subjectively guilty?

The fact that this series of questions has never before been treated together and in detail provides the reason for attempting to treat so vast a subject. The answers to these questions will provide a clearer insight into the role and necessity of the Church in the world.

2. A History of Catholic Treatment of Indicative Holiness

The history of the treatment of the holiness of the Church as an indicative miracle by Christian writers is not one of mere transcription. The problem facing each era was not the same. The chief objective of the writers of some eras was to treat Catholicism against a background of paganism; in others, against a background of heresy.

In the first few centuries of the Christian era, Christian writers directed much of their attention towards pagans and paganism. Heresies, to be sure, even powerful ones, rose up and had to be dealt with. But many of the educated non-Catholics with whom Christians came in contact were not heretics, but rather were vacillating between paganism and Christianity. In their writings, Christians placed ethics in the foreground, explaining its origin and nature. They contrasted Christian and pagan ethics, illuminating the superiority of Christian morality. They thus used Christian ethics to signalize the divine origin of the Christian Church.

Christians emphasized this indicative aspect of their morality during this early period. *The Didache*,[9] St. Justin,[10] Origen,[11] Lactantius,[12] St. Cyril of Jerusalem,[13] St. Augustine (in his *City of God*),[14] and many others appeal to the holiness of the Church as one of the primary reasons for embracing Christianity. They bring out each of the three aspects of her holiness: that of her teaching, founder, and members, and cite each as having real indicative value.

None of them set out to treat the subject methodically and extensively. For the most part they simply wove it into their treatment of other subjects. In setting forth the unity of God, they would contrast Christian worship with pagan idolatry. In setting forth Christian respect for human life, they would contrast it with pagan hecatombs.

They appealed to a universal moral law, a natural law which bound all men, as a criterion in establishing the nature of true holiness. This law could be arrived at by using right reason to study the nature of man in his environment. All human laws were judged according to their correspondence with this law.

As time went on, Christianity became universal in Western

Europe. The pagans vanished. The Western world became almost entirely Catholic. Catholic writers turned their attention away from paganism and concentrated on trying to bring the Catholic people themselves to follow more closely the ideals set forth by the Church.

The marks of the Church were accepted. Her sanctity was unquestioned. There was no need to prove it. Christian writers ceased to emphasize the indicative mark of sanctity or the other marks of the Church. This remained true from the fifth to the fifteenth century.[15]

In the fifteenth and sixteenth centuries, with the rise of the errors of Wycliffe, Huss, Luther, and Calvin, interest was reawakened in the marks of the Church. In particular, Catholics pointed to the notes of catholicity, unity, and apostolicity as designating the true Church.

Holiness could not be used so effectively as the other notes. In most points, the heresiarchs of this new era generally retained Catholic moral principles intact. They concentrated their objections on dogmatic questions. The discrepancy between Catholic and Protestant holiness was far less than it had been between the Catholic and the ancient pagan morality. And early Protestants claimed not their heresiarch but Christ for a founder, and thereby avoided criticism of the holiness of their founder.

Their lack of catholicity, unity or apostolicity was much more easily grasped than their lack of sanctity. Consequently, Catholic writers tended to concentrate on those notes.

When Catholic dogmatists of this period did discuss the note of sanctity, the criterion chosen was not the natural law, as it had been when dealing with the pagans, but the Bible. The holiness of the Church was proved primarily on the grounds that the Church taught specifically Christian and Biblical precepts and counsels (v.g., virginity) whereas the heretics sometimes did not. The members of the Catholic

Church, too, were affirmed to be closer to Biblical standards than were the Protestants.

This same approach has been used by Catholics down to our own times. Modern Catholic dogmatists[16] have treated the marks of the Church in the same way as those in the sixteenth century. In the last few centuries paganism has been unknown in the West. Only heresy and schism furnish a background. As a result, Catholic writers have developed the arguments based on unity, apostolicity, and catholicity, the three notes which tell most effectively against the early stages of heresy and schism. And when they do treat the mark of holiness, they contrast the holiness of Catholicism only with that of heretical and schismatical groups, and omit any extensive treatment of paganism.

Very recent changes, however, in the religious environment of the West, require us once more to adapt our treatment of the holiness of the Church. The number of "liberal" Protestants has greatly increased. The moral code of this group is much closer to paganism than is the code of the earlier "fundamentalist" Protestants. Improved methods of communication, moreover, have brought the pagan sections of Asia and Africa into much closer contact with the West.

These changes indicate that the Catholic approach to the holiness of the Church must again be modified. It is no longer sufficient to treat the holiness of the Church only against a background of fundamentalist Protestantism and schism. Studies of the indicative value of the holiness of the Church must now be made against a background of Protestantism, schism, and paganism.

These modifications, in turn, will bring the discussion of indicative holiness back from the shadows, and into the front rank of the vital tasks of the apostolate. This will occur for two reasons. First, the differences between Catholics and non-Catholics in the West are no longer chiefly dogmatic. There are now major differences on moral points as well.

These new-found differences need to be analyzed and evaluated. Secondly, more intimate knowledge of the pagan religions of the East has given rise to two questions: Are there major differences between the moral code of Christianity and those of the great pagan religions? And, if so, what is the significance of these differences?

To solve these problems of holiness in religion, it is necessary to revert to the criterion of holiness used by the early Fathers, the criterion of natural law. The Bible, which has served the West for so long as the universally accepted source of holiness, is now rejected or ignored by many. Not only modern pagans, but even many modern Protestants do not recognize the Bible as the supreme source of morality revealed by God Himself. Therefore, we must shift to a criterion of morality which is independent of this revelation. This other criterion, the natural law, is, as we shall see, the law of conscience written by God in the hearts of men. It does not require a previous knowledge of the Bible for its discovery.

PART I

Holiness of Teaching

CHAPTER ONE

Natural Law in General

1. *The Rational Foundation of Natural Law*

The natural law is just one facet of God's law or plan directing all creatures. God gave each of the other creatures (animate and inanimate) in the universe a certain nature and certain proper modes of acting. So too with man.

For inanimate creatures God set down laws such as those which have been partially described by scientists as the laws of gravity, of centrifugal force, of momentum, etc. These laws may be, in some cases, only vaguely understood and described by scientists, but they are relentlessly obeyed by the inanimate objects. The earth moves in its established path around the sun, a rock sinks in water, according to some plan set down by the unfathomable wisdom of God.

Vegetable and animal life too are subject to laws set down by God when He created them. Vegetable life has been given the faculties of nutrition, growth, and reproduction. Animal life has in addition sensation and locomotion. All these faculties are exercised according to certain laws. Plants absorb their food and grow according to a very specific and detailed plan imposed on them by their Creator. Animals, too, use their faculties according to instincts or patterns set down for them by God. Sometimes these patterns are very elaborate. A wax-worker bee constructs a cell in the form of a hexagonal prism terminated by a pyramid of rhombs. Each bee constructs her cell in exactly the same way as her fellow workers. Even the angles of the cells are the same.

The entire life cycle of plants and animals runs, machine-like, according to a pattern of action and reaction. Law rules every plant and animal. Every plant and animal acts in obedience to the law governing its nature.

Like all the rest of creation, man has been destined by God to act according to certain laws.

Human nature is the same in all men, and has been from the beginning of history. As far as archeology can determine, human nature has been homogeneous from the time man first appeared on earth.[1] There are certain faculties which are possessed by men in all societies. And there are certain relationships between men which occur in all societies. These faculties and relationships induce corresponding natural obligations. To use these faculties as they should be used and to observe these relationships is morally good and necessary. To pervert or abuse these faculties or to warp these relationships is morally evil and forbidden by nature.

For example, the power of speech has as its proper object the reproduction in audible words of the thoughts which are contained in the speaker's mind. This has its consequences in morality. To use the power of speech to speak the truth is according to nature and therefore morally right. To use it to lie is a perversion of nature and therefore morally wrong.

Similarly, the nature of man requires a long period of nurturing and education before he is able to act independently. Consequently, every man is naturally required to honor those who have cared for him in his youth. To fail to pay this honor is a perversion of the order of nature and therefore morally wrong.

A study of the various faculties of man in the context of

his relationships will reveal certain basic natural laws of morality. These laws apply to all men in so far as they possess the corresponding faculties and enter into the corresponding relationships. These laws, taken together, are called natural law.

Other special precepts may be added by a given society to the natural law because of particular circumstances in that society, but there will be basic rules which apply to all. Every man, because he is a man, is bound, according to the universal order willed by the Creator, to live in accordance with his own nature.

The natural law is an unwritten law, first promulgated to men not in the Bible or any other written document, but in their hearts. Men who have never heard of the Bible can come to a knowledge of the various precepts of this law. This knowledge is not innate. It is derived by a process of reasoning, by examining human nature in its relationships and from them deducing a moral code.

Infants and insane persons, who have not the actual use of their reason, cannot therefore know this law. They are not held responsible for their violations of it. All those, however, possessing the use of reason, who are men, rational animals in the complete sense, are bound by the law.

2. Natural Law and Positive Law

Before going more deeply into natural law as it applies to various classes of men, we must set forth the precise relationship between natural law (the law of conscience) and the various other systems of law in the world, both religious and secular. These latter systems of law are called, collectively, positive law.

Positive law is distinguished from natural law in that it does not arise entirely from the conscience of the subject but from some external manifestation, oral or written.

Natural law requires that men live together in some form of organized society. But (with man weakened by original sin) an organized society in which everyone followed only his own conscience would be impossible. This would be chaos. Many would not follow their consciences. Many others would be confused by special moral problems arising in their particular environment. Natural law by definition only regulates those things which all men have in common.

Positive laws are necessary in all societies to apply the general norms of natural law to the special circumstances of each society. Natural law commands, for example, that innocent lives be preserved. But traffic laws and the laws for pedestrians in busy cities will be different from those in rural areas.

Positive laws also are necessary to remind wayward citizens of their previously existing obligations in natural law (v.g., that stealing and perjury are wrong). Positive laws also enable a society to formulate penalties for violation of those laws of conscience which tend to undermine society, and to provide further rewards for virtue.

Positive law, then, should be founded on natural law. Positive laws derive their morality from natural law. They are either good or evil depending on whether they are in agreement with natural law.

Positive laws are good because they either restate or determine natural law, or provide inducements for its observance. Levin says, "I was told that [I must love my neighbor and not oppress him] in my childhood, and I believed it gladly, for they told me what was already in my soul."[2]

Positive laws are evil when they are opposed to natural law: by tolerating a practice which is forbidden in natural law; by forbidding something which is tolerated; or by adding unnecessary and oppressive burdens to moral life.

Natural law, then, constitutes the ultimate standard by which all positive laws are to be judged good or bad, right or wrong. This applies not only to positive secular or civil law, but to positive religious law as well.

It is in this sense, and for these reasons, that natural law can be used as a criterion in evaluating the moral codes of the various religions of the world.

3. The Teaching of the Major World Religions on the Existence of Natural Law

As a first step in studying the relation of religious law to natural law, it will be well to see what the various religions say about natural law itself. What they say for or against natural law will not be a strict proof of the existence or non-existence of this law. The strict proof of the existence of natural law lies in the demonstration given above based on the fact that there is general order in the universe and specific uniformity in the human race. External testimony, however, can serve to confirm the existence of natural law.

The major religions of the world are unanimous in affirming the existence of natural law.

Christianity has always accepted the concept of natural law. On many occasions, Christ was explicit on the point. He placed the natural law, the law of God, above any man-made law. He denounced the Pharisees for abrogating a precept of the natural law by devising, on their own authority, a contradictory law. "Well do you nullify the commandment of God, that you may keep your own tradition! For Moses said, 'Honor thy father and thy mother.' . . . But you say, 'Let a man say to his father or mother, "Any support thou mightest have had from me is Corban"' (that is, given to God). And you do not allow him to do anything further for his father or mother. You make void the commandment of God by your tradition, which you have handed down; and many such like things you do" (Mark 7:9–13).

St. Paul, speaking of the idolatrous pagans, gave one of the classic Christian expositions of natural law: "For the wrath of God is revealed from heaven against all ungodliness and wickedness of those men who in wickedness hold back the truth of God, seeing that what may be known about God is manifest to them. For God has manifested it to them. For since the creation of the world, his invisible attributes are clearly seen—his everlasting power also and divinity—being understood through the things that are made. And so they are without excuse seeing that although they knew God, they did not glorify him as God or give thanks. . . . And as they have resolved against possessing the knowledge of God, God has given them up to a reprobate sense, so that they do what is not fitting, being filled with all iniquity, malice, immorality, avarice, wickedness; being full of envy, murder, contention, deceit, malignity; being whisperers, detractors, hateful to God, irreverent, proud, haughty, plotters of evil; disobedient to parents, foolish, dissolute, without affection, without fidelity, without mercy. Although they have known the ordinance of God, they have not understood that those who practice such things are deserving of death." "For whoever have sinned without the Law will perish without the Law." But "when the Gentiles who have no law do by nature what the Law prescribes, these having no law are a law unto themselves. They show the work of the Law written in their hearts. Their conscience bears witness to them, even when conflicting thoughts accuse or defend them (Cf. Rom. 1:18; 2:29)."[3]

According to St. Paul, then, even those who have never heard the revealed words of God still are bound by a moral law. This law is fixed for all men and is written in their hearts. It forbids idolatry, avarice, envy, etc., to all men. Those who disobey its precepts are "deserving of death" and subject to punishment by God.

The later Church writers[4] are unanimous in teaching the same doctrine.

The non-Catholic testimony is strikingly similar to the Catholic. Although paganism is at the furthest ethical extreme from Catholicism, even it agrees with the Church on this point. The greatest religious leaders and ethical thinkers of all times have taught the existence of natural law.

The *Hymns of the Rig-Veda* of ancient Hinduism proclaim that "the law (Rta) pervades the whole world and all gods and men must obey it."[5] Later Hindus reaffirmed what had been stated in the *Hymns of the Rig-Veda*: "Natural law . . . is identical in all faiths and is common to all mankind."[6]

The Jews, for their part, both ancient and modern, "did not fail to distinguish between commandments and prohibitions which were, we may say, of natural obligation, recognized by the reason and conscience of all right thinking men . . . and statutory laws given to Israel alone."[7]

And Buddha (d. 483? B.C.) taught that "the moral law is not the chance intervention of an exceptional mind or (even the dogma of . . . revelation but the necessary expression of the truth of things." In the *Dhammapada*, we find clear evidence of Buddhism's understanding of natural law and of its position as the source of ethical norms.

"They who forbid when there is nothing to be forbidden and forbid not when there is something to be forbidden, such men . . . enter the evil path. They who know what is forbidden as forbidden and what is not forbidden as not forbidden, such men enter the true path."[8] "After Buddha . . . the belief in the permanence and universality of natural law became almost an instinct of the Indian mind."[9]

Confucius (d. 479 ? B.C.) refers to the "absolute standard of righteousness."[10] And the great Confucian Scripture, *The Works of Mencius*, shows an accurate insight into the philosophical origins of natural law: "Every faculty and relation of man must have its laws."[11] Confucius presented his teaching only as a reflection of the law of nature. "The doctrine of our master [Confucius] is to be true to the principles of our nature."[12]

Plato affirmed that some laws, like that commanding respect for parents, are universal laws and are observed everywhere in any country.[13]

Aristotle says, "Equity is that natural justice which exists independently of human laws" and also "If the written law tells against our case, clearly we must appeal to the universal law and insist on its greater justice and equity."[14]

According to Cicero, "There is a true law, right reason, consonant to nature, coextensive with the race of man, unchanging and eternal. . . . It is not allowed us to make any alteration in that law: we may not take away any least portion of it; nor can we repeal it as a whole. Neither senate nor people have power to release us from our obligations in its regard. We need not search for some one to explain or interpret it. We shall not find one law at Rome, another at Athens: one now, another hereafter; but that law, one, everlasting and immutable, is binding on all races and at all times: and there is one common Master and Lord of all, God. He it is who drew up this law, determined its provisions, and promulgated it."[15]

Seneca held that "Nature produced us related to one another since she created us from the same source and to the same end. She engendered in us mutual affection and made us prone to friendships. She established fairness and justice."[16]

Though Mohammed does not emphasize the role of the natural law, he does hold the proposition which is basic to acceptance of a natural law: that all men have one and the same nature. "So set thy purpose [O Muhammad] for religion as a man by nature upright—the nature [framed] of Allah, in which He hath created man" (sura 30:30).

Thomas Jefferson in 1816 wrote that "Our legislators are not sufficiently appraised of the rightful limits of their power; that their true office is to declare and enforce only our natural rights and duties and to take none of them from us."[17]

Catholics and the greatest ethical thinkers among the non-Catholics, then, agree. A natural law exists. It is based on human nature itself. And it binds men of all times and in all places.

To be sure, there have been many non-Catholics who have denied the existence of a natural law. Even in the time of Plato there were many pagans who denied the natural law and held moral law to be mere convention.[18] But these people were the ones whom Plato and the others were refuting. The great ethical thinkers saw the error in indifferentism and were unanimous in proclaiming the unity of mankind and announcing a universal moral law.

Thus, if a person denies the existence of the natural law, he will maintain an awkward position on two counts. He must oppose the ethnological theory of the unity of the human race. And secondly, in denying the existence of the natural law he finds himself contradicting not only Christ and Christianity but also the greatest non-Catholic ethical thinkers (thinkers who in some cases were completely cut off from the others of their number).

4. The Similarities among Moral Codes

Confirmation of the existence of the natural law, however, is not derived simply from testimony concerning its theoretical existence. These theoretical statements are themselves confirmed by the existence in fact of striking similarities among the moral laws of disparate peoples.

A Christian who studies the ethical codes of non-Christian religions is frequently amazed at the degree to which they resemble one another and Christianity. The great ethical writers of ancient Greece and Rome, like Plutarch, Seneca and Marcus Aurelius, answer a mountainous variety of moral questions in almost the same way that a Christian would answer them. As far as the bulk of their thought content goes, their works could have been written by Christians. Plutarch's *Morals*, Seneca's *Moral Essays* and *Moral Letters* and Marcus Aurelius' *Meditations* contain brilliant remarks on such virtues as patience, modesty, sobriety, and courage, and have aroused the admiration of many Christians. This is especially true of Seneca. His insights into the nature and practice of virtue are often not only in agreement with the teaching of Christianity but are also recognized by Christians as extremely penetrating and apt.

Nor are Plutarch, Seneca, and Marcus Aurelius the only pagans whose ethical principles approximate almost entirely those of Christianity. It is true also of the other great pagan moralists. The ethics of the *Laws of Manu* in Brahmanism, of Buddha, or Confucius, and of Mohammed, all resemble to a surprising degree the ethics of Christianity.

They may differ in the manner of phrasing these laws. On respect for elders, the *Laws of Manu* say, "For the vital airs of a young man mount upwards to leave his body when an elder approaches; but by rising to meet him and saluting he recovers them."[19] The Bible has "Rise up before the hoary head and honor the person of the aged man: and fear the Lord thy God. I am the Lord" (Lev. 19:32).

They may differ in the emphasis given to a particular virtue: Islam emphasizes external forms of worship more than Christianity does. In the same way, the Chinese religions emphasize tokens of respect for elders more than does Christianity.

They may also differ in the earthly rewards and penalties affixed to the observance or non-observance of the laws: in the Koran an almost Draconian penalty is attached to stealing. "As for the thief, both male and female, cut off their hands" (sura 5:38).

Behind these and other variations, however, the basic moral principles remain constant. Brahmanism and Christianity both teach us to respect our elders. Islam and Christianity both teach the necessity of some external manifestation of worship of God. Islam forbids stealing, so does Christianity.

When we compare Christian ethics with those of any of the great pagan philosophies, we shall find many more similarities than discrepancies. What is commanded in Christianity very often will be commanded in pagan philosophy. What Christianity prohibits, so will the pagans. What Christianity recommends but does not command, so too will the pagans. Moral codes are more similar than many men realize.

5. *The Significance of the Dissimilarities*

There are exceptions. Sometimes Christianity finds herself disagreeing with other religions on basic moral issues. Sometimes she will teach a moral principle which most other religions also accept but some qualify or reject entirely. And then, even less often, we find cases where she holds a particular moral principle which most of the other religions reject. The pagan religions, too, disagree among themselves.

These exceptions, however, can seem to be more numerous or significant than they really are. Some men have set forth certain teachings of pagan religions as diametrically opposed to those of the generality of the other religions when in fact such opposition does not exist. Others, finding a true discrepancy, exaggerate it.

For example, surveys have revealed that almost all, if not all, societies of men have arrived at a conviction that there is personal reward or punishment awaiting men in the next life. Some men have pointed to the Buddhists as a major exception to this.[20] The Buddhists, they say, do not expect personal reward or punishment in the next life. They hope for *Nirvana,* a state of annihilation.

But the Buddhists, they note, form a very large segment of mankind. And if a very large segment of mankind disbelieves in a future personal reward and punishment, men cannot be said to be unanimous on the point.

The initial premise here is false for two reasons. First, in practice, the majority of individual Buddhists consider *Nirvana* as unattainable for them and hope only for a lesser reward promised in the next life to faithful Buddhists.[21] This reward is a personal one with earthly pleasures and is called the Buddhist heaven. Secondly, even *Nirvana* itself cannot truly be described as strict annihilation.[22] The Buddhist teaching on *Nirvana* corresponds roughly to the Christian description of the spiritual joys to be found in heaven. Where Christianity describes these joys in a positive manner, as the joys of contemplation and love of the Creator, Buddhism describes them negatively, as the absence of pain and desire.

Thus Buddhists in general, together with the rest of mankind, have a fundamental expectation of a future personal sanction. In effect, the Buddhist teaching on the point does not contradict natural law, and does not swell the ranks of the exceptions to it. In a similar manner, many other pagan teachings which are cited as aberrations are less so than is often supposed.

In some cases, however, a teaching of a particular religion does deviate fundamentally from that of most of the others. Even here, upon occasion, the discrepancy is exaggerated. The teaching of the Church on chastity, the virtue regulating the sexual appetite, is a case in point. The Church strongly recommends and praises chastity both inside and outside of marriage. Certain writers have declared that the Church stands alone here, that non-Christians are in complete ignorance of any concept of chastity. Leclercq observes that they have concentrated so heavily on describing some of the more sensational dissipations of the pagans that they give the impression that these people lived in a constant state of erotic frenzy.[23]

In reality, nearly all the non-Christians recognized the ideal of chastity and encouraged its observance. All the major groups, both in the East and in the West, placed restrictions on the use of the procreative impulse. Those who have praised sensuality or have advocated free love in the major civilizations, Christian and non-Christian, have been on the outer fringe and have not gained a fundamental and widespread acceptance by the members of their respective societies.[24] They promote novelty for its own sake. Control of the sexual instinct, whether one is married or not, has been encouraged by the generality of mankind. Debauchery is recognized as a vice and chastity as a virtue.

The difference is one of degree. Christianity is more strict than virtually all non-Christian groups. The various pagan religions may duplicate Christian teaching on some aspects of chastity, but in some other aspects, fall short, each in a different way. Christianity has given chastity a prestige unknown to the non-Christians.[25] She has emphasized the need for this virtue more than the other religions have. Nevertheless, there is no total disagreement between the two groups on whether there exists the virtue istelf of chastity.

True differences, then, between Christian and pagan teachings on certain fundamental moral questions have often been exaggerated.

From the foregoing sections, some important conclusions can be drawn in relation to the discrepancies between Christian and non-Christian moral teaching. There is not widespread disagreement between the religions of the world in relation to every point of morality. It is not as if on every ethical point on which the majority of religions agree, there were a substantial minority who disagreed. Rather, there are many points of moral law on which almost the entire human race agrees. Moreover, a close study of the points on which there seems to be widespread disagreement causes many of the discrepancies to melt or even disappear, and the number of points on which there is virtual unanimity, to increase.

6. *The Sanction of Natural Law*

A natural law, then, certainly exists. This leads to a further question. Does this law have any rewards and penalties attached to it or is it merely a theoretical law without any sanction of its own? Civil officials attach rewards and penalties to the civil laws to encourage their observance and discourage their violation. Has God attached any rewards and penalties to the natural law which has its origin in Him?

Reason shows us that God, in fact, has attached two sanctions, or sets of rewards and penalties, to the natural law. One of these sanctions acts in this life, the other in the next. God has placed a powerful sanction on the natural law which acts in this life. Many delude themselves that this is not so. They think that apart from the penalties which may be attached to it by civil society, vice is all delight in this life; and that apart from the rewards which may be granted for it by civil society, virtue is all asperity. They imagine that if one is willing to forego the civil rewards of virtue and at the same time if one can escape civil punishments for vice, the advantages in this life are all in favor of vice. Thus if there were no civil rewards or punishments attached to a given virtue and its contrary vice, there would be no earthly reason to practice it.

A close inspection, however, shows that God has, indeed, attached a threefold sanction in this life to the observance of the natural law. The three parts of this sanction act independently of any civil sanctions for the same virtues and they have been classified under the headings "essential," "natural," and "moral."

The first earthly sanction of natural law has been classified as essential because of the intrinsic connection between the observance of natural law and this sanction. Virtue, by itself, brings great peace and joy to the soul springing from an interior conscience approving good deeds.[26] The Wolsey who had finally turned to God could say,

> I feel within me
> A peace above all earthly dignities,
> A still and quiet conscience.[27]

Vice, on the contrary, unnerves the soul by the twinge of a guilty conscience. The faces, words, and actions of those who violate the natural law often reveal that their conscience, an internal enemy, an unavoidable and highly unwelcome guest, is always there to mingle gall with the nectar they are drinking. Conscience stings at the time of the sin. More than that, however, its sting remains. Even the most depraved man must spend long intervals of time without being able to commit sin. The actual commission of sin can only punctuate his day. Its major portion must be spent alone with his thoughts, plagued by the thorn of conscience.

Secondly, some goods are naturally connected with a virtuous life, and some evils with a sinful one. This arises from the very physical constitution of man, the result of the combination in human beings of a body with the soul. "For virtue, self-control, and temperance in particular, that is a just moderation in the enjoyment of earthly goods, by their very nature, strengthen the forces of the body, preserve its health, free it from many pains and ills and prolong its life. Vice, on the contrary, naturally produces in the body the opposite effects. It weakens its vigor, injures its health, causes many pains and sicknesses, and hastens death.

Intemperance, says the old proverb, has killed more men than the sword."[28]

Thirdly, some goods accompany virtue, and some evils accompany vice, morally. The impression that our virtues or vices make on our acquaintances will, reflexively, often bring further goods or evils back to us. Virtue produces the esteem, love, and confidence of other men, whilst vice generally begets their contempt, aversion, and distrust.[29]

The threefold sanction in this life, then, is visible in its effects. This visible sanction, in turn, however, demonstrates the existence of an invisible sanction, one which must exist in a future life.

The sanction of natural law in the present life is imperfect. The joys of an upright conscience, physical well-being, and a good reputation can never be commensurate in the case of heroic virtue. What earthly reward is received by the saints who forfeit all things and sacrifice life itself rather than transgress God's law, as was done by the seven Maccabean brothers and their mother, and by the millions of martyrs who have died for Christ?

Then again, natural rewards may be insufficient even in the case of ordinary virtue. Sometimes these rewards can be, for the most part, absent in the life of one who is observing the natural law. Physical suffering can come upon the innocent. At times, an innocent man can pass an entire lifetime without enjoying a good reputation. In some cases, virtually all of the earthly rewards for virtue can be lacking.

Neither are earthly natural punishments sufficient in many cases to keep men from breaking God's law. Many commit sin frequently while fully aware of its natural penalties in the present life. In many cases, earthly punishments for sin are overcome and evaded. The vehemence of remorse is not generally increased in proportion to man's depravity, and the number of crimes he commits. In the hearts of the most depraved, remorse is often almost totally absent.

Many, too, live comfortably, in good health, and with honor, though sunk in vice.

The rewards in this life for virtue are often insufficient. The earthly penalties attached to sin are frequently the same.

Yet God is just. He will always fully reward virtue and fully punish vice. But those virtuous men who leave the world after a lifetime of physical afflictions and undeserved scorn certainly have not been fully rewarded. The wicked who leave the world after a lifetime of undeserved felicity have not been fully punished. Therefore God must grant some rewards to the virtuous and mete out some punishments to sinners in a life after death.

This is not a conclusion arrived at only by Christians. St. John Chrysostom says "Jews and Christians, Greeks and Romans, pagans and believers, in short, all classes of men, are in perfect accord in acknowledging the imperative necessity of a future retribution."[30] Some individuals and some small groups may disagree, but the generality of mankind in all places and at all times has been convinced that there are rewards and punishments of some kind awaiting men in a next life. The rewards depend on the level of virtue attained in this life. The severity of the punishments depends on the degree of moral guilt of the sinner. Thus far, then, men are agreed. Few would contradict the conclusions, at least, of the foregoing proof.

The duration of the sanction in the next life, however, is a very much disputed point. All religions agree that man in some way is to live on after death. Societies disagree, however, on the duration of this future life. Some say that the rewards and punishments in the next life are eternal;[31] others, that they are only temporary.

The necessity of strictly eternal sanction, however, can be proved by the demonstration of two propositions.

First, an eternal sanction is just. The discussion of the

justice of eternal sanction really centers on the question of the justice of eternal punishment. (Few strenuously dispute the justice of an eternal reward.) That eternal punishment is just is shown by the following line of reasoning. A grievous culpable violation of natural law is an offense against God, the Maker of that law. And the greater the dignity of the person offended, so much greater and more grievous is the offense. In the case of a deliberate violation of natural law the person offended is God, who possesses infinite dignity, while the offender is only a finite being, infinitely inferior to Him. It follows that in every grievous sin we find an injury and contempt that are in a certain manner infinite. Therefore, a punishment in some way infinite is due such a sin.

Such a punishment cannot be infinite intensively, because finite creatures are not capable of suffering infinite pain. . . . The penalty, therefore, "to be equal to the gravity of the offense, must be infinite in duration, that is, eternal." Eternal punishment is, therefore, just.

Secondly, an eternal punishment for at least some violations of natural law is necessary. "If we take into account man's fallen nature, the violence of his passions, the intoxicating allurements of sensible goods, particularly the enticing pleasures of the flesh, and the hardships at times encountered in the practice of virtue, we cannot but be convinced that temporary penalties, however prolonged, do not offer men motives sufficiently strong to induce men to observance of the divine law in all the circumstances in which they may find themselves during the period of their . . . probation on earth. This is shown by the criminals themselves, who to give full scope to their disordered passions, strive to persuade themselves and others that future punishments, if they exist at all, at least are not eternal" and "that the souls of the wicked" either "will be annihilated, or, after due atonement, will be admitted to enjoy perfect happiness in the next life." St. Jerome remarks "The most perverse belief, that hell's pains are to have an end, completely destroys the fear of God, and makes easy to men the career of sin."[32]

The only fully adequate sanction, then, is one which can be eternal. But if the only adequate moral sanction is based on a fiction, if there is no eternal reward nor eternal punishment in fact, God's truthfulness would be in question. God would be cheating man if He arranged things in such a way that the only adequate sanction is the hope of eternal reward and threat of eternal punishment, and did not at the same time provide these eternal rewards and punishments. But God does not deceive man. Therefore there must be both an eternal reward for the observance of natural law, and an eternal punishment, hell, for at least some of the more serious violations of it.

The exact nature of heaven and hell need not concern us here: whether they are places or simply states of existence; whether they include bodily pleasures and pains or not; whether they include intellectual rewards and punishments. We confine ourselves to the propostion that there exist eternal rewards and penalties in the next life in recompense for moral activity in this. Virtue in this life will bring eternal rewards in the next. Serious and deliberate violations of the law of God which remain uncorrected in this life will bring eternal punishment.

God has placed two sanctions on the natural law, one affecting this life, one the next. These two sanctions support one another. A single virtuous act can be motivated by advertence to both of these sanctions. Sometimes, either one of these sanctions taken separately might be insufficient in the case of a given individual to develop a certain necessary virtue. In such a case, he would have an obligation to advert to both of these sanctions and provide himself with a double motive.

The two sanctions of natural law, however, are not absolutely equal in potential motivating force. The sanction of the next life is essentially stronger and primary; the sanctions in this life are auxiliary and add to the invisible but stronger sanction in the next life a visible and more rapid sanction in this.

How do the two sanctions of natural law apply to man-made (positive) religious law? If the religious law agrees with natural law, there is no difficulty. The sanctions of natural law then apply to the religious law. But what if the religious law on some points contradicts natural law?

In such a case, both sanctions of natural law can continue to operate. A sin against natural law which results in bodily or mental disease will continue to do so in a given society even though the religion of that society tolerates or condones the sin. And the eternal sanction can also operate. That is, it is possible for a sin, which under natural law deserves eternal punishment, to continue to do so in a given society even though the society tolerates that sin. This latter possibility is contingent upon one thing: that this serious violation of the natural law is culpable.

7. Knowledge of Natural Law

The question of whether a man can observe the rules of his own religion, and at the same time culpably and seriously violate one or more precepts of the natural law, brings us to the question of our knowledge of the natural law.

On the basis of knowability, the principles of the natural law have been divided into three groupings: primary principles, primary conclusions, and secondary or remote conclusions.

The primary principles include: "Good is to be done, evil avoided"; "Do not do to others, what you would not have them do to you"; "God is to be worshiped"; "Benefactors are to be honored"; "No injustice is to be done," etc. These principles are not derived from other principles. They are *per se* evident. It is from them that all other principles are derived.

The primary conclusions are derived immediately, easily, and obviously from the primary principles. Primary conclusions include: "Honor thy father and mother"; "Thou shalt not steal," and in general those things contained in the ten commandments (except the determination of the Sabbath).

The remote conclusions are deduced only by a more or less elaborate process of reasoning from the primary principles and primary conclusions. The remote conclusions include: "Articles which are found must be returned"; "Injuries whenever possible are not to be rectified by private revenge but by a civil procedure"; "Usury is unjust"; "Polygamy, lying, abortion, fornication, and direct suicide are always wrong," etc.

The phrase "more or less elaborate" used in describing the process of reasoning in arriving at the remote conclusions is of significance. The remote conclusions are not equally difficult to arrive at. This is evident even in the examples given above. Some are more remote and obscure than others. The prohibitions of usury and of all lying are both remote conclusions of natural law. Both require an elaborate process of reasoning to come to their knowledge. Yet the process of reasoning required to arrive at a knowledge of the malice of all usury is less intricate than that required to know the malice of every lie. Both prohibitions are equally valid but not equally knowable.

All precepts of the natural law, then, the primary principles, the primary conclusions, and the secondary conclusions are knowable, and can be discovered by unaided right reason. The differences among the three categories of precepts lie only in the facility with which they can be known.

8. *Ignorance of Natural Law*

Looking at the same problem negatively, to what extent is ignorance of the natural law possible? Those who do not have the use of reason—infants, feeble-minded, and insane —are, by definition, unable to discover natural law for themselves. They cannot discover these principles without help from others. Their only means of knowing the propositions of the natural law is through the instruction of others. If they lack this instruction, they will be ignorant of the true teaching of nature.

But what about those who are in possession of the use of reason? Do they always arrive at the knowledge of all the principles and conclusions of the natural law?

We know that many who possess the use of reason do violate natural law. Sometimes, going further, certain men endowed with the use of reason even teach principles which contradict the principles and conclusions of natural law. Secondly, we know that many who do these things do so in ignorance. Many men break some precepts of natural law without having full awareness of the malice of their acts. Similarly, some lawmakers who formulate a positive law which is in opposition to natural law are not fully aware of their error.

St. Augustine cites the story of a woman who apparently broke the natural law in ignorance. Her husband was in prison awaiting execution because of an unpaid debt. She had no means of paying the debt and saving his life. A certain depraved and wealthy man learned of the situation, and offered to pay the debt if the woman would have intercourse with him once. She went to her husband and asked his opinion; he commanded it to be done.

Of this case, St. Augustine says that this woman seemed to herself to be under obligation to do what in fact was forbidden by natural law.[33]

St. Thomas says that the Germans, mentioned by Julius Caesar, permitted theft and did not consider it wrong, though theft is expressly contrary to natural law.[34]

In these cases, there certainly was at least some ignorance, but was the ignorance culpable or inculpable? Can there be inculpable ignorance of the natural law and if so, to what extent? To find the answer to these questions, it is first necessary to study the nature of culpable and inculpable ignorance.

Ignorance is culpable when it is vincible, i.e., when a person does not attempt to remove it with the diligence possible and obligatory under the circumstances. The diligence need not be the maximum effort which is physically possible at a given time. There need be only "moral" diligence, i.e., that effort "commensurate with the importance of the affair in hand, and with the capacity of the agent, in a word, such as a really sensible and prudent person would use under the circumstances."[35]

Vincible ignorance is always culpable. But this culpability can vary depending on the reason for it. Ignorance which is induced by a deliberate and formulated intention to remain ignorant is more culpable than ignorance which arises from simple neglect. The culpability of ignorance arising from simple neglect can also vary, depending on whether little effort or no effort at all was made to remove it.

Ignorance is inculpable when it is invincible, i.e., when the person is unable to remove his ignorance even after using "moral diligence."

Both vincible and invincible ignorance of the natural law are possible. But this possibility will vary according to the type of precept: primary principle, primary conclusion, or secondary conclusion.

Of the supreme principles of the natural law, no man

possessed with developed powers of reason can be in ignorance, either invincible or vincible.[36] No adult, either deliberately or otherwise, can blot out from his mind knowledge of the fact that "good is to be done and evil avoided," or of any other primary principle. It is impossible for a man in this world to say with sincerity: "Evil, be thou my good."[37] While depraved men have mistakenly considered a given evil act to be good, no one maintains in principle that evil as evil is to be done. Ignorance of the primary principles of natural law is altogether impossible in a person who has the use of reason.

This is not true, however, of the primary conclusions. There can be either vincible or invincible ignorance of these conclusions in one possessing the use of reason.

There can be vincible ignorance of primary conclusions. The primary conclusions, unlike the primary principles, do not force the mind to assent to them. It does require at least some "moral diligence" to learn of them. One can deliberately blind oneself to these laws. This self-deception can go quite far. It is possible for a man to be in bad faith on one of these precepts even though he categorically assures us of his good faith.[38] Externally he proclaims his innocence but internally, in the depths of his heart, he knows he has never bothered to study the problem fully.

There can also be invincible ignorance of the primary conclusions. This is likely to occur in those societies where laws or customs tolerate the violation of one or more of these conclusions. In such a society, a person could be in invincible ignorance of the malice of an act which is opposed to a primary conclusion of the natural law. There is one very important qualification of this, however. Though people can be in invincible ignorance of the primary conclusions, no one who has a developed use of reason can remain in this state of invincible ignorance for a long period of time.[39] These primary conclusions are too obvious for an adult to remain in ignorance of them for a long time without coming sooner or later to have good reason to suspect, at least, that he himself is in error.

Of the remote conclusions, there can also be both vincible and invincible ignorance.[40] But the invincible ignorance of these conclusions can last a very long time.

Even a person who grants that ignorance of the natural law is confined within the above limits can still have an exaggerated idea of the practical extent of inculpable ignorance of primary and secondary conclusions of natural law.

Many would grant that lengthy invincible ignorance of the primary conclusions would not be possible for people possessing developed powers of reason. But, noting the phrase "developed power of reason," they would raise this further objection: "Do not most of those who violate the primary conclusions of the natural law, especially those who live in societies which tolerate these violations, actually lack developed powers of reason? For this reason, are not most people who break these rules, *de facto,* in invincible ignorance?"

Similarly, with regard to the remote conclusions, many might feel that these conclusions are so remote that invincible ignorance of them (apart from knowledge of revelation) is not only likely, but unavoidable. Many would be inclined to hold that many of these conclusions are reached by such an intricate process of reasoning that no one without the aid of revelation could possibly arrive at them.

We shall study each of these exaggerations of the extent of ignorance of primary and secondary conclusions of natural law, treating the secondary conclusions first and reserving the primary conclusions for later.

9. *Instances of Agreement among the Christian and Non-Christian Religions on Secondary Conclusions of Natural Law*

The student of comparative religion unfolds case after case of pagans who are cut off from the Judaeo-Christian revelation and yet who offer as their own some of the remote conclusions which are also taught by the Biblical religions. Perhaps one of the most surprising aspects of comparative religion is the extent to which pagan religions duplicate Christianity, not only on primary conclusions but also on these very obscure points of natural law, the secondary conclusions.

What follows is a series of maxims uttered by non-Catholic ethical thinkers. These men were out of touch with Christian teaching. Yet their maxims sometimes approximate or duplicate the remote conclusions of the natural law, and as such, are also found in Catholic teaching. Though not all these conclusions are equally remote, some, at least, require such an elaborate process of reasoning to discover their validity that, apart from the knowledge that a non-Catholic does teach them, we might be tempted to think that they are the exclusive property of Christianity.

Seneca echoes St. Paul's teaching (Rom. 3:8) that the end never justifies the means. In his *Exhortations*, Seneca says, "But it makes no difference with what intention you act when the act itself is vicious."[41] And speaking in particular of the use of irrational anger as a means of correcting or restraining the wicked, he utters the principle: "It is not right to correct wrongdoing by doing wrong."[42] And many years before St. Paul, Plato had said that though many disagreed on the point, to do wrong for whatever purpose was always evil and dishonorable.[43]

Through the centuries, orthodox Christians have defended the proposition that man's sins are never due to temptations that are simply beyond his capacity to overcome them. "God is faithful and will not permit you to be tempted beyond your strength, but with the temptation will also give you a way out that you may be able to bear it" (1 Cor. 10:13). Here again, Christianity is not alone. Marcus Aurelius says, "Nothing happens to any man which he is not formed by nature to bear."[44] Confucius asks, "Is anyone able for one day to apply his strength to virtue? I have not seen the case in which his strength would be insufficient."[45]

A firm purpose of amendment is not only desirable but is necessary before sins can be forgiven. Sorrow alone is not enough. Brahmanism, one of the early forms of Hinduism, gives an explicit statement of this relationship between sorrow and purpose of amendment. "He who has committed a sin and has repented, is freed from that sin, but he is purified only by [the resolution of] ceasing [to sin and thinking] 'I will do so no more.' "[46]

In the definitions of the various virtues and vices, the non-Catholic philosophers are at times close to Christianity even on details of natural law. In running through the various virtues and vices for the purpose of comparing religions, in this section as well as in the subsequent ones, we shall group the virtues and vices under the following headings: religious assent, moral effort, benevolence, and the ten commandments. The first three headings are natural virtues which correspond to the three theological and supernatural virtues of faith, hope, and charity. We shall not use the words faith, hope, and charity to refer to these natural virtues in order that we may not mislead the reader into thinking that we are speaking of the corresponding supernatural virtues.

There are some remote conclusions relating to the three virtues of religious assent, moral effort, and benevolence, which are agreed upon by Catholics and non-Catholics.

Christian theologians have described what would be an absolute minimum of religious assent for those who have never heard of Christianity. Non-Christians must at least accept a personal God who is both Creator and Remunerator in the next life. In sura 5:69 of the Koran, Mohammed lists those groups who can be saved. In doing so he gives his minimum requirements of religious assent for Moslems and certain non-Moslems. "Lo! those who believe, and those who are Jews, and Sabaeans, and Christians—Whosoever believeth in Allah and the Last Day and doth right—there shall no fear come upon them, neither shall they grieve." Mohammed not only inculcates in his followers each of the elements of minimal religious assent, but he also agrees that these elements and nothing more are, in fact, minimal.

The natural virtue of moral effort regulates the exertion of energy in the pursuit of the other virtues. All men must make this personal effort for virtue, and not allow themselves to remain passive toward temptation. No state of mind and no set of religious convictions excuses one from doing good works or avoiding sin. Nor will membership in any religious group or any amount of help from friends entirely obviate the necessity of personal good works. Christianity emphasizes the need for moral effort as much as or more than any other major religion. This same note of emphasis, however, on the need for personal effort, seems to be struck in the *Laws of Manu*. "Single is every living creature born; single he passes into another world; single he eats the fruit of evil deeds; single, the fruit of good."[47]

The word benevolence, as we shall use it, refers to love of neighbor. Christ taught that the norm of love of neighbor is to be love of self. "Love thy neighbor as thyself" (Luke 10:27). Buddhism also relates love of neighbor to love of self. Buddha said, "I have never yet met with anything that was dearer to anyone than his own self. Since to others, to each one for himself, the self is dear, therefore let him who desires his advantage not harm another." Buddhism teaches that "we should cultivate our emotions so that we feel with others as if they were ourselves. If we allow the virtue of compassion to grow in us, it will not occur to us to harm anyone else, any more than we willingly harm ourselves."[48]

On the giving of benefits, Seneca makes the proper distinctions brilliantly. "It is necessary to give certain benefits openly, others without witnesses—openly, those which it is glorious to obtain, such as military decorations or official honors and any other distinction that becomes more attractive by reason of publicity; on the other hand, those which do not give promotion or prestige, yet come to the rescue of bodily infirmity, of poverty, of disgrace—these should be given quietly so that they will be known only to those who receive the benefit. . . . Otherwise the motive is ostentation."[49]

The necessity of giving alms is inculcated by all major religions. Christ specified that alms were to be given in secret and that the penalty for not doing so was loss of merit. "When thou givest alms, do not sound a trumpet before thee as the hypocrites do in the synagogues and streets in order that they may be honored by men. Amen I say to you, they have received their reward. But when thou givest alms, do not let thy left hand know what thy right hand is doing, so that thy alms may be given in secret; and thy Father, who sees in secret will reward thee" (Matt. 6:2–4). The *Laws of Manu* say: "When he has bestowed [a gift], let him not boast of it . . . [the reward of] a gift is lost by boasting."[50]

What is true of the virtues of religious assent, moral effort, and benevolence in this matter is also true of the ten commandments. Details of Christian ethics pertaining to the ten commandments are sometimes duplicated by non-Christians.

The first commandment, "I am the Lord thy God; thou shalt not have false gods before me," in general prescribes monotheistic worship.

In the worship of the Moslems, there is one prayer that is central. It is an essential part of all Moslem worship, both public and private. No solemn contract or transaction is complete unless it is recited. This prayer has been called the Lord's Prayer of the Moslems. It is taken from the Koran and comprises the first sura or chapter of this book. The entire prayer is especially noteworthy in that it could also be recited with profit by a devout Christian. There is nothing in it which is repugnant to orthodox Christianity. It runs: "[In the name of God, the beneficent, the merciful.] Praise be to God, Lord of the worlds, the beneficent, the merciful. Owner of the Day of Judgment, Thee [alone] we worship; Thee [alone] we ask for help. Show us the straight path, the path of those whom Thou hast favored; not [the path] of those who earn Thine anger nor of those who go astray."

With some conclusions derived from the second commandment, "Thou shalt not take the name of the Lord thy God in vain," all would agree; other conclusions based on this commandment, however, have been disputed.

On the matter of oaths, for instance, everyone accepts that oaths in general are binding. The binding force of a judiciary oath, however, when telling the truth would result in harm to oneself or one's relatives, has been seriously disputed. Many, too, have questioned the validity of a promissory oath taken under duress, or taken to commit a sin. In these special cases there is a conflict between the binding force of an oath and some other right or obligation. The correct solutions can be classified as remote conclusions of the natural law.

Mohammed correctly solves the first type of special case by teaching that man must tell the truth under oath not only in general but also even when personal loss, ties of blood, friendship, etc., might prompt him to waver. Considerations such as family ties do not excuse us from truth under oath. "Observe justice when ye bear witness before God, although it be against yourselves, or [your] parents or [your] kindred, whether [the case be of] a rich man or a poor man. . . . So follow not passion lest ye lapse [from truth] and if ye lapse or fall away, then lo! Allah is ever informed of what ye do" (sura 4:135).

There are certain special qualifications to the binding force of a promissory oath. The simple fact that a promissory oath has been taken does not mean that the person who has taken it is bound. Confucius rightly points out that a person who has been forced to take a promissory oath is not bound to observe it. "An oath under duress is disregarded by the gods."[51]

Similarly, Islam holds that a promissory oath to do what is sinful is not binding before God.[52]

The third commandment, "Remember that thou keep holy the sabbath day," is the only commandment which does not deal directly with a primary conclusion of natural law. Under the third commandment, however, can be placed the laws of nature pertaining to public or social worship. Men in general are required at least to offer some kind of worship to God.

However, the necessity of authority on this point might be disputed in good faith. Should each individual be allowed complete freedom to follow the dictates of his own emotions in the worship of God, or should there be some common regulation of this worship?

Plato rightly answers that men should be free to choose the form of worship that appeals to them, but that this freedom should not be anarchy. It should be supervised. Not everyone's inclinations will guide him infallibly into a fitting and decent manner of worshipping God. Not all men should be "allowed to practice religious rites (of their own devising). . . . No man shall have sacred rites in a private house. When he would sacrifice, let him go to the temples and hand over his offerings to the priests and priestesses, who see to the sanctity of such things. . . . The reason of this is as follows:—Gods and temples are not easily instituted, and to establish them rightly is the work of mighty intellects. And women especially, and men too, when they are sick or in any kind of danger, or again on their receiving any good fortune, have a way of consecrating the occasion . . . promising shrines to gods, demigods, and sons of gods . . . and will fill every house and village with them. . . . The law has also regard to the impious, and would not have them fancy that by the secret performance of these actions—by raising temples and by building altars in private houses, they can propitiate the gods secretly with sacrifices and prayers."[53]

The fourth commandment, "Honor thy father and thy mother," requires determination in special cases where there is a conflict with another principle.

What if parents were to command their children to commit a serious sin against natural law? Which takes precedence—obedience to parents, or avoidance of the sin? Christianity says it is the latter. But Plutarch, too, speaks approvingly of a certain Acrotatus who had refused when his parents commanded him to join in some unjust action.[54]

The fifth commandment, "Thou shalt not kill," deals directly with murder. The direct killing of an innocent person is wrong.

Christianity teaches that this prohibition is absolute, that under no circumstances may an innocent person be killed directly. This strict Christian teaching is not entirely without parallel even among the pagans. Seneca cited (if only to try to refute them) certain men of his time who believed that suicide was never justifiable. These men, according to Seneca, "maintain that one should not offer violence to one's own life, and hold it accursed for a man to be a means of his own destruction; we should wait, they say, for the end decreed by nature."[55]

And regarding the guilty, what about those who have previously inflicted injury on another? Is revenge licit? The

Lord said, "If someone strike thee on the right cheek, turn to him the other also; and if anyone would go to law with thee and take thy tunic, let him take thy cloak as well; and whoever forces thee to go for one mile, go with him two. . . . Love your enemies, do good to those who hate you, and pray for those who persecute and calumniate you" (Matt. 5:39–44); "Bless those who curse you" (Luke 6:28). Certainly many have disagreed with Christianity on this point. "An eye for an eye" is perhaps the prevailing axiom among most men. It is, however, startling to find that some of the pagans did come remarkably close to the teaching of Christ on the point. Plutarch says "To revenge an injury and to do an injury . . . both . . . originally proceed from the same deficiency and weakness."[56] Marcus Aurelius says "It is thy duty not to be disturbed or to show anger toward those who are angry with thee."[57] Going farther east, we find even more striking parallels. Where Plutarch and Marcus Aurelius merely prohibit anger toward enemies, some in the East command love. A Buddhist writing declares, "Hatreds never cease by hatred in this world. By love alone, they cease. This is an eternal law."[58] Brahmanism teaches, "Let him [the ascetic] patiently bear hard words, let him not insult anybody, and let him not become anybody's enemy for the sake of this [perishable] body. Against an angry man let him not in return show anger, let him bless when he is cursed."[59]

The virtue of temperance has implications not only for the soul but also for the body. This relationship of temperance to bodily well-being brings temperance under the fifth commandment.

Pagans have not confined themselves simply to recommending temperance in general terms. More specifically, some have made accurate and forceful statements on the various effects, even in this life, of both temperance and its contrary vice. The *Laws of Manu* give one of the earthly motives for temperance: "He who desires happiness must . . . control himself."[60] Other pagans present earthly deterrents to intemperance. Homer said, "There is no satiating the greedy paunch."[61] Seneca writes, "Gluttony, drunkenness and other indulgences . . . kill by giving pleasure."[62]

The sixth commandment, "Thou shalt not commit adultery," like the others, contains many remote principles which are not the exclusive property of Christianity. Here again are some which we are wrongly accustomed to think of as being alien to all forms of paganism.

Christian teaching on the nature and stability of marriage is echoed by some pagan writings. Christ taught that marriage is completely indissoluble by human authority. "Have you not read that the Creator, from the beginning, made them male and female, and said, 'For this cause a man shall leave his father and mother, and cleave to his wife, and the two shall become one flesh?' Therefore now they are no longer two but one flesh. What therefore God has joined together let no man put asunder" (Matt. 19:4–6). The *Laws of Manu* say "Thus [says the Veda], and [learned] Brahmans propound this [maxim] likewise, 'The husband is declared to be one with the wife.' "[63] Though Hinduism allows divorce,[64] we still find a strong statement on the stability of marriage. "Let mutual fidelity continue until death; this may be considered as the summary of the highest law for husband and wife."[65] Among the West African Fulah, if a man repudiates his wife the women attack him *en masse*.[66] And certain primitive peoples prohibit divorce absolutely.[67]

On rights and duties within marriage, Christianity teaches that contraception is not only wrong in general, or in most cases, but in all cases. Orthodox Judaism teaches the same.[68] Every method of contraception is forbidden and in all circumstances.[69]

Some pagans, too, agree with Christianity on the relative value of virginity and marriage. Both Christianity and almost all non-Christian groups praise marriage. Christianity holds, however, that virginity undertaken for love of God is even superior to marriage (Matt. 19:10–12; 1 Cor. 7:7–8, 17, 25–7, 32–4, 37–40). But this idea of the superiority of virginity is by no means the exclusive property of Christianity. Among the ancient Romans, the vestal virgins took a vow of perfect chastity for thirty years. They were free to marry after the thirty years but they very rarely did so.[70] They were in a position of honor in the state. An idea of the esteem in which they were held can be obtained from the fact that even the great Seneca calls them the "noblest maidens."[71]

Plato makes several accurate judgments on remote conclusions of the natural law which fall under the seventh commandment.

The seventh commandment, "Thou shalt not steal," prohibits theft and cooperation in theft. Thus not only the thief himself, but also those who have commanded, or counseled, or participated in any way in the theft embrace to some extent the malice of the sin. Similarly, he who knowingly receives goods which are stolen is at least partially guilty. The exact extent of the guilt of a receiver of stolen goods is probably only a remote conclusion of the natural law. Plato rightly says that he who knowingly receives stolen goods is equally guilty with the thief. "If any one knowingly receives anything which has been stolen, he shall receive the same punishment as the thief."[72]

In cases where theft has already been committed, the seventh commandment prescribes restitution by the guilty party to the one who has been robbed. Many principles relating to restitution can be classified as remote conclusions of natural law.

On one such case, Plato makes an accurate distinction.

He was speaking of principles concerning the practice of slavery, which was common in his day. But what he says of the buying and selling of slaves shows a correct understanding of the detailed principles of natural law on buying and selling in general. He says, "If a man sells a slave who is in a consumption, or who has a disease of the stone . . . or some other tedious and incurable disorder of body or mind, which is not discernible to the ordinary man, if the purchaser be a physician or trainer, he shall have no right of restitution. But if a skilled person sells to another who is not skilled, let the buyer appeal for restitution within six months, except in case of epilepsy and then the appeal may be made within a year."[73]

The eighth commandment, "Thou shalt not bear false witness against thy neighbor," prohibits, in a general way, besides slander, the sins of detraction, contumely, etc.

In slander, a lie is involved. A fault is imputed to another when it does not exist in him. In detraction, there is no lie. The fault, in detraction, either truly exists or at least is thought to exist in the other person. There are special cases in which revealing the faults of another is licit. One of these is correctly noted in the Koran: "God loveth not that evil should be noised abroad in public speech except where injustice hath been done" (sura 4:148). One who has been seriously wronged by another may reveal the other person's faults as a means of obtaining justice.

Contumely consists in unjustly dishonoring another person in that other's presence. The *Laws of Manu* correctly apply this general prohibition to a special case. "Let him not even though in pain [speak words] cutting [others] to the quick."[74]

The ninth and tenth commandments, "Thou shalt not covet thy neighbor's wife" and "Thou shalt not covet thy neighbor's goods," prohibit sins of thought. All would agree that the simple intention to commit a sin is itself a sin. Many, however, have been in doubt concerning a further question: What about those who relish internally the malice of an external sin, but without making the intention of ever positing the sinful act or omission itself? Few non-Christians have agreed with Christ that such thoughts are sinful.[75] In Islam, however, there are at least some who feel that sin can be involved in such thoughts.[76]

There is not, then, a vast number of remote conclusions of the natural law which are absolutely unknown to non-Christians. Those ethical teachings which we often think of as the exclusive property of Christianity can in fact be found among at least some non-Christian peoples.

These teachings of the pagans on obscure points of natural law are not to be understood as completely identical in all details with the teaching of Christianity on these same points. There are discrepancies in detail. They are more approximations to than duplications of Christian teaching on these points.

Nevertheless, the surprising fact remains that the remote conclusions of the natural law, even some of those which are the most difficult to uncover, can be and have been discovered by non-Christian philosophers and religious leaders, at times even without the aid of revelation.

There are many remote conclusions which are widely known, not only to Christians but also to non-Christians. The ancient Roman religion,[77] Brahmanism,[78] Islam and other non-Catholic religions have legislated against usury, for instance. Ignorance of these conclusions is not necessarily almost universal.

The fact that a prescription of natural law is classified as remote does not mean that it is unknowable and unknown without revelation. Even the most remote conclusions have been discovered by philosophers who have had no contact

with the Bible. And other less obscure but still remote conclusions have been known by a great number of non-Christians. To be sure, invincible ignorance of them, even for a
long time, is possible. But invincible ignorance of these remote precepts need not be taken for granted in all pagans.
Some pagans who violate even these obscure conclusions of
natural law may be doing so knowingly and in bad faith.

Many of the secondary conclusions of natural law, then,
have been and are known by great numbers of pagans. But
there would seem to be one upper limit to the knowledge of
the remote conclusions by those out of touch with revelation:
as yet, no non-Christian individual (or group) has been discovered who knew the entire gamut of the remote conclusions of the natural law. Many remote conclusions have
been known by many non-Christians. Even most remote
conclusions have been known to some pagan philosophers.
But as yet, no one who knew them all has been found among
the pagans.

To sum up the discussion of invincible ignorance of secondary conclusions, invincible ignorance of these conclusions
can be exaggerated. Some erroneously suppose that without
revelation no one can discover any of these conclusions by
the use of reason alone. In fact, however, pagans without
revelation can and have discovered many of these conclusions. And many pagans, knowing these moral laws, will be
judged by God according to whether or not they observe
them.

Still, invincible ignorance of these remote conclusions is
possible even for a long time. And no pagan as yet has been
found who, without the use of revelation, has discovered
them all.

From the above summary, a striking possibility arises: a
man without revelation could violate many remote conclusions of natural law during his life, and remain in invincible

ignorance of the malice of these violations during his entire lifetime; thus, conceivably, he would die blameless before God (i.e., subjectively or formally innocent) with respect to these violations, even though he had been objectively or materially guilty of them.

CHAPTER TWO

Primary Conclusions of Natural Law

1. *The Potential Significance of Primary Conclusions*

As important as the secondary conclusions are, the primary conclusions could be far more so. The primary conclusions of natural law are not discovered by a more or less difficult process of reason; they are discovered easily. A person can have invincible ignorance of them for a time; but it is impossible for one who has developed reasoning powers to remain in invincible ignorance of them for a long time. It is this last phrase which can make the primary conclusions of natural law assume tremendous significance. The fact that many men can remain in invincible ignorance of secondary conclusions even for a lifetime diminishes somewhat the importance of these secondary conclusions as natural laws binding all men regardless of the society in which they live. They bind all men theoretically, but not all in practice. But men cannot remain in such lengthy invincible ignorance of the primary conclusions. Primary conclusions are not laws which bind all men only theoretically, but are laws which do so subjectively and in practice. All men must in time come to a knowledge of them and must observe them when they do learn of them.

From this last statement two significant conclusions follow:

The fact that all men must, in time, come to a knowledge and acceptance of these primary conclusions gives us a universally acceptable criterion of holiness. The primary conclusions of natural law are so evident that not only Catholics but all men who are honestly trying to find truth accept them as valid moral laws. Thus, on a theoretical level, we have a criterion by which all such men can distinguish a holy religion from an unholy one: a holy religion is one whose moral laws are in agreement with the primary conclusions of natural law; and an unholy religion is one which tolerates (or commands) the violation of one or more of the primary conclusions of natural law.

Secondly, the fact that all men must observe the primary conclusions of natural law gives a pressing reason for the Catholic apostolate in any society which tolerates the violation of a primary conclusion on a wide scale. Such toleration encourages many men to fall into sins of whose malice they cannot remain unaware for a long time. And if they do fall into these sins and remain in them for a long time, they will be guilty. If this guilt is serious, they will be subject to eternal punishment in the next life. Such men are in grave need of the teaching of the Church. For the Church, by inculcating firmly the necessity of the observance of all the primary conclusions of natural law, will add the human voice of the missionary to the voice of conscience, informing these men that their society erred in not warning them to avoid their sins.

The force of the two significant conclusions above, however, depends on several factors. First, what are the primary conclusions, and are they sufficiently detailed so that they do find their way into codes of moral law, so that some societies are in the embarrassing position of having some law or laws on the books which tolerate the violation of a primary conclusion of natural law, or are these conclusions mere platitudes? Secondly, how specific can we be in defining "a long time"? Thirdly, is "developed powers of reason" a phrase which includes most men, or does it, on the contrary, exclude them, thus, in effect, releasing most men from the binding force of the primary conclusions? Fourthly, to what extent can the guilt of violating primary conclusions be serious? And fifthly, to what extent do non-Catholic religions tolerate the violation of primary conclusions of natural law?

The significance of the primary conclusions as a criterion of holiness and as a motive for Catholic evangelization depends on the answers to these questions. The remainder of Part I of this book will endeavor to answer them in so far as it is possible.

2. *A List and Explanation of Some Primary Conclusions*

Before defining the meaning of "developed powers of reason" in this context, it is necessary first to see in detail what is expected of the reasoning faculty: What are some of these primary conclusions of natural law, and why do we say that they are so obvious?

First of all, when we say that they are obvious we do not mean that all men can easily formulate these conclusions in precise language, nor do we mean that all men can easily formulate in detail all the reasons why these conclusions are valid. Many men may not be able to give a detailed list of reasons and may not even be able to put the conclusions themselves into words. But all men (i.e., those with a developed use of reason) will have these conclusions implanted in their hearts. These conclusions will be obvious to them, even though they are unable to express them in words or to frame the reasons for them.

The list of primary conclusions which follows is by no

means intended to be exhaustive. It will be confined to a selection of some of the primary conclusions which previous Catholic writings have already identified as such.

To confine the list within these limits, of course, exposes it to the objection that the conclusions are derived not from right reason but from the arbitrary teaching of Catholics on the point. Suffice it to say that the Catholics who have previously presented these conclusions did so, not arbitrarily, but because they were obvious to all who possessed developed powers of reason. This will be evident when we see the conclusions themselves in detail.

The reason, however, for limiting the list in this way is that since this is the first time such a list has been compiled, extra caution is justifiable. Secondly, even the smaller list serves our purpose of providing a practical and necessary criterion of holiness for all men. Later studies will, I hope, develop and expand this list.

A. RELIGIOUS ASSENT

The first of these primary conclusions is the obligation of acceptance of the existence of God. (The natural virtue which consists in the fulfillment of this obligation we shall call "religious assent." The term religious assent is equivalent to the concept of a natural faith. But because of the danger of confusion of natural faith with supernatural faith, we shall avoid using the words faith and belief, and use in their place "religious assent," and "acceptance of God.") Religious assent is required of all men. There are many questions about the nature of religious assent on which men may sincerely disagree. It is evident, however, that all men must acknowledge one God who is both Creator and Remunerator.[1]

This prescription, as we have defined it, deals directly with thought and only indirectly with action. The carrying out of this intellectual acknowledgment of God into acts of worship of Him is governed directly by the first and third commandments and not by the virtue of religious assent.

The primary conclusion "All men must acknowledge one God who is both Creator and Remunerator" has a great many implications.

The word "acknowledge" distinguishes religious assent from simple opinion. A firm assent is required. A simple opinion that God exists is not enough. Opinion allows reasonable doubt. In the act of religious assent, there can be no reasonable doubt. Religious assent is a firm assent with no admixture of reasonable doubt.

The notion of religious assent can be treated positively or negatively. Positively it relates to the making of the internal act of religious assent. This positive act of religious assent is required of all reasoning men.[2]

We shall, however, treat this primary conclusion of natural law chiefly from a negative point of view. There are a great many sins of intellect which are directly opposed to this primary conclusion requiring religious assent.

First, atheism is forbidden by it. Atheism is the complete denial of existence of any Creator or Supreme Being.

Atheism can arise from a refusal to accept the existence of anything which cannot be perceived by the senses, from a refusal to accept anything superior to man, etc.

A person who is reductively an atheist is one who admits a God but denies that this God is a person, i.e., has intellect and will.[3] For such a person, God is a thing or a force, not an intelligent self-directing person.

One variation of atheism is pantheism. According to pantheism, God and the world are one. All earthly objects are not really distinct from one another nor from God but are nothing more than a manifestation of Him. They are God. Similarly, human personality is merely an illusion; the individual man is merely one fragment of the Divine Being.

God is not a person, an intelligent Creator and Governor. God is an infinite substance or self-evolving energy, forever changing and advancing and helpless to determine the direction in which the advance shall take place. No strict pantheist can have the minimum requirements for true religious assent.[4]

Atheism and pantheism consist essentially in a denial of the existence of any being superior to man. The error here is obvious. No brainless "it" put order in the universe, and even if this error were not obvious to our intellects, our hearts would still tell us of the existence of the Superior Being.

Those who deny one or more of the principle attributes of God (providence, wisdom, goodness, eternity, etc.) also are in opposition to this primary conclusion of natural law.[5] These errors, like those of atheism and pantheism, are repugnant both to the human intellect and the promptings of the human heart, and hardly need refutation. All men can easily perceive that a God who creates without a plan or good purpose in mind is no God at all. And such a creation is meaningless. Those who deny this use reason to show everything is without reason. According to a primary conclusion of natural law on religious assent, men of good will may differ on the exact nature of God's plan for His creatures and the exact position of man in this plan, but they may not remain in good faith and deny that there is at least some plan and that according to it He governs the universe and directs the course of human affairs with a definite purpose and with a beneficent design.

The word "Remunerator" in the statement of the primary conclusion above is also of importance. The word does not refer to a merely earthly remunerator.[6] It brings into the concept of religious assent the idea of the next life. God will reward the good and punish the wicked in the next life. And one who thinks of God's justice exclusively in terms of this life is not fulfilling the precept. This error can be called "annihilationism." All reasoning men can easily see that justice is not always perfectly carried out in this life, that on the contrary many good men receive little or no reward in this life and many evil men receive little or no punishment here. (See treatment of this p. 16.) To look to this life alone for God's rewards and punishments is to deny that He is a just Remunerator. To deny that He is a just Remunerator, is to deny that He is a Remunerator at all. All reasoning men can easily see that God is an all-just Remunerator and that therefore He must reward and punish, to some extent at least, in a next life.

However, this does not mean that all men will easily be able to discover that heaven and hell are eternal or to discover the nature of the rewards and punishments. Merely because we can prove that the sanction is eternal, for example, does not mean that all men of good will must reach the same conclusion. This conclusion is not obvious. Men can disagree on the duration and nature of future reward and punishment, and still not be opposed to the primary conclusion that God is a Remunerator. Opposition to this primary conclusion is brought about by a complete denial of all future rewards and punishments.

The concept of a Remunerator refers to the future life. It also, of its nature, implies that reward and punishment are personal. The person on earth who performs acts deserving reward or punishment will himself receive this reward or punishment in the future life. His conscious self will perdure into the next life. One who accepts immortality but only that type of immortality which consists in a reabsorption resulting in complete annihilation of personality and person, obviously does not truly accept future reward and punishment. For such a person, there is really no future reward or punishment.

Similarly, one who admits personal immortality but denies

that there will be rewards and punishments of any kind in the next life has no faith in God as Remunerator. And the same is to be said of one who admits personal immortality but holds that God will reward all and will punish no one in the next life. God must be a just Remunerator.

The above errors, atheism, pantheism, etc., consist in a denial of some essential element of the primary conclusion: "All men must acknowledge one God who is both Creator and Remunerator." But there are other ways of opposing this conclusion apart from a complete denial of it. These are the various forms of agnosticism. An agnostic does not deny that God is One, Personal, etc. He simply claims ignorance and deliberately and completely suspends judgment on one or more of these points. He makes no act of religious assent. A person can be an agnostic by claiming ignorance of whether God exists, of whether God is a person, a Creator, or a Remunerator. Any one of these forms of agnosticism is, like atheism and the other sinful opinions above, opposed to a primary conclusion of natural law. The hearts of all men with developed powers of reason tell them of the existence of God who is the One Creator and Remunerator. To refuse to make any decision on this, just as to deny it altogether, is to act contrary to an awareness of a supreme being present in all men.

Atheism, pantheism, agnosticism and the other errors listed above seem to be more characteristic of civilized and educated men.[7] Even among this latter group, these errors are not usually characteristic of an entire society. They are the misconceptions of individuals. One man or a small group of men will hold themselves to be more "enlightened" than the others in their society, and in opposition to the conviction of the vast majority, will embrace some such error as atheism or agnosticism. To be sure, some large groups, sometimes even a group of primitive peoples, have been accused as a group of adhering to these errors. Buddhists have been accused of atheism; Brahmanism, of pantheism, etc. But on close inspection it has been observed that in each case, these errors have not sifted down into the rank and file. Though the theoretical teaching of the moral system of the society might be atheistic or pantheistic, in practice the majority of the members of these systems do not adhere to these errors.

There are other errors which are opposed to this primary conclusion of natural law relating to the existence of God, however, which are found more frequently among primitive peoples than among the civilized.

The first of these is polytheism, or acceptance of many independent gods. The word independent is crucial in distinguishing polytheism from monotheism. That religious concept in which there are many gods but in which all but one of these gods are considered as being absolutely dependent on and subject to one supreme God is not polytheism in the sense in which we are using the term. Frequently such a religious concept is described as polytheism, but this description is somewhat misleading. Basically such a teaching is monotheistic. One God is supreme, and other beings which are called "gods" are really no more than creatures entirely subordinate to the supreme God.

Polytheism as it is understood here will refer only to those creeds in which there are many gods, each *independent* of each other and each with complete and unqualified dominion over its segment of nature. This "strict polytheism" could have one god ruling the sea, another ruling vegetable life, another the stars, etc. It could have various gods ruling each of the virtues, or the passions, or even the vices, and considered as the source and director of these. It could have some gods ruling categories of earthly events: war, peace, travel, etc. Strict polytheism is opposed to the primary conclusion of natural law requiring all men to acknowledge the existence of God.[8]

Strict polytheism is, at its root, atheism. All men can easily see that if there is no supreme God ruling all things, then there is no Creator or Organizer at all. If there is no Being who rules all men and all spirits, then all is chaos.

The second religious error common among primitive peoples is that of fetishism, the attributing of divinity or of divine powers directly to some creature which can be perceived by the senses. Fetishism ascribes divinity to the heavenly bodies (i.e., the sun, stars, planets, etc.), to other inanimate objects, or to vegetable, animal, or even human life. Fetishism is distinguished from polytheism, above, in that in polytheism the divinity is not considered as attached in some way to a particular physical object. Fetishism embraces creeds which consider that independent gods or divine powers inhabit the sun, moon, stars, stones, mountains, manmade idols, rivers, trees, animals, men, etc.

Strict fetishism would restrict various independent gods each to certain material objects. The note of divinity is considered as inhering in the material object. Sometimes the god is thought to be so confined to the object that it is impossible for him to escape.

Sometimes, in strict fetishism, even the greatest of the independent gods can be considered as restricted to a material object. This appears to be true of the sun-god of ancient Egypt. Some Egyptians considered the visible sun in the sky to be the only residence of the supreme god in their pantheon. Most often, however, the fetish is not thought to contain the greatest god but one of the lesser independent gods.

Strict fetishism (like strict polytheism) would refer to acknowledgment of fetishes which are thought to have independent jurisdiction over some field of the activity of creatures, or of fetishes which are thought to possess one divine attribute to the exclusion of the other divine attributes. Thus, an object which is thought to have intrinsically the power to heal all diseases in a divine and instantaneous manner would be a fetish in the strict sense. In the history of man, almost every substance on earth at some time or other has been said by some peoples to have this power.[9]

Strict fetishism is basically so alien to Western culture to-day that it seems almost subhuman. One asks, "How is it even possible?" "How can its origin and continuance among so many peoples in history be accounted for?" There are many motives for strict fetishism. Some of these are: an exaggerated admiration for the power and grandeur of natural creatures or for the beauty of man-made objects; the fact that unlike monotheism it permits a feeling of superiority of man over god; simple sluggishness in overcoming the effects of fetishistic instruction; desire for novelty; etc. Strict fetishism is not a psychological impossibility.

The error of fetishism is more obvious even than that of polytheism. The same reasoning which exposes the error of polytheism does so for fetishism. In addition, there are still other factors which make fetishism a more difficult sin to commit. To convince oneself that a group of rocks, sticks, or trees contains independent gods requires a more violent abuse of the faculty of reason than to do so of a group of imagined extra-material spirits. The manifest error of fetishism has been described in the Bible. (Here we are using the Bible not as an inspired authoritative source of dogma, but only as a human expression of the manifest error of fetishism.) In the Old Testament, the book of Wisdom has: "But all men are vain in whom there is not the knowledge of God: and who by these good things that are seen could not understand him that is. Neither by attending to the works have they acknowledged who was the workman: But have imagined either the fire, or the wind, or the swift air, or the circle of the stars, or the great water, or the sun and moon to be the gods that rule the world. With whose

beauty, if they being delighted, took them to be gods. . . .
But unhappy are they, and their hope is among the dead"
(Wisdom 13:1–3,10).

In the New Testament, St. Paul says "For the wrath of
God is revealed from heaven against all ungodliness and
wickedness of those men who in wickedness hold back the
truth of God, seeing that what may be known about God is
manifest to them. For God has manifested it to them. For
since the creation of the world his invisible attributes are
clearly seen—his everlasting power also and divinity—being
understood through the things that are made. And so they are
without excuse, seeing that, although they knew God, they
did not glorify him as God or give thanks, but became vain
in their reasonings, and their senseless minds have been
darkened. For while professing to be wise, they have become
fools and they have changed the glory of the incorruptible
God for an image made like unto man and to birds and four-
footed beasts and creeping things" (Rom. 1:18–23).

St. Gregory of Nyssa specifies the precise manner in which
those who believe in fetishes become "vain in their reasonings." "Seeing that they, with their untrained and narrow
intelligence, were disposed to look with wonder on the
beauties of nature, not employing the things they beheld as
a leader and guide to the beauty of the Nature that transcends them, they rather made their intelligence halt on
arriving at the objects of its apprehension, and marveled at
each part of the creation severally—for this cause they did
not stay their conception of the Deity at any single one of
the things they beheld, but deemed everything they looked
on in creation to be divine."[10]

This analysis of the error of those believing in fetishes
can be applied to the violation of all the other primary conclusions of natural law. To remain in ignorance of any
primary conclusion for a long period of time, one must "make

his intelligence halt," and precisely in this act does his reasoning become vain.

All reasoning men can easily come to a knowledge that the sun, the fire, the birds, and other material, limited objects are not independent gods. No man can be inculpably ignorant for a long time of the malice of strict fetishism. Strict fetishism, then, even though it is seemingly embraced by many people, is opposed to a primary conclusion of natural law.

B. MORAL EFFORT

The primary conclusion of natural law relating to the virtue of moral effort is a natural consequence of that relating to religious assent. Men must not only acknowledge the existence of God; they must strive to discover and obey any laws He may have laid down for men.

One way in which this primary conclusion can be opposed is by a complete denial of the value and necessity of moral effort. Such a denial was put forward by a Spanish priest named Michael Molinos in the seventeenth century. (It might be thought that the Hindus and Buddhists, with their doctrine of denial of desire, would deny entirely the necessity of moral effort. But, as we have noted previously, this is not true. As a group, the members of these religions very definitely have a notion of the necessity of effort in moral life.) Michael Molinos set forth his doctrine, not as a move toward a more lax code of morality, but ostensibly as a step toward perfection. He taught that to arrive at the state of perfection and perfect love for God, it was essential to lay aside all self-love to such an extent that one became indifferent to one's own spiritual progress, salvation, or damnation.[11] All personal moral effort should be suppressed. One should forget self and concentrate on God to the extent that one no longer made a conscious effort for virtue but placed oneself in the hands of God to be carried through moral life completely under inspiration from Him. The human agent was to remain passive, allowing God to do the active work of carrying the soul through temptation.

This error is a species of presumption. (Here we are speaking of presumption in the context of natural law, not of the theological virtue of hope.) Presumption, as the word is used here, will refer to any suspension of moral effort due to spiritual overconfidence. The overconfidence of Molinos' teaching lies in exaggerating the strength and frequency of God's unsolicited graces. Another form of presumption would be that caused by overconfidence in one's reward in the next life.

The primary conclusion that all men must use moral effort is not only opposed by presumption, but also by despair. In despair, one abandons hope for any reward in the next life and therefore abandons moral effort as useless. The sin of despair is a defect of confidence. Despair does not refer to a momentary or unreasoning fear of abandonment by God, but to a permanent conviction of this abandonment. Despair can arise through any of a variety of motives. A man can despair through a conviction that God will not forgive him, because of the number or gravity of his sins. He can despair because he feels that he has previously and unalterably been destined by God for punishment in the next life, regardless of his actions in this life.

Failure to use moral effort, whether this failure arises from presumption or despair, can easily be perceived as evil. Regardless of his state of soul, everyone can easily perceive the error of abandoning the struggle to persevere and to improve. And if this error is not seen immediately, time will expose it to view by bringing out its necessary effect: the disintegration of virtue.

C. BENEVOLENCE

Just as all men are bound by a primary conclusion of natural law to religious assent and moral effort, so too all men are bound to have the virtue[12] of benevolence. It is an obvious conclusion of natural law that we should love God, ourselves and our neighbor and that we should express this love to those in need by performing the corporal works of mercy (feeding the hungry, sheltering the homeless, etc.) in so far as we are able. Love of neighbor should be for his own sake, not for what we can gain from him. The relation of love of self and of neighbor to natural law has not been dealt with extensively by Catholic theologians. In particular, the answer to the question, "Who is my neighbor?" has never been definitively explained in terms of primary and secondary conclusions of natural law. Certainly, some details of the answer to this question would be only secondary or remote conclusions. Because of the unsettled nature of the relationship, however, we shall not attempt to develop it here. Suffice it to say that it is a primary conclusion of natural law that all men must have love for themselves and also love their neighbors and help those in need. And hatred of self or of neighbor is forbidden by that same conclusion.

D. FIRST COMMANDMENT

Again, the list of primary conclusions given above does not exhaust the number of primary conclusions of natural law associated with the virtues of faith, hope, and charity. The same will be true of the list of conclusions associated with the Decalogue, below. The list is intended to be no more than fragmentary.

The first commandment of the Decalogue is a negative one. It prohibits the worship of false gods. One of the primary conclusions associated with this commandment is a corollary of the one above pertaining to faith. By the precept of faith, every man capable of reasoning is forbidden to assent to polytheism or fetishism of any sort. By the first commandment, every man capable of reasoning is forbidden to put this assent into practice by the sin of idolatry. Idolatry is the actual worship of a false god, whether this god is thought to be immaterial or whether it is thought to be contained in a material object. (Idolatry, as the term is used here, does not require that the god worshiped be visible.)

Idolatry is not identical with polytheism or fetishism. In these last sins, there is belief in false gods. In idolatry, there is worship of them, that is, positive acts of honor and submission are made to the false gods.

Idolatry may or may not include the sins of polytheism or fetishism. If it does, there is worship of a false god, to which god divinity is deliberately attributed. If it does not, the god is worshiped, not as a god, but for some extrinsic motive, v.g., to manifest hatred of the true God who is recognized, or as a means of gratifying some depraved impulse. In his customary strong and blunt fashion, Tertullian gives us his ideas on what some of these latter impulses might be. In his *On Idolatry*, written about 211 A.D.,[13] he says, "The principal crime of the human race, the highest guilt charged upon the world, the whole procuring cause of judgment, is idolatry. For, although each single fault retains its own proper feature, although it is destined to judgment under its own proper name also, yet it is marked off under the general account of idolatry. . . . You may recognize in idolatry: adultery and fornication; for he who serves false gods is doubtless an adulterator of truth because all falsehood is adultery. So too, he is sunk in fornication. For who that is a fellow-worker with unclean spirits does not stalk in general pollution and fornication? And thus it is that the Holy Scriptures use the designation of fornication in their upbraiding of idolatry. . . . Idolatry does fraud to God by refusing to Him, and conferring on others, His honors; so that to fraud it also conjoins contumely. . . . In [idolatry] also are the concupiscences of the world. For what solemnity of idolatry is without the circumstance of dress and ornament? In it are lasciviousness and drunkenness; since it is, for the most part, for the sake of food, and stomach, and appetite that these solemnities are frequented. . . . In it is mendacity, for its whole substance is false. Thus it comes to pass, that in idolatry all crimes are detected."[14]

Sometimes, then, idolatry is committed in direct injury to God, either by choosing to worship false gods as gods or by worshiping them out of hatred for God. In other cases idolatry is an insult to God only in an indirect manner, where some other sin (drunkenness, fornication, etc.) is directly sought after in worshipping idols and where there is no direct intention to insult God. Either way, the sin is committed freely and culpably. (We prescind, however, from treating a third possibility, where a monotheist is forced by a civil government to worship idols but who internally withholds himself from consent to any worship.)

The malice of idolatry, as we have defined it, cannot remain unknown to any reasoning man of good will. Idolatry is opposed to a primary precept of natural law.

E. SECOND COMMANDMENT

The second commandment, like the first, is a negative one. Where the first prohibits the worship of false gods, the second prohibits irreverence against the true God. Sins of irreverence against God are: temptation of God, blasphemy, perjury, and violation of a vow.

The first of these, temptation of God, is any word or deed by which a person challenges an attribute of God. In the strict sense (the sense we will be using here), temptation of

God has its origin in lack of faith, i.e., when a person doubts the reality of some divine attribute and proposes to put God to the test, as it were, to settle the doubt (v.g., for a farmer to neglect to cultivate his crops as a means of testing the existence of God's providence, or for a man to ask for a miracle as a condition *sine qua non* of his acknowledgment of the existence of God). Temptation of God, at least in the strict sense, can easily be seen by all men to constitute a grave insult to the Creator.

Blasphemy is contumely directed against God, or against creatures precisely because of their relationship to God. As the word will be used here, blasphemy refers only to those cases where contempt of God is intended, and not where the irreverence consists in the use of God's name as a mere exclamation or expletive. The contumely must be deliberate and in some way premeditated.

Irreverence against God can be committed by attributing to God some unbecoming quality (v.g., by saying that God plays favorites), by denying to God some perfection that does belong to Him (v.g., by proclaiming that He is not just or that He does not exercise providence over his creatures), by speaking the truth about God sarcastically or contemptuously, etc.

Blasphemy presupposes monotheism. It is possible for a pagan to insult his gods without being blasphemous. If a pagan insults gods, knowing in his heart that they are false, he is not a blasphemer.

True blasphemy is directed against the one true God, and fully deliberate blasphemy against one's God and Creator can easily be seen to be a perversion.

Perjury is the violation of an oath. In an oath, God is called upon to witness the truth of what is said. An oath is assertatory when God is called upon to witness the truth of a simple statement of fact. An oath is promissory when God is called to witness a promise or resolution.

In a vow, a free promise is made to God concerning a good which is possible and which is a greater good than its contradictory. A vow differs from a promissory oath in that in a vow the promise itself is made directly to God, and in a promissory oath the promise itself is made to someone other than God.

Perjury and the violation of vows can be committed for many reasons, v.g., to save the life of oneself or of another, to avoid inconvenience, to obtain wealth, or to show one's contempt for God and religion. As far as primary conclusions of natural law are concerned, however, at least one thing is certain: if the perjury or violation of the vow is committed with the specific intention of insulting or showing one's contempt for God, there is an evident violation of natural law.[15]

F. THIRD COMMANDMENT

The first two commandments of the Decalogue are negative. The third is positive. In the first two, the obstacles to true worship are removed; in the third, true worship is established. The third precept of the Decalogue commands men to worship the One God. As a primary precept of natural law, it can be phrased, "All men are bound to give both interior and exterior worship to God frequently."[16]

In worshiping God, we both honor Him and submit ourselves to Him. For true worship both the notes of honor and submission are necessary. Honor is the manifestation of respect or reverence for God. But in worship, there must be more than honor; honor can be paid to equals or inferiors. There must also be an act of submission by which we explicitly recognize our dependence on God and freely subordinate ourselves to Him whom we honor.

The failure to pay due worship to God is called religious indifference. Religious indifference is not to be confused with doctrinal indifference (failure to see the need of doctrines as a stabilizing force), or ethical indifference (failure to see the need of any set moral code).

The primary act of worship of God is adoration. Adoration is the conscious and explicit acknowledgment of God's infinite greatness and our utter dependence on Him. Here the motive of worship is God's greatness itself.

But it is not to be thought that adoration is the only form of true worship. In prayer, too, we worship God. Here, though, the worship is implicit. Explicitly in prayer we are either seeking something from God for ourselves or for someone else, or thanking God for some benefit already received. But true prayer does include an implicit act of honor and submission to God. Recognizing His existence and His providence, we acknowledge our dependence on Him in the benefits we receive. True prayer is itself an act of adoration.

Acts of adoration and prayers of petition or thanksgiving are all acts of worship whether they are expressed in a definite formula of words or not. Thus one can worship God whether he uses formulas taught to him by others or composed by himself, or whether he simply fixes his mind on God and submits to Him without formulating his thoughts in words at all.

An act of worship is not the same as an act of religious assent. In religious assent, we make an intellectual act of recognition of the excellence of God and of His position as Creator and Remunerator. In worship we add to religious assent an act of the will submitting ourselves to Him.

Among those who totally lack the virtue of religion are those who have no faith in the one God and consequently fail to worship Him. More properly though, religious indifference is predicated of those who have faith in God but fail to worship Him.

Complete failure to worship God can arise out of simple sloth, or from a rationalization.

There has been a variety of attempts to rationalize away

the worship of God. Some (v.g., Kant) have denied the necessity of worshipping God because they have convinced themselves that positive virtue consists entirely in doing good to man. One must avoid disrespect for God, but there are no positive obligations toward Him. No one who does attempt to worship God will ever gain merit by it, or gain what he asks for by virtue of the prayer itself. All worship, in itself, is fruitless. Moreover, all who do worship are guilty of indulging in superstition. All worship is superstition.

Others prescind from worship. It is enough to believe in God, they say. An occasional intellectual recognition of the existence of God as Creator and Remunerator is sufficient. There is no need to make a further act of the will submitting oneself to Him.

Still others (v.g., Schleiermacher) fail to worship God because they refuse to understand what true worship is. Worship, they say, is an experience of awe in the presence of something infinite and mysterious. It is more an emotion than an act of the will. It is a feeling that one receives, more than something given to God. This last group, too, fail to make positive acts of submission to God.

These are only a few of the rationalizations of failure to worship God. There have been many others, and many combinations of the ideas given above.

The obligation to worship one's Creator is so obvious that it is almost instinctive. When men turn their minds toward their Creator, almost involuntarily they include in their thoughts some act of honor and submission. It requires a positive act of the will to refrain completely from these acts of worship over a long period of time. As St. Paul says, worship is an obligation which arises in our hearts.

Reason can confirm the judgment of the heart in testifying to the obvious necessity of making acts of worship of God. The existence of this obligation can be illustrated by a parallel obligation. All men with the use of reason admit the obligation of honoring their parents or guardians. All would recognize as monstrous the person who, having been carefully nurtured and educated, upon reaching adulthood, left home, never once during his entire life to return or pay his respects in any way to those who had cared for him in youth.

The same is true of God, but even more so. The Creator has provided us with our principle of life, our soul. He sustains us in being all our lives. It would certainly be monstrous for us never to honor Him, but deliberately and completely to ignore Him during our entire lives. It is clear that all are bound to make at least internal acts of worship.

Not all men, of course, will be able to formulate these and the other reasons why they must worship God. But they will come to the same conclusion. The need for making positive acts of honor and submission to one's Creator is so obvious that it can almost be called instinctive.

In the statement of the primary conclusion above, we read that "at least internal acts of worship" are required. But is anything further needed? Is it also necessary to make acts of worship externally?

Internal worship is that in which only the mind acts; there is no physical or bodily participation (v.g., kneeling or movement of the lips) in the mental act of worship of God. (Some would dispute that strictly internal worship is even possible—since, they say, thought inevitably causes some minimal physical activity in the vocal cords or elsewhere.) External worship is that in which the body takes part in some way.

It is important that the external worship we are speaking of be distinguished from public or social worship, in which one man associates himself with other men in paying homage to God. (We prescind here from the question of the necessity of social worship by a primary conclusion of natural law.) External worship can be carried on either in public or in private. It consists in movements of the lips, the act of kneeling, bows, prostrations, etc., or in all of these.

External worship is required by a primary conclusion of natural law. Man, by nature, is not a disembodied spirit, nor is the soul his only essential part. His nature is composed of both body and soul, and they interact. The soul naturally works through the body. Thoughts, originating in the soul, tend to express themselves in external facial expressions, gestures, and attitudes of body. People vary in the extent to which they give external expression to their thoughts. But never to give any outward sign of a thought which is repeatedly brought to mind over a long period of time would require a positive act of repression. A man who frequently worshipped God interiorly would have to make a positive act of repression to prevent this worship from ever manifesting itself exteriorly.

And, *a posteriori,* internal worship will fail if it is not externalized. Man's thoughts tend to wander if they are denied their natural expression. The man who does not allow himself to worship God externally will soon find himself ignoring God altogether, both exteriorly and interiorly.

It is impossible for a reasoning man to remain in invincible ignorance for a long time of the necessity of both internal and external worship of the one God. Failure to make acts of internal and external worship is due either to conscious bad faith or to willful ignorance.

The manner in which this internal and external worship is to be given is not determined by the primary conclusion of natural law. Provided it is reverent, the natural law does not prescribe the exact way in which this honor is to be expressed. Formulas of prayer may vary widely. The actions may vary. One may use a ritual or a set form of prayers and gestures; another may worship impromptu. The Christian making the Sign of the Cross, the Moslem performing his *salát,* and the Buddhist turning his prayer wheel, if their actions are performed with the intention of honoring the one God, are all fulfilling this prescription of natural law.

Similarly the exact time, choice of day or hour, and the duration of each act of worship are not prescribed by natural law. Some men may prefer to make explicit acts of worship frequently but briefly during the day, and thus span the entire day with them. Others may choose to make only one or a few such acts but to make them more lengthy. Of the latter, some may choose the morning, others noon, others another part of the day to make these extended acts of worship.

Then, too, natural law does not prescribe any special time of the week or year for special observances. Some may choose the last day of the week, others the first, etc., for a special observance. Men may vary in their choice of days of the month, or of the seasons, or of the year, or in their choice of months or seasons or years themselves for special times of worship.

However, in the statement of the primary conclusion of natural law relating to the worship of God, there was the word frequently. Is one act of worship of God in a lifetime sufficient, or must this worship be offered frequently?

St. Thomas gives us the basis for an answer to this. He says, "There is in man a natural inclination to set aside a certain time for each necessary thing, such as refreshment of the body, sleep, and so forth. Hence, according to the dictate of reason, man sets aside a certain time for spiritual refreshment, by which man's mind is refreshed in God."[17]

The Latin word for refreshment, *refectio,* used by St. Thomas above, has the meaning of "food and rest." St. Thomas, then, draws a parallel between man's need for eating and sleeping, and his need to worship God. It is not without significance that each of the necessary functions of the body, cited by St. Thomas as parallel to the need of the soul for worship, are of very frequent occurrence. All of them must be performed much more often than once in a lifetime, and even much more often than once a year. They are daily necessities. Everybody generally needs daily refreshment and sleep.

Of its nature, the worship of God must be frequent. A man who worships God only occasionally and has deliberately ignored God for a long period of time, praying neither internally nor externally during that entire time, has no real concept of his dependence upon God. True worship implies that acts of worship play a real and vital part in one's life. All men must habitually live "under God" and continually acknowledge their dependence upon Him. The frequency of this worship may vary: some worshiping Him literally "without ceasing"; others recurrently. The species of worship, too, may vary: some worship being motivated by a direct desire to adore God; other worship, in the form of prayer, owing its origin to some human need. But whatever its degree of frequency or whatever its species, the worship of God must be frequent enough so that it plays a real and vital part in our lives. Anything less is simply religious indifference.

It is difficult or impossible to say precisely how often one must worship interiorly in order that the worship of God be a real and vital part of one's life. It would seem safe to say, however, that if a person found himself worshiping God interiorly or exteriorly only once or twice a year, that the worship of God would be no real and vital part of his life.

The extent of one's social or public worship is frequently a good criterion of the extent that one worships interiorly and exteriorly in private. Real faith and real orientation toward God tend almost necessarily to lead to expression of this in public in union with other men. The person in whose life the worship of God plays a real and vital part tends to gravitate toward the church, synagogue, mosque, or other place of public worship.

Thus the frequency of public worship—on the part of one who has the opportunity to take part in it (i.e., is not crippled, and lives in a community with other monotheists, etc.)—can be a good criterion of the frequency of interior and exterior worship in general. It would seem that one who has the opportunity to worship God socially and yet fails to attend any public religious service of any kind more than once or twice a year can be presumed to be violating this precept. In such a case, it can be presumed that there is no frequent interior or exterior worship of God and that the worship of God plays no vital role in that person's life.

It is evident to all adults that they must worship God, and worship Him frequently during life. Those who fail to do so cannot remain in invincible ignorance for a long time. It is a primary conclusion of natural law that all men worship God frequently, both interiorly and exteriorly.

G. FOURTH COMMANDMENT

The primary conclusions of natural law associated with the virtues of religious assent, moral effort, and benevolence, and the first three commandments of the Decalogue, in so far as they pertain to an obligation toward God, (i.e., excluding benevolence in so far as it pertains to our neighbor) are absolute. That is, there are no special circumstances under which an adult could remain in invincible ignorance of them (as they are defined above) for a long time. Prolonged ignorance of any of these conclusions by an adult must be culpable regardless of the circumstances.

The reason for this is that our obligation to acknowledge and honor God, at least internally, is easily seen to outweigh any conceivable conflicting obligations to any of His creatures. Conflicts can easily be resolved. It is very difficult, if not impossible, to have a very noble motive for an act which is opposed to the fulfillment of an obligation toward God. The motives for internal idolatry, deliberate blasphemy, neglect of even the private worship of God, can hardly compete with the motives for the contrary acts.

This is not true of the primary conclusions of natural law associated with the last seven commandments of the Decalogue. The last seven precepts of the Decalogue are directed toward fellow men. The precepts themselves are universal (v.g., Thou shalt not commit adultery—One may *never* justifiably kill an innocent man directly), but not obviously so.

They are universal because of the teaching of revelation and the demonstration of right reason. But the demonstration of right reason is not easy or obvious. The conflicts cannot always be resolved easily. This is so because the conflict is not always between a divine right and a human right as in the cases above, but between one human right with another human right. Can one commit adultery in order to save a life? The correct answer to such questions can be found by right reason, but only after much study and thought. The fact that these precepts should be universal is only a secondary or remote conclusion of natural law.

As primary or obvious conclusions of natural law, these precepts cannot be expressed in universals. They must be conditioned. But certain obvious qualified principles can still be formulated in connection with the last seven precepts of the Decalogue.[18]

It is possible to be in invincible ignorance for a long time of some special applications of the last seven precepts of the Decalogue, but not of the general principles themselves. No adult can remain in invincible ignorance of them as general principles, though many can be ignorant of the fact that they are absolute and of universal application. The universal application of many of these principles is only a secondary conclusion of natural law and as such can be unknown by an adult in good faith for long periods of time.

The fourth commandment covers, in general, the relations between those in authority and their subjects.

The primary conclusions of natural law relating to the obligations of children to their parents are an expression of the command "Honor thy father and thy mother." It is an obvious conclusion of natural law that all children must love, reverence, and obey those parents, or, in their absence, guardians, who rear them.

They must love them both internally and externally, wish them well and give signs of this love. This love must not be that which we would have for equals or inferiors; it must include reverence for them as superiors. They must be revered and also obeyed. This obligation of obedience applies to all licit commands which pertain to their upbringing, and it remains as long as the child abides under the authority of the parents or guardians.

The obligations of love and reverence are permanent. The duration of the obligation of obedience will vary among different societies because of the varying times set by them for the emancipation of the child.

The general duties of love, reverence, and obedience are clear to all those with the use of reason. But these duties need not be apprehended as absolute. An adult could, when faced with some concrete cases of conflict, be in invincible ignorance for a long time on this matter. He could, in some cases, think that his obligations toward his parents had ceased for some very serious reason, even though in fact they had not ceased, and still be in good faith.

But all men must know the general principle and that it would take at least a very serious reason for these obligations to cease. Thus it would be impossible for an adult of any nation, who had been conscientiously and lovingly reared by his parents or guardians, to refuse to return love or reverence in any way to them, and still remain in good faith for a long time. Similarly, a child who had been conscientiously and lovingly reared by his parents and yet hoped for the death of those parents for no other reason than to inherit their estate, or who insulted them because of some affliction brought on by age or some other cause, would be committing an obvious sin; and in no case and in no society could such a person be in good faith for a long time.

Parents and guardians, for their part, must love their children and provide for their corporal and spiritual education. This obligation is self-evident. Nature itself clearly demands it.[19] No extensive process of reasoning is required to arrive at a knowledge of these obligations.

Parents are held to love their children both with an internal love of benevolence and by showing this love externally.

Corporal education includes the provision of the necessities of life, and of the means whereby to provide for themselves upon reaching adulthood, etc. These things must be provided according to the ability and social status of the parents, and the circumstances of the society.

Spiritual education means training in the things of the soul, those things whether of doctrine or morality which are necessary for a virtuous life. This education is given in three ways: by instruction, by example, and by the correction of mistakes.

The obligations of parents, like those of children, are so obvious that no reasoning person can for long be invincibly ignorant of their existence. All are aware of the fact that at least it would take a grave reason to excuse a parent from the observance of one of them. Even primitive peoples would condemn the parent who, without a just cause, showered all his love on one of his children and was indifferent to or despised the others. So too would they condemn the parent who, through avarice, dissipation, or simple indifference, failed to provide his children with any of the things required for their corporal and spiritual education.

Primary conclusions of natural law also regulate authority in the state. Obligations of reverence, obedience and responsibility exist in the state as well as in the family.

It is evident to all that citizens must cooperate toward the common good. In particular, this means giving legitimate civil superiors due reverence, obedience, and loyalty. Respect must be paid to those in legitimate authority. Obedience must be given to all honest and just preceptive laws pertaining to the civil order. Loyalty must be granted to those civil superiors who preserve the common good. Those who for a slight reason, v.g., vanity, desire for power, etc., instigate a rebellion or seriously and deliberately dishonor a civil government which does, *de facto*, preserve the common good, would certainly be violating this precept.

It is equally evident to all reasoning men[20] that, for their part, those entrusted with civil authority are bound to preserve the common temporal good, and that they are bound to do so in such a way that spiritual goods are not endangered. The common good refers to the good of all groups, not of some small faction in the state. The persons who possess civil authority have these obligations: to combat temporal evils such as famines, plagues, widespread poverty, etc.; to promote and preserve as far as they are able a high standard of ethical morality and economic prosperity; and to distribute responsible offices to the worthy, and penalties to those guilty of injustice. A civil official who makes no attempt to ward off avoidable temporal evils, or who, through favoritism, nepotism, or graft bestows not just honorary titles, but offices involving the exercise of real authority to incompetent men, would certainly be violating this primary conclusion of natural law.

In practice, there are very few religions which tolerate the violation of any of the aforementioned primary conclusions relating to the fourth commandment. Westermarck notes, for example, that all people (with very few exceptions and in very special circumstances) recognize that children must care for parents in their old age.[21] With regard to the obligations of parents, he says that two duties so universal and so evident that they are rarely mentioned are: the duty of the mother to bring up her children supposing they have been permitted to live; and the duty of the married man to protect and support his family.[22] And with regard to the obligations of those in authority, he observes that unreasonable and indiscriminate cruelty does not characterize public justice even of savages, and that their punishments are imposed according to the crime.[23]

The primary conclusions mentioned above, relating to the fourth commandment, are so obvious then, that for the most part, no one even begins to try to refute them.

H. FIFTH COMMANDMENT

The chief primary conclusion of natural law associated with the fifth commandment states that "direct killing of an innocent[24] person is at least generally illicit."[25] No one can be in good faith for a long time and defend the position either that murder is an indifferent matter, generally licit, or that it can be justified by anything less than very grave reasons.

The *absolute* prohibition of the direct killing of an innocent person is not a primary, but a secondary or remote conclusion of natural law. Thus a person could remain in invincible ignorance for a long time of the malice of such killing under very special circumstances, v.g., abortion to save a mother's life.[26]

In considering the direct killing of an innocent person as

a violation of a primary conclusion, a special problem arises. This problem centers about the phrase "invincible ignorance for a long time" as it applies to this conclusion. In the primary conclusions of natural law which have been mentioned previously, the phrase "for a long time" presents no serious difficulty because the acts or omissions in question admit of being carried on over a long period, v.g., religious indifference for a period of five years. Here, however, in the matter of killing, we have an act which is ordinarily fairly brief. How then are we to understand the phrase "for a long time" in relation to murder?

First of all, this question does not militate against the fact that the general malice of murder is, in itself, easily discoverable. It merely raises the question of whether, in a great many instances where murder is committed for a slight cause, there might not be time enough for an adult to make a correct decision on what would otherwise be an easy problem.

There are two ways in which, even in cases of murder for a slight reason, a "long time" could elapse giving the murderer sufficient time to make this easy moral decision accurately. First, if the murder were planned a long time in advance, the murderer would have had enough time to make the necessary judgment. Secondly, assuming that the murder was committed on the spur of the moment, if the murder were of such a nature that it could be repeated several times on new victims (v.g., abandoning infants, but again only for slight reasons), enough time might elapse after the first killing so that the murderer could easily come to suspect his error and be able to correct it before carrying it still further. In either case, as soon as he realizes this error, if he continues in his plans to murder an innocent person for a slight reason, he is no longer in good faith.

It is virtually impossible to be very specific in applying these principles to concrete cases, and to list in detail those circumstances under which the malice of murder could be easily perceived by all adults. On the other hand, if nothing is said on the application of these principles, there is the danger that someone could draw the erroneous impression that they are entirely theoretical, and that, in practice, all types of murders could be committed in good faith.

In view of this latter consideration, some applications will be made, but with the understanding that they are minimal, and that many more could be made. Many more circumstances could be cited in which the malice of murder is obvious to all adults.

The general malice of abortion, killing of an unborn infant, is easily known by all adults. Its malice might not be easily apprehended when it is committed for the purpose of saving the mother's life.[27] But this is not true in the case of much less serious reasons such as killing the unborn infant in order to free oneself from the ordinary burdens involved in raising the child, or in order that, freed from the expenses of raising the child, luxuries can be purchased with the money saved.

The same is true, *mutatis mutandis*, of abandonment of infants.[28]

Parricide has been justified under certain circumstances in some societies.[29] Some societies, perhaps in good faith, have had the custom of killing parents when the parent is old and the tribe or society is nomadic or hardworking. Under these conditions, it was regarded as a kindness to give the parents death rather than continued overwork.[30] No society, however, in good faith gives a sweeping permission for parricide. At least a very serious reason is required. All adults know parricide is wrong, at least in general.

A duel for the purpose of avenging a very serious injury might be entered into without knowledge of its sinful nature.[31] One might have invincible ignorance of the malice of such a duel for a long time. But no adult can be in invincible ignorance for a long time of the malice of provoking a duel when the purpose for provoking it is merely to gain glory, to avenge a very slight insult, or for some other trivial object.

The dictator who feels he has the right to put to death with impunity any citizen he wishes, even without a trial, cannot be considered just.[32] The same is to be said of the parent who believes he holds an absolutely unconditional power of life and death over his children.

Those who freely fight and kill for sport fall under this same precept. (By qualifying this expression with the word "freely," we mean to prescind from those who take part in such combats under compulsion. We are only referring here to those who voluntarily enter such contests.) Gladiatorial combats are forbidden. In ancient Rome, we read that many of the gladiators who fought in the arena volunteered for this privilege. Under the republic, these volunteers came from the lowest orders of the free-born citizens. Under the empire, equites, senators, and even at times women, fought in the arena by their own choice.[33] No one of these volunteers, if he were in his right mind, and if he had had time to give it sufficient thought, could have entered the arena in good faith, without some knowledge that what he was doing was a hideous thing and in serious violation of the moral law of conscience.

The fact that the Roman gladiatorial contests were conducted on a scale unequaled in history makes contemporary Roman testimony of special value in determining whether revulsion against such combats is naturally common to all men. If on the site where such contests were extremely common and a part of everyday life, there were still serious outcries against them, we can conclude that wherever they are found men will easily come to know in some way the malice of them.

Seneca deplores the contests of his day, saying, "Many

an object of reverence in the eyes of man is now slaughtered for jest and sport; and [men] . . . are thrust forth exposed and defenseless; and it is a satisfying spectacle to see a man made a corpse."[34] Seneca objects to these contests on the ground that they arouse sadism in the spectators. Thus, even shows of gladiators who are condemned criminals are immoral. "Nothing is so damaging to good character as the habit of lounging at the games. . . . By chance, I attended a midday exhibition, expecting some fun, wit, and relaxation—an exhibition at which men's eyes have respite from the slaughter of their fellow men. But it was quite the reverse." (During the luncheon interval condemned criminals were often driven into the arena and compelled to fight for the amusement of the spectators who remained throughout the day.) "These men have no defensive armor. They are exposed to blows at all points and no one ever strikes in vain. . . . [In these bouts] the spectators . . . always reserve the latest conqueror for another butchering. . . . You may retort: 'But he was a highway robber; he killed a man!' And what of it? Granted that, as a murderer, he deserved this punishment [but] what crime have you committed, poor fellow, that you should deserve to sit and see this show? In the morning they cried 'Kill him! Lash him! Burn him!' . . . And when the games stop for the intermission, they announce: 'A little throat-cutting in the meantime, so that there may still be something going on.' "[35]

Pliny, too, raised his voice against these contests.[36] Thus it is revealing to see pagans, who may not have given all the possible reasons against it, still able to see the grave malice in killing for sport, at a time when such killings were at their height.

Suicide presents a special problem. Suicide was not only tolerated and openly advocated by some of the greatest of the pagan ethical thinkers, but many of them actually followed their own advice and committed it themselves: Socrates, Cato the younger, Seneca, etc. In the case of most of the tolerations of violations of primary conclusions of natural law which we have treated before or shall treat, the great thinkers either tolerated them by silence, by failing to condemn them, or, if they openly allowed them, they did so with some apologies. But if these great men, each keenly aware of the natural law, openly and unashamedly advocated suicide, how can we say that the prohibition of suicide is in any sense a primary or obvious conclusion of natural law?

It is revealing to note that these great thinkers did not advocate suicide indiscriminately. For them there were only a limited number of reasons which justified it. If it was committed for reasons other than these, it was to be considered immoral. Socrates said that suicide was licit when the law of the state required a man to do it, when a man has met some painful and inevitable misfortune, or when he suffers from irremediable and intolerable shame, but not when it is committed from sloth or want of manliness.[37]

Seneca says, "If the body is useless for service, why should one not free the struggling soul? . . . I shall not abandon old age if old age preserves me intact for myself; but if old age begins to shatter my mind, and to pull its various faculties to pieces, . . . I shall rush out of a house that is crumbling and tottering. I shall not avoid illness by seeking death, as long as the illness is curable and does not impede my soul. I shall not lay violent hands upon myself just because I am in pain; for death under such circumstances is defeat. But if I find out that the pain must always be endured, I shall depart."[38]

These and other[39] citations show that the greatest of the ancient Greeks and Romans did not approve of suicide for every cause. In fact, suicide was generally held to be licit only when a person met a catastrophe which could not be remedied. None of these men allowed suicide as an escape from ordinary difficulties met with in every life or even as a means of escaping extraordinary misfortunes which could be remedied.

Even with these restrictions, the attitude of the Stoics toward suicide has been described as "extremely lax"[40] when compared with the teaching on suicide in other religions and philosophies. Other major religions are more strict. If the Stoics could and did see the general malice of suicide, so too can the others. All men, then, can easily arrive at a knowledge of at least the principle that suicide is wrong as a general rule and that no slight reason would justify it.

The distinction made by the philosophers above can serve as a basis of the distinction here. Those adults who deliberately and in full possession of their faculties commit suicide out of cowardice or as a means of escaping the ordinary difficulties of life cannot do so in good faith. On the other hand, it is at least possible for a man to commit suicide in good faith when his motive is to escape an otherwise irremediable and overwhelming affliction.

What is true of suicide is true of euthanasia. An adult might be in invincible ignorance of the malice of killing a man dying in agony, but not for a long time of the malice of killing innocent people who are experiencing the ordinary trials or pains of life.[41]

In all this, it is necessary to keep in mind that the possibility of invincible ignorance even in the very difficult cases would be remote for a person living in a Christian society or in any other society which forbade these crimes absolutely. Invincible ignorance, even in extreme cases, would be likely only in societies where no one taught the absolute prohibition of these crimes.

The fifth commandment also forbids sins of thought and word which lead to acts of violence. Some evident prohibitions under this heading would be such sins as envy, malice, malignity (by which everything is accepted and explained in its worst light), and quarrelsomeness. Also included would be the sin of loving no one but oneself.[42] Ignorance without fault and for a long time of the malice of these sins would be impossible, at least when they are committed for slight reasons.

The need to take ordinary precautions to preserve one's health is also an evident conclusion of natural law relating to the fifth commandment. And to the extent that intemperance endangers health, it is wrong. Gluttony and drunkenness are sins whose malice is easily perceived by all.[43]

I. SIXTH COMMANDMENT

Central to the precepts of natural law relating to the sixth commandment is the notion of marriage. Within marriage there are certain rights; outside of marriage these rights do not exist. From human nature, we can deduce certain laws determining the nature and stability of marriage.

Existence of a Conjugal Union

The natural law demands a permanent union of man and woman for the proper continuance of the human race. Men and women may be united only after they have made an agreement to remain together permanently. To enter a union which is understood by the parties to have no permanent binding force at all would evidently be wrong at least in most circumstances.

Such unions are called either fornication or adultery. Fornication is voluntary sexual intercourse between unmarried persons. Adultery is intercourse between a husband or wife and another person. In adultery, either one or both parties may be married to another.

All men can easily perceive the malice of fornication in general. Men of developed reason in all societies have recognized the need for the institution of marriage, of a permanently binding union of man and woman. The malice of simple cohabitation without any intention whatsoever of remaining together is evident to all men. The need of promising permanent fidelity at the outset of carnal intercourse is almost instinctive. As St. John Chrysostom says: "For we have no need to learn that fornication is an evil thing, and that chastity is a good thing, but we know this from the first."[44]

There can, however, be invincible ignorance, even for a long time, of the malice of fornication in some special circumstances (v.g., in a society that legalizes prostitution).[45] But this ignorance would occur even more rarely than in the case of the other primary conclusions of natural law.[46] Grave reasons, which might justify fornication for a long time in the minds of those without revelation, arise less easily than in the case of many other violations of primary conclusions.

What has been said on fornication applies *a fortiori* to promiscuity. At one time, some writers held that in the early history of man, the malice of promiscuity was completely unknown. They say that originally there was no such thing as a family. Men and women lived promiscuously without the faintest idea that what they were doing was wrong, and without any idea that family life was necessary. This theory has been shown to be without foundation. Later and more thorough researches show that in the history of man there have been no substantiated instances of wholesale promiscuity.[47] Knowledge of the need for family life of some sort has been found in every society which has been studied from this point of view.

Adultery too, at least in general, is forbidden by a primary conclusion of natural law. In adultery, the parties ordinarily make no true contract of permanent fidelity which all adults can see is necessary before having marital relations.

To be sure, in some very special cases (v.g., adultery by

mutual consent where there is a serious reason such as desire of sterile couples for an heir), a given couple might be in invincible ignorance of the malice of adultery for a long time. But, on the other hand, adultery committed for a slight reason (v.g., simple gratification of desire for change and novelty) cannot be committed in good faith for any great length of time by an adult.

Fornication, promiscuity, and adultery are evidently opposed to reason. Either the parties will not or cannot promise permanent mutual fidelity. The partners in every act of carnal intercourse must be willing and able to promise fidelity which is in some way permanent. These sins allow no such promise. And man instinctively recognizes that without such a promise of fidelity, intercourse is wrong.

Properties of marriage:

Unity

Here, we assume that some sort of permanent family tie is necessary, and examine the various possible ways of putting together a family. These are four: group marriage (a tie among a small closed group of men and women, each of whom would have, either simultaneously or successively, marital rights with all the others), polyandry (the union of one woman with several men), polygamy (i.e., polygyny, the union of one man with several women), and monogamy (the exclusive union of one man and one woman).

Group marriage can be resolved into a combination of polyandry and polygamy. And what will be said of these last two forms of marriage can be applied to it.

Polyandry is rare. It is almost non-existent in civilized peoples. Among those primitive peoples who practice it, its "usual form is fraternal; that is, several brothers agree to have one wife. The main reason for this arrangement is poverty: each brother being too poor to have his own wife, they agree to have one in common." Another cause is an environment in which the husband must be away from home for a long period of time and "where it is not safe to have a woman alone. In this case, he agrees with other men to act as husband during his absence."[48]

Then again, it often arises simply from an excess of males. In some areas, this excess of males is due to female infanticide or its equivalent (serious neglect of infant daughters).[49] In certain other areas where incest is frequently committed, an abnormal excess of male births has often been noted, lending support to the theory held by some that there is a cause and effect relationship here.[50]

"As far as direct evidence goes, it is only in a few areas that polyandry is or has been practiced by a considerable number of the population."[51] Two areas where it is extensively practiced are the Himalayan region and Southern India.

Polyandry is opposed to a primary precept of natural law.[52] At least among primitive peoples the polyandric woman tends to become sterile. Polyandry, too, is an "inevitable source of bitter jealousy, strife, and domestic discord. No child can be properly reared in such an atmosphere."[53] Polygamy as well as polyandry, as we shall see, causes familial strife. But the discord caused by women who are forced to share one husband is puny compared with that where several men are forced to share one wife. Another and not the least of the evil effects of polyandry is the fact that the paternity of children can be very dubious. Where this is so, none of the men involved is likely to nurture and rear a child that may not be his own. Because of this, the offspring of polyandrous unions usually have to provide for themselves.[54]

In polyandry, then, the primary end of matrimony, the procreation and education of children, is greatly impeded, and harmony between the spouses is similarly obstructed.

Though not all the reasons against the practice will be obvious to everyone, enough of the evils of polyandry will be so evident even to primitive men that no one of them who has developed powers of reason can be in invincible ignorance of the general malice of polygamy for a long time.

Some statements have been made concerning Tibetan polyandry which seem to refute this last conclusion.[55] Polyandry is very common in Tibet. Some have said that polyandry has also been universally justified by the natives of that country. Tibetans, they say, have neither the knowledge nor even the suspicion that polyandry is wrong. But if polyandry is universally and unquestioningly justified in any large area, this would at least seem to militate against the statement that the general malice of polyandry is evident to all adults. If its malice is evident to all, at least some men, even in backward areas, should *de facto* have discovered this malice. Thus if indeed the malice of polyandry is completely unknown in Tibet, polyandry would not seem to be forbidden by a specifically primary precept of natural law.

But these statements have not been proved. In fact, not a few of those who have visited Tibet have found that polyandry was widely recognized as sinful by the natives themselves. Baber was "frequently told by Tibetans that polyandry did not exist to any great extent among the better classes of society; and many learned and worthy lamas assured him that it is a sinful practice, solely attributable to the very lax morality of the people, and by no means a recognized institution."[56] The early Christian missionaries gathered the same impression of popular disapprobation of polyandry as did these lamas.[57]

It is very possible, however, that in those areas of Tibet or elsewhere where there is, indeed, extreme poverty, or where other grave reasons are verified, that at least some of those who practice polyandry could remain in good faith for a long time.

Polygamy is rather common in that it is found among a great many pagan societies. But within each society, strict polygamy, from the nature of things, is not usually practiced on a very wide scale.[58]

In a study of the various primary and secondary conclusions of natural law, perhaps one of the most surprising aspects of Catholic teaching is that polygamy is classified under natural law under a different heading from her apparent twin sister, polyandry. Catholic theologians teach that polyandry is opposed to a primary conclusion of natural law. But polygamy, which would seem to be essentially the same as polyandry, is held by these same theologians to be opposed only to a secondary conclusion of natural law. The malice of polyandry they say, is obvious to all adults, that of polygamy is not.[59]

This distinction seems at first glance to be an exercise in hairsplitting. Why should there be a vast difference between the morality of the union of one woman with several men and that of one man with several women?

Upon closer examination, the reason appears. The evils of polygamy are seen to be far less serious than those of polyandry. In both polygamy and polyandry there is naturally friction between the competing spouses. But many of the other evils of polyandry are eliminated in polygamy. Most important, the essential care and protection of the father for his children are safeguarded in polygamy where they are not in polyandry. In polyandry, paternity is often uncertain, and all the fathers often, on these grounds, neglect to provide for the child of their wife. In polygamy, paternity is certain and the father as a matter of course will assume the responsibilities of providing for the newborn child.

Polygamy, then, much more than polyandry, safeguards one of the primary purposes of marriage, the education of the children. Polygamy, however, does necessarily tend to promote certain evils: familial discord, neglect of fatherly care for all children, excess of unmarried men, etc. But its evils are not always flagrant and evident to all, as are those of polyandry.

Adults can be in invincible ignorance even for a long time of the malice of polygamy under a wider range of circumstances than in the case of polyandry. Here again, though, there are limits. Even a polygamous union must be directed in some way toward the good of the family unit. But when its purpose is nothing else than gratification of lust, its malice cannot be unknown by a man of good will.[60] This would be verified more frequently in the case where polygamy is not a matter of a few wives but of a great many. The man with a harem of 50 or 100 wives or more, whose wives are considered as exclusively his, would find it difficult to justify himself in his heart. To be sure, such men are rare. But this number of wives has been reached and even exceeded. Westermarck mentions certain rich men and kings in Africa who had 70, 600, and according to some reports, 7000 wives.[61]

Monogamy is commanded by natural law. In several ways, nature shows us that marriage should at least ordinarily be restricted to one wife and one husband. First, the percentages of men and women in the world are roughly equal. And many of the natural evils of the other forms of marriage, even of polygamy, are eliminated in monogamy. The terrific family discord which is generated almost inevitably even in polygamous families[62] is cut to a minimum in monogamy. If there is discord in monogamous families, it is the fault of the parties themselves, not of the institution.

That nature itself leads man to see that monogamy is the normal form of marriage is confirmed by anthropological surveys: "Monogamy is the only form of marriage permitted among every people. Wherever we find polygamy, polyandry, or group marriage, we find monogamy side by side with it."[63] Many societies forbid polygamy, polyandry,

group marriage, or all three of these, but none forbids monogamy. Even "most polygamous or polyandrous unions (themselves) are modified in a monogamous direction; with one,
usually the first married, being the chief and the others only
auxiliary or secondary."[64] "The general rule (in polygamy)
is undoubtedly that one of the wives holds a higher social
position than the rest or is regarded as the principal wife."[65]

Indissolubility

Here the term divorce will refer to that type of dissolution of the marriage bond which includes the right of remarriage while the first partner is still alive. We shall not
deal with mere separation, i.e., the temporary or permanent
separation of the parties without the right to remarry.

It is evident to all adults that because of the many evils
that flow from divorce, there must at least be a serious reason
for dissolving the marriage bond and marrying another. It is
equally evident that any system which allows divorce for
very slight reasons is opposed to right reason. But what
would be examples of systems of divorce which fall into this
last category?

The first such system would be one which uncondition-
ally allowed "temporary marriages." Temporary marriages
are entered into with the understanding by both parties that
the marriage is not to be permanent, but is to last only for
a predetermined period of time. At the end of this time, the
marriage is *ipso facto* considered to be dissolved, and both
parties free to marry someone else. If there were no judicious
and extensive restrictions of time or circumstance whatsoever
placed on laws (or customs) tolerating temporary marriages,
these laws would be evidently opposed to right reason.

The second such system would be one which unqualifiedly
tolerated the dissolution of marriage intrinsically. Marriage
is dissolved intrinsically when the spouses themselves break

a previously contracted marriage bond independently of the approval or permission of any third party. In this system of divorce, the parties are not required to go to court or to any kind of judge who has the power to grant or refuse the petition. They are free to break the bond of marriage at any moment and at their own discretion. If, indeed, the laws or customs of a given society tolerate such an intrinsic dissolution of marriage on any grounds, without restriction, these laws or customs are obviously evil and opposed to a primary conclusion of natural law.[66] On the other hand, if the intrinsic dissolution of marriage is allowed only for grave reasons which would apply only in a very limited number of cases, there could be invincible ignorance of the malice of the practice, and it would be opposed only to a secondary conclusion of natural law.[67] The practical possibility, however, of a workable system allowing only limited intrinsic dissolution of marriage is slight. By definition, no one supervises and controls the granting of divorces except the parties to the marriage themselves. And where they are thus given the chance, the parties not infrequently will divorce each other for objectively slight reasons, even though the law itself does not sanction it. In practice, limited intrinsic divorce degenerates into unlimited divorce.

The third such system would be one which allowed the unlimited extrinsic dissolution of marriage. Marriage is extrinsically dissoluble when a divorce may be granted after a decision by a third party: a judge, or other official or group of officials. The parties are considered to have no right to remarry until this third party has given his approval or permission.

If the laws of a given society allow extrinsic dissolution even for slight reasons, then these laws are in opposition to a primary precept of natural law. Divorce for a slight cause, even when it is granted by a third party, is clearly opposed to right reason.[68] On the other hand, if the granting of divorce by a third party were restricted to certain special and serious causes (v.g., when one of the spouses is sterile, or in case of adultery) the evils of this system would not be quite so evident. It would be opposed only to a secondary or remote conclusion of natural law.[69]

There are not a few evils consequent upon divorce which, taken together or singly, make it evident that at least nothing less than a very serious reason would justify divorce.

Divorce, like polyandry and polygamy above, renders the education of children more difficult. In practice, it is rare even when a widow or widower remarries for the new spouse to get along well with the children of the former marriage. "What will happen when the new partner is faced with children whose father or mother is still alive, and with certain exceptions, still in relation with him or her? The children will be a reminder of the earlier union; nay more, they will remain a bond between former husband and wife." The new spouse may, of course, be of an uncommonly noble nature and accept this without reacting against it, but this would be the exception. Any plan, then, of establishing peace and order in a household by bringing in a new spouse frequently ends in causing greater friction between children and parents than before.

Divorce also tends somewhat to impede the procreation of children. In a divorce "the position of a woman whose husband has driven her to give him his liberty is indeed to be commiserated. She has sacrificed to him her freshness and good looks: . . . She has a just claim to be cherished and supported by him . . . saddled perhaps with young children, [she] is hardly in a position to form a favorable union."[70] And the fact that the presence of young children makes future unions more difficult leads to the avoidance of children in those societies where marriage may be dissolved.[71] The wisest course will be "to avoid the responsibility of maternity. Thus the purpose of marriage is frustrated: and the race, the good of which it is designed to promote, reaps no benefit from it."

Divorce tends to lower the dignity of women in a society, for divorce puts them in danger of being abandoned after serving the passion of men.[72]

Divorce tends to defeat still another purpose of marriage: the development of affection and unity of mind and heart between husband and wife. When ultimate separation is possible, the two partners cannot give themselves unreservedly to each other. Each must bear in mind that the present state of things is provisional. Common sense dictates to them that rash commitments should be avoided, so that should a severance come, it would not involve the total shipwreck of life. The full identification of interests is not to be thought of.

Nor can anything be more destructive of conjugal love than the possibility of divorce. Love calls for confidence. Where divorce may occur, confidence can hardly exist. In its place there will be a constant sense of insecurity. Suspicions and jealousies will never be long dormant. And they will be ten times more vehement than where marriage is indissoluble, because divorce itself furnishes an additional motive to inconstancy. "It is also to be remembered that where the bond is known to be lifelong, the partners are provided with a strong motive to put a speedy end to those misunderstandings which must inevitably spring up from time to time."[73] "Where divorce is possible, the thoroughly selfish party will refuse to curb his willfulness, knowing that he can get out of a bad situation by divorce."[74]

Divorce breeds divorce. "When a marriage turns out ill, and the parties have reason to regret that they ever linked their lots together, this unhappiness is often chiefly imputable to the recklessness with which they took the step. Only too frequently does it happen that young people rush into marriage without forethought, without duly weighing the immense importance of the issue. Who can wonder at the failure? And who can doubt that the possibility of ultimate divorce will be an immense encouragement to such marriages?"[76] Recklessness, which is the primary cause of unhappy marriages, is itself far more likely under a system which tolerates divorce.

And divorce, to a certain extent, encourages crime. Where the commission of crime is the only legal way of gaining freedom from the marriage bond, crimes will sometimes be committed for just that purpose. The counterobjection against this is that the inhibition of divorce also incites to crimes: those of adultery, prostitution, etc. In answer to this objection, it can be said that these difficulties are not adequately met by legalizing the adultery and allowing the adulterer to marry his paramour.

Divorce hurts society as a whole. Joyce expresses this clearly: "Family life is the foundation on which society and civilization rest. Where the family is lacking in unity, in love, in high ideals, the whole of society will soon feel the effects. There will be a lower tone, a meaner outlook, a diminished achievement. Decadence will have set in: and so long as divorce prevails, no effective remedy will be possible."[77]

There are, of course, evils which arise in a social or religious system which limits divorce. To the extent that divorce is forbidden, there will be more and more spouses yoked to unworthy partners with whom married life is impossible. Separation is possible; but remarriage is not. Even the innocent party is forbidden to start afresh and contract a new marriage. But, on the other hand, the evils of unlimited divorce are far greater. The latter affect society as a whole. The evils of limited divorce "are purely personal. They are no more injurious to society as a whole than are,

v.g., the pains of the sick in a hospital." As opposed to unlimited divorce, limited divorce will make for the greater
number of happy persons and the fewer unhappy ones.
"Society may justly claim that the public good should in
such a case prevail over private convenience. Though the
individuals concerned deserve all possible commiseration, yet
it is far better that they should endure the heavy trials
which have befallen them, than that the community should
be exposed to the incalculable evils which [unlimited] divorce would inevitably bring."[78]

This leads to the following conclusions: All adults can
see the evils of unlimited divorce. And unlimited divorce is
opposed to a primary precept of natural law. Divorce for
anything but a very serious reason is clearly opposed to right
reason.

But what about a system of limited divorce (i.e., a system in which divorce can be granted, but only for serious
reasons)? Is this, too, clearly opposed to right reason? Limited
divorce is, indeed, opposed to right reason and natural law,
but not obviously so.

It is opposed to right reason in that wherever a system
of limited divorce is instituted, human weakness will gradually discover more and more reasons justifying divorce and
ultimately will allow it for any cause. In practice this has
been the case.[79]

But this is not evident. The knowledge that limited divorce will almost inevitably disintegrate into unlimited divorce ordinarily requires a great deal of experience. It is
possible then, for those in backward areas to be in invincible
ignorance for a long time of the evils of such a system. Individual citizens in a backward area could conceivably obtain a divorce and remarry in a case of adultery, and still be
in good faith for a long period of time. Even lawmakers in
some areas could enact legislation which for the first time

allowed divorce and remarriage in certain special cases (adultery, sterility, etc.) and still be in good faith for a long time. Experience might never show them that even limited divorce is opposed to right reason. Limited civil divorce, then, is opposed to a secondary, not a primary conclusion of natural law.

The conclusions of reason are confirmed in practice. The most lax forms of divorce, i.e., temporary marriage and unlimited intrinsic and extrinsic divorce are in no areas generally held to be institutions leading to heroic virtues. On the contrary, they are at most only tolerated. Some groups do indeed blind themselves to the malice of these crimes, but their blindness is not complete. They do see some evil in them. Islam, for example, is one of the religions which is most lax on the matter of intrinsic divorce, allowing it for any cause. But even here, Mohammed is reported to have uttered the paradox: "The most detestable of the things allowed by Allah is divorce."[80]

Other Sins Opposed to the Sixth Commandment

All nations agree that incest, marital relations between close relatives, is opposed to natural law. They disagree in their understanding of what constitutes a close relative in this context.

Blood relationship can be traced in two ways: in a direct line, a series of persons, one descending from another (v.g., grandfather and mother and son), and in a collateral line, a series of persons who descend not one from the other, but all from one common ancestor (v.g., aunt and brother and sister).

Some nations forbid marriage only between the closest of relatives; other nations forbid marriage between even distant ones.

The Church prohibits marriage between all those related in a direct line, and collaterally, all those up to and including second cousins. Parts of this prohibition arise from a primary conclusion of natural law. The prohibition of marriage and marital relations, apart from a very serious reason, between father and daughter or mother and son originates from a primary conclusion of natural law.[81] This does not refer to stepfathers and stepdaughters, to stepmothers and stepsons, or to foster parents and their wards. This prohibition refers only to marital relations between a parent and any of his natural offspring, whether the offspring are themselves legitimate or illegitimate.

On the other hand, the prohibition of marriage between such relatives as first cousins, uncle and niece, and even between brother and sister is not a primary conclusion of natural law, but at most only a secondary one.

Reason shows that marriage between parent and child is evidently wrong for two reasons. *A priori,* in marriage there exists an equality between the spouses, and it tends to make them intimate companions. But nature itself places a parent and child in the relationship of superior and subject. To warp this relationship by carnal intercourse between parent and child is naturally repugnant to all men.

The effects of such marriages show its evils. Marital unions between parent and child frequently are sterile or else produce weak or deformed children. The likelihood that such unions will be sterile or will result in defective children is far greater than where the parents are unrelated. Westermarck cites certain studies which reported that insane, deaf and dumb, or epileptic children born of incestuous unions are far more frequent than from unrelated parents.[82]

The prohibition of incest, especially of that between parent and child, has been very common throughout history. Few peoples even attempt to deny that marriage between parent and child is forbidden.[83] Two of the rare instances of such toleration are among the ancient Persians and Assyrians.[84] Most people, Christian or pagan, when they hear of an instance of a marriage between parent and child, concur with Plutarch's reaction to the marriage of Artaxerxes and his own daughter. Artaxerxes, Plutarch said, was "overriding all the principles and laws by which the Greeks hold themselves bound, and was regarding himself . . . as supreme arbiter of good and evil."[85]

Something must be said here of the sins of sodomy, solitary pollution, and marital onanism or contraception. All three are opposed to a primary conclusion of natural law. Protracted invincible ignorance of the general malice of them is impossible.[86] But where there is a grave reason (v.g., pollution for medical purposes, or contraception where childbirth is foreseen to be certainly a great risk to the life of the mother), it is possible for invincible ignorance to arise and to remain for a long time.[87] However, even in these exceptional cases, invincible ignorance need not be presumed. And Vermeersch seems to indicate that there can be no invincible ignorance at all of the malice of voluntary pollution.[88]

Intuition will show the malice of these sins. The argument from reason against them at times has been obscured by the use of the word "unnatural" in reference to them. The word "unnatural" is too ambiguous. "Perversion" is better. All these sins are perversions. The malice of each is the same. The reasons for condemning one are the same as for condemning the others. Try to exculpate one and you have approved the others. Secondary reasons against them can be adduced: v.g., contraception tends to cause sterility, and also tends to cause a gradual disintegration of mental balance, especially in women.[89] But the primary indictment is that sodomy, pollution, and onanism are simply perversions. The statement made by Plutarch over 1800 years ago

in reference to sodomy can be applied to all three: They are
"in defiance of nature . . . and contrary to the end of vene-
real pleasure."[90]

J. SEVENTH COMMANDMENT

The seventh commandment, "Thou shalt not steal," pertains to debts between one individual and another individual
and not to obligations between the society and the individual.
In particular, it protects the individual's right of ownership
against the encroachment of another individual.

No adult can remain for a long time in invincible ignorance of the malice of theft. As a primary conclusion of natural law, the seventh commandment can be phrased in general terms: Except for at least a very serious reason, stealing
is sinful.[91] Stealing can be defined as the taking of a thing
against the reasonable will of its owner. The phrase "against
the reasonable will" indicates that in some cases property can
licitly be taken from someone without actually having received his consent, expressed or implied. It would not be
theft, for example, on the part of a starving man to take a
loaf of bread from another who would not miss it, even if
this other would refuse to give the bread willingly to the
starving man.[92] But the phrase "against the reasonable will"
is not an elastic clause. Under most circumstances, owners
do have a "reasonable" right to their property. Men with the
use of reason can easily know this. And no adult can remain
in invincible ignorance for a long time of the general malice
of taking another's property.[93]

On the relation of particular application of the seventh
commandment to primary conclusions of natural law, Vermeersch has an interesting comment. Speaking of the possibility of invincible ignorance of natural law, he says "There
are not a few conclusions which are not remote and yet

which, at least outside of the matter of justice, can be unknown by many for a time; this ignorance can be extended (augeri) because of evil customs."[94]

This phrase, "at least outside of the matter of justice," implies that in questions of justice invincible ignorance of natural law is less likely than in other moral questions. In using the word justice Vermeersch might be referring both to the debts existing between the community and individual and to the debts of one individual to another. More probably, though, he is referring only to the latter. In either case, he is indicating that the obligations of justice between one individual and another can and should be understood more completely than the obligations induced by many of the other virtues. Even many details connected with the rights of ownership, the rights induced by contracts, and the obligations of restitution are in very many cases evident to primitive peoples.

One reason why justice occupies a special place in natural law is that, more than any other virtue, it is most apt to be carefully and accurately regulated by society. Very often civil laws will prescind to a great extent from the obligations of citizens to practice virtues like religious assent, moral effort, worship, etc., leaving citizens either individually or in groups to find for themselves the proper courses of action. But the defining and establishment of justice are the primary objects of the laws of every well-ordered state. Long ago, Plutarch said "Justice is the king's first business."[95] In more recent times and in our own country, George Washington said, "The administration of justice is the firmest pillar of government."[96] According to Daniel Webster, "Justice is the ligament which holds civilized beings and civilized nations together. Wherever her temple stands, and so long as it is duly honored, there is a foundation for social security and general happiness."[97] The very life of a state depends on whether justice is observed.[98] Some other virtues can be weak, and society can limp along. But without clear ideas of justice, there is chaos.

Every lawmaker will devote the utmost care to points of justice. Any errors that he makes on important matters of justice will raise a great outcry and thus will almost inevitably tend to be corrected in one way or another. As a result, the laws of virtually every society will deal in detail with justice and the bulk of the major laws (i.e., those affecting a great number of people), and also will be in very close harmony with natural law.[99]

Thus, in most matters of justice, men have, in addition to their conscience, the civil law pointing in the right direction. In the case of other virtues, this is less often so. As a result, in matters of justice, invincible ignorance for a long time will be that much less likely.

Only very rarely have men attempted to defend the position that stealing is licit on a wide scale. Ancient Sparta is sometimes cited as an instance of a society where stealing was accepted as morally good. It is true that in Sparta stealing was allowed and even encouraged. This was not a sweeping permission. Stealing was allowed and encouraged only in those who were being trained to fight, and even then only within certain limits. Young boys were encouraged to steal food in order to make them cunning foragers in war.[100] For them, stealing food was training in a skill. If they were caught in the act, they were punished. Thus, stealing was allowed, but only when it involved certain articles and under certain circumstances. Spartans still knew and proclaimed the malice of stealing in general.

K. EIGHTH COMMANDMENT

The eighth commandment forbids the giving of false testimony against our neighbor and thereby safeguards the

virtue of veracity. This virtue is violated both by telling un-
truths and by unlawfully revealing what is true. The following sins are clearly opposed to this virtue: Lying, detraction
and calumny, contumely, rash judgment, and the violation
of secrets.[101]

Here again, at least the general principles should be evident to all,[102] even though there may be honest error in
some special cases.[103] One such special case might be a lie told
in order to procure an advantage for oneself or for another,
which does not injure anyone else. It is possible to remain in
invincible ignorance of the evil of a lie or even perjury for
the legitimate defense of oneself or another. A virtuous man
might be convinced that in cases where false charges are
brought against him, it is licit to attempt to exonerate himself by use of a lie.[104]

But in other cases prolonged invincible ignorance is impossible. Lies where the motive is ignoble (v.g., for the purpose of swindling another, or gaining a large sum of money
to which one would otherwise have no right, or for reasons
of envy or ambition) cannot be justified in good faith.

Reason shows that lying, at least in general, is evil. The
purpose of the faculty of speech is the communication of
our ideas. A lie frustrates this end. And if lying is allowed
unqualifiedly, good order in society as a whole is impossible.

Detraction, contumely, rash judgment, and the breaking
of personal secrets violate a man's right to his reputation. In
all these, a person either knows or thinks he knows a defect
of another, and without serious reason destroys the other's
reputation. But men have a right to their reputations. The
peace and good order of society demand this. "And a good
reputation is worth more than great riches" (Prov. 22:1).
To destroy it, whether such action is deserved or undeserved,
requires at least a serious reason.

A notion of truth and of falsehood has been possessed by
all men. The unrestrained liar is condemned among all

peoples.[105] Similarly, the idea of reputation, both good and bad, is common to all men.[106]

L. NINTH AND TENTH COMMANDMENTS

The ninth and tenth commandments deal with sins of thought: sins of lust and greed.[107] The general malice of these sins is known even to non-Christians.[108]

Sins of thought can be classified as efficacious and inefficacious. Efficacious sins of thought include the intention to perform the imagined sin. Inefficacious ones exclude this intention.

It is evident that one cannot have invincible ignorance for a long time of the malice of efficacious desires to perform actions known to be sinful.[109] That is, if an adult intends to commit a sin, this intention itself is sinful, and is culpable even if through some accident the intention is never carried out. In our contemporary dramatic shows, we frequently hear of plots wherein an employee intends to embezzle a large sum of money from his place of work, and upon receiving a windfall from some other source, in great haste retracts his plans to steal. Such a man is at least to some degree guilty of being a thief, and can easily be known as such by those in ignorance of revelation.

Reason shows that both virtue and sin require an intention. Moral good or evil does not consist in external conformity or nonconformity alone. Morality resides primarily in the internal act. Therefore, if a complete and decisive internal moral decision is made, we must also already have merit or sin even before any external act is performed. There can be simple thoughts which are either meritorious or blameworthy.

These statements, however, in so far as they pertain to primary conclusions of natural law, refer only to cases where the intention is truly firm and truly efficacious. They do not necessarily refer to those situations where a man is hesitating in his intention to commit sin. Nor do they refer to cases where tentative plans are made and the decision is voluntarily retracted before they are carried out.

With regard to inefficacious sins of thought, in those which lack any desire to put them into execution, there is a distinct possibility of lengthy invincible ignorance.[110]

M. SUMMARY

In summary, we can list some of the violations of primary conclusions of natural law as follows: atheism, pantheism, annihilationism, agnosticism, polytheism, fetishism, despair, presumption, hatred for God, hatred for self or neighbor, idolatry, temptation of God, blasphemy, perjury, violation of vows, and religious indifference, internal or external.

Other sins are at least in general clearly opposed to natural law, and an adult may remain for a long time in invincible ignorance of their malice only in special cases and for very serious reasons. Such sins include irreverence, disobedience, irresponsibility, murder, abortion, abandonment of infants, dueling, suicide, envy, malice, malignity, quarrelsomeness, selfishness, fornication, adultery, polyandry, temporary marriage, intrinsic dissolution of marriage, extrinsic dissolution of marriage, incest between parent and child, perversion, stealing, lying, calumny, detraction, contumely, rash judgment, violation of secrets, and efficacious sins of thought.

One of the most unfortunate requirements in the composition of this or any other list of primary conclusions is that the counsels must be omitted. The counsels of poverty, virginity, and religious obedience provide some of the most beautiful aspects of holiness. But any judging of holiness from the point of view of primary or obvious conclusions of natural law must omit any detailed expression of these counsels precisely because the validity of these counsels is not obvious to all adults. Many in good faith can question the virtue in renouncing all earthly possessions, in a life of virginity, etc. Detailed statements of these counsels belong at best to secondary conclusions of natural law, and so, regrettably, they must be omitted from this list.

3. The Phrase "for a long time"

No adult can remain in invincible ignorance of the primary conclusions of natural law for a long time. Extended ignorance of them by an adult arises either proximately or ultimately from bad faith.[111]

The phrase "for a long time" indicates that invincible ignorance of these primary conclusions can be present for a limited period of time. A person can tentatively justify in good faith violations of the primary conclusions. But as time passes, experience will shower him with irrefutable evidence that his first judgment was indeed wrong, and that he must henceforth act contrary to his previous custom. If at this point he does change his way of life, he is guilty of no sin. But if, at this point, out of motives of passion, sloth, encouragement from others in sin, etc., he deliberately refuses to examine this further evidence, and closes his mind to all thought of change, his ignorance, if it still can be called ignorance, becomes vincible. And as long as he remains in this last state, the man is a sinner before God.

The length of time required for an individual to realize an error he has made in a matter falling under a primary conclusion will, of course, vary. Many who violate these conclusions are never in invincible ignorance. They either know or seriously suspect the error of their decision from the very moment of making it.

Many others, never having considered a given problem very deeply, being suddenly forced to make a decision, may on the spur of the moment make the wrong one; but afterwards, instinct or reflection will show them their initial error.

But generally speaking, invincible ignorance of primary conclusions will not last indefinitely. When one commits one of the sins listed above, invincible ignorance will not, under normal circumstances, last a full lifetime. There will come a time when the idolater, murderer, agnostic, etc., will realize or seriously suspect his error. Either the repeated commission of the sin itself or the visible accumulation of evil effects will show the error.

But within what limit of time can we presume that this realization or serious suspicion of error will take place? Can we set any limit less than simply the span of a normal lifetime? It is impossible, first of all, to set any limit which will give us certainty. We can only establish a presumption. It would seem safe to say that for most of the precepts, both negative and positive, ignorance can be presumed to cease being invincible within a year of the time when an error was first made by a reasoning person. Thus, if an adult on a given date chose to profess atheism or agnosticism, within a year from that date, he could, in general, be presumed to have seen or seriously suspected his error. The same could be said for a man who committed murder for a slight reason (v.g., out of sadism), or divorced his wife for a slight reason, or failed to worship God externally. Granted, in some extreme cases, invincible ignorance of the evident malice of these sins could last longer than a year, but generally the ignorance would end before that time.

4. The Phrase "developed powers of reason"

The discussion above has been qualified by the phrases "in those who have developed powers of reason," "in those whose minds are fully developed," "in adults," or "in men." All these phrases refer to the same idea.

In themselves, these words and phrases are elastic. "Developed powers of reason" means one thing to the board of admissions of a postgraduate school of law, and quite another to the mistress of admissions of the first grade of a grammar school. In each case, the meaning of the phrase depends upon what is expected of the reasoning powers in each situation. So too, here.

But in the context of natural law, what does the phrase "one possessing developed powers of reason" or the word "adult" mean? The word "adult," as we are using it, has been defined by Lombardi. "By the word adult, we mean the man who here and now can distinguish between the concepts of moral good and evil, and who in some way perceives that he must do good and avoid evil. It does not matter whether or not he can indicate with precision all those actions which are truly good or evil according to the natural law; still less does it matter whether he regulates his life according to such a detailed rule; what is necessary is that he shall have the knowledge of the moral imperative, and that in some way he shall perceive it as absolutely binding upon himself. Only on this condition will he be able to act in a fully human way, as a responsible man, and therefore deserve the name of adult in the full sense."[112]

According to Lombardi, then, the way in which we determine whether a person's mind is fully developed (in the sense used here) is to find first, whether the person has a knowledge of right and wrong and can distinguish the two, and second, whether he sees that he himself has the obligation to do good and avoid evil.

This definition of an adult is not unreasonable in the context of primary conclusions of natural law. By definition, the primary conclusions can be discovered without great mental ability or labor. They are so obvious that they are almost instinctive. Give a person enough reason to be able to perceive the difference between right and wrong and to perceive that he has an obligation to do what is right, and he has been given enough reason to perceive with ease the primary conclusions of natural law. We hold that Lombardi's definition of the word adult in this context is a natural consequence of the way in which the primary conclusions themselves have been defined.

The implications of Lombardi's definition are great. Most important is the fact that he does not require any more than he does. Certainly, no formalized education would be necessary to qualify as an adult under this definition. Nor is there required any detailed moral instruction. A person who can distinguish between right and wrong and knows he must do good is, morally speaking, by that fact, an adult, and a person who has developed powers of reason. As a consequence, in the light of what has been said above, such a person is held responsible for the observance of the primary conclusions of natural law.

But granting that those who are bound to observe primary conclusions of natural law are all those who can distinguish right from wrong and recognize a moral imperative, exactly what types of persons fall into this category? What types of people are able to distinguish right from wrong and recognize this imperative? Who are adults in the sense used here, and who are not?

Among the number of those who lack the use of reason as defined here would be infants; those who chronologically are not infants but who have been feeble-minded from birth (v.g., idiots, and perhaps imbeciles); those who are permanently insane;[113] and those who have never[114] developed their reasoning powers because of some early physical accident such as a head injury or a disease affecting their brain during infancy.

The foregoing applies to special classes of individuals within every society. There are certain categories of exceptional individuals within every society whose reasoning powers have not developed. But what about entire societies? Is it possible for such defective development to occur not only in exceptional individuals in a given society, but also to occur in all or almost all of the members of any entire society? This has, at least to all appearances, taken place. In South America there exists at least one small tribe, nearly all of whose members are feeble-minded. In this tribe, it is not a case simply of the existence of depraved customs, or of a simple lack of any education as we understand the word, but one of mental deficiency. Missionaries have found it next to impossible to make any impression on the minds of its members. The cause of the feeble-mindedness is clear: the tribe is isolated, and has been for generations. There neither is nor has been any intermarrying with members of any other tribe. Intensive inbreeding for years has gradually brutified the people's minds. Here, then, is a society which even as a society would seem to be excused from observance of the primary conclusions of natural law.

In the above instances of lack of development of reasoning power, both in parts of a society and in whole societies, the failures were due to some positive malfunctioning in the brain itself. The brains of the permanently insane and the permanently feeble-minded have by definition some inherent operative defect. But what is to be said of the possibility of a lack of development of the use of reason in minds which are basically sound? To what extent have persons possessing basically normal minds failed to become moral adults simply because of a grossly defective education? We shall answer this question using as a point of departure the important recent attempt by Cardinal Billot to solve it.

Speaking of the matter of faith, Cardinal Billot gave extensive treatment to the question of the definition of the term adult. Seeking a way to avoid the conclusion that many pagans must be considered damned because of lack of minimal faith, Billot developed the following theory: Simple faulty education can prevent human beings from ever reaching moral maturity. Moreover, there are, in fact, "very many" people to whom this applies.

The extent to which he pushes this theory is surprising. There are many, he says, who are physically and even intellectually adult in all that concerns temporal matters and earthly life, but who are morally immature. Thus, he admits the likelihood of the existence of many "apparent adults," not only among backward, but also among civilized peoples. For Billot, even those who have reached their full intellectual development in the sphere of mundane affairs can be morally immature and therefore not responsible.[115] A man could go through sixteen, twenty or more years of schooling, become a capable executive or even a college professor and still be a moral infant. And, in Billot's experience, this was not a mere possibility, but a probability, verified extremely often.

Short of completely excusing all sinners, Billot pushes the idea of moral infancy just about as far as it can possibly go. For him, a great many men have not the developed powers of reason of which we speak in the context of natural law; a great many in virtually every society, whether civilized or not, would not qualify as adults. And consequently, the number that he would excuse from observance of the primary conclusions of natural law would seem to be very large.

What foundation is given by Billot for his theory? He declares that there exists a duality in the faculty of reason. The complete faculty of reason is composed of a "lower reason" by which men consider earthly things, and a "higher reason" by which they ascend to divine things and to God, the Lord of the universe. Not that man has two distinct faculties of reason, but that there are two different functions of one and the same faculty.[116] "He believes that only a few are capable of developing fully their higher reason without the aid of instruction from others. He thus ended by considering it possible that many (at least among the unbelievers, whose religious education is the most deficient) succeed in developing only the lower type of reason."[117]

Billot holds, then, that large numbers of those who have been endowed with basically normal minds, have, because of a grossly defective education, failed to become moral adults.

In criticism of Billot's theory, it is necessary to refer to our definition of moral adult: An adult in the context of primary conclusions of natural law is one who is able to distinguish right from wrong and who accepts the moral imperative. The question, then, resolves itself thus: To what extent can defective education, whether in a civilized or uncivilized society, prevent a person who has a basically sound mind from being able to distinguish right from wrong, or from accepting the moral imperative?

Experience[118] shows us that at least the vast majority of civilized people *de facto* satisfy the definition of moral adult. They know at least that right is different from wrong and that they must do what is right. And being adults, they cannot be excused *en masse* from the observance of natural law. Errors which they make in regard to primary conclusions of natural law are due either to culpable negligence or to malice.

But what about a less extreme position: that of applying Billot's theory to barbarous peoples but not to civilized ones? Granted that we cannot excuse the civilized world *en masse* from the observance of natural law, are there not large numbers of primitive people who lack developed use of reason simply through the absence of any education worthy of the name?

At first glance, an affirmative answer to this question would not seem illogical. There exist many tribes and even nations who have been cut off for eons from virtually all contact with civilization, either Eastern or Western. These people have been left almost alone in forming their conscience. In many cases, they appear so backward that there is good reason for assuming that they lack the quality that distinguishes man from animals, the use of reason. And this not because of any defect of brain power but because of simple intellectual stagnation. The brain seems to vegetate, used for nothing more than the animal functions of sensation, memory, imagination, etc. Unlike Billot's theory, where the mind is supposed to work amorally but still with some rationality, here we seem to have a complete lack of reason from all points of view. The minds of such people are considered by some to be the same as those of imbeciles or idiots.

There are not a few who, having seen the depraved morals and the concomitant brutish minds of certain primitive tribes, have held this last opinion privately. In print, however, they are very cautious on the point. Some will present the problem, setting forth reasons pro and con, but giving no solution. Rarely will any one positively uphold the opinion in print.[119]

There are several reasons, however, why it is false. First, so mild an opinion leaves us with a paradox. According to it, those with the most vicious customs, the primitive peoples, are the ones most free from sin. At the same time, that part of the world that is elevated from the mire is the only part that provides inhabitants for hell. The reward for bringing a society out of barbarism is hell for many of its members.

But there is another, and a more basic, objection to the mild opinion. The question of the extent to which primitive peoples fail to reach adulthood is fundamentally an anthropological one. *De facto*, do large numbers of pagans lack a moral sense or do they not? Do they have a concept of right and wrong and apply it to themselves, or not?

Westermarck provides a very interesting answer to this question. "Custom, or moral regulation, goes back without any doubt to a very remote period of human history. We do not know any primitive people which has no customs; and as one shall see from what follows, savages often express their indignation very clearly when someone violates their customs."

Various pieces of evidence, he continues, show that culturally inferior races have some idea of justice. And the supposition that remorse is unknown among them is not only unfounded, but is contradicted by the facts. To suppose that primitive people are entirely without any conscience is to put oneself in contradiction to the inference that one can draw from the great respect which they have for their customs—and in contradiction also to the explicit statement of travelers who have studied this question. He cites, among other things, an interview between one such traveler and some Bechuanas in South Africa.

"Do the Bechuanas have a conscience?"

"Yes, all of them have one," they replied.

"And what does it say to them?"

"It remains tranquil when they do good, and tortures them when they commit sin."

"What do you call sin?"

"Theft, which one commits while trembling, and murder, of which one can purify oneself again and again but which always leaves remorse."

Westermarck discusses the reasoning of Lord Avebury[120] who held the opposite opinion, and was convinced that modern barbaric peoples seem to lack almost entirely any concept of morality. Lord Avebury stated that he had been led to this conclusion by "the remarkable absence" of repentance and remorse among many backward peoples. We shall cite the various reasons Lord Avebury gives for his opinion, and then give Westermarck's criticism.

Lord Avebury quotes one author who stated that among the Comanches of Texas, "no individual action is considered as a crime, but each one acts according to his own judgment, unless a superior authority, like that of the chief, acts upon him." He cites another writer who says: "Indians have no concept of morality at all." And among the Basutos (in South Africa), according to Casalis, morality "depends so completely on the social order that any political disorganization is immediately followed by a state of degeneracy that only the re-establishment of political order can correct." The same can be said of Central Africa and elsewhere. Thus at Djenne (in West Africa) and in the neighboring region, "each time that a village is deprived of its chief, the inhabitants no longer recognize any law: anarchy, disorders, confusion reign immediately, and all work ceases until the naming of the successor." The Damara (Southwest Africa) "seem to have no perceptible idea of good or evil." The Tasmanians (Australia) "lacked any moral outlook or impressions." Eyre said of the Australians that they have no "moral sense of that which is just and equitable in the abstract"; and that a missionary would have had a great deal of trouble in inculcating the idea of sin in these people. The Kacharis have "no words in their language for sin, piety, prayer, repentance"; and speaking of another tribe indigenous to India, Campbell observes that they are considered to be deprived of any moral sense.

Lord Avebury cites another witness according to whom the expressions of the inhabitants of the Pacific archipelago of Tonga for vice and virtue "are equally applicable to other things." The South American Indians of Gram Chaco (part of Paraguay and Bolivia), according to the missionaries, "make no distinction between good and evil, and consequently have neither fear or hope of sanction in the future life, nor any terror of any supernatural power."

Of these points, Westermarck says that many of them do not presuppose at all the absence of moral sentiments. The statements relating to the Comanches signify only that among them individual liberty is great. And the social disorder which strikes various peoples during times of political disorganization indicates a feeble political cohesion and also a certain discordance between moral ideas and their practical application. In Morocco also, he says, the death of the Sultan is immediately followed by a quasi-perfect anarchy; but this does not prevent Moroccans from continuing to recognize the moral regulations of the Koran, and even more rigid rules stemming from ancient customs.

As to the Basutos, Casalis expressly states that they have the idea of moral evil, and that they represent it in their language by words which mean ugliness, or shame, or indebtedness or incapacity; Arbousset heard a Basuto cry out upon the pronouncement of an unjust sentence, "The judge is powerful, therefore we are silent; if he were weak, all would cry out at injustice."

Moreover, it is possible for a people to lack any abstract concept of the theoretical nature of justice and of moral "ideas" (in the strict sense of the word) and still be able to distinguish in concrete cases between good and evil, between just and unjust.

Chauncy expressly says of the Australians that they have a very keen sense of justice. And the most recent authorities on the Central Australians observe that if their moral code does differ radically from ours, still "one may not deny that their conduct is regulated by this code and that every known violator is treated with certainty and severity." Those who live in the archipelago of Tonga, according to Mariner, "in their ideas of honor and justice do not differ appreciably from ours. The difference is one of degree: they consider certain things more honorable than we do, and others as much less." Elsewhere, he says that "the ideas of the people of Tonga on honor and justice are sufficiently defined, firm and universal," even if they do not always put them into practice. Westermarck adds that it is strange to hear that the American Indians have no concept of morality. He cites Buchanan as an example of one who affirms that they have a "strong and inbred sense of justice."

Westermarck then observes, "When the missionaries or travelers deny to certain savage peoples any moral ideas or sentiments, they seem to be thinking in terms of ideas or sentiments similar to their own." For many savage and barbarous peoples we have direct testimony that they possess a sense of justice. Speaking of the Andaman Islanders (near India), Man writes that: "Certain traits that one can observe in their relations with us would justify the belief that they do not absolutely lack a sense of honor, and they have a vague idea of what justice implies."

Colonel Dalton reports that among the Korwas in India, when many people are implicated in the same misdemeanor, they are most careful to assign to each one his exact part and no more; the oldest of the group invariably assumes the greatest responsibility because he is presumed to have had greater knowledge. The Aleuts, according to Veniaminof, are "naturally prone to be just." Kolben, who is at present recognized as a sure authority, wrote of the Hottentots: "The rigidity and celerity of their justice are points where they surpass anything in Christianity." Missionaries have been surprised that among the Zulus "in spite of the absence, during ages, of all revealed truth and of all suitable religious instruction, there still remains so much mental integrity, capacity to discern truth and justice, and consideration for these principles in their everyday dealings with one another."

Westermarck goes on to cite similar testimony pertaining to other primitive peoples in Africa and to the Bedouins.[121]

What we have seen can be rather surprising. Here are peoples who are in many cases cut off from civilization, and who in many cases have customs which even in report curdle the blood of a civilized man. Many of these customs are opposed to primary conclusions of natural law. And because of their gross lack of suitable training, we might be tempted to think that they are equivalently imbeciles and therefore excused from the observance of the natural law.

But, on the contrary, we have seen that these people, as a group, do have a knowledge of good and evil, can distinguish the two, and realize that they have an obligation to choose good. They thus have sufficiently developed powers of reason to be classified as moral adults and to be held responsible for the observance of at least the primary conclusions of natural law.

To be sure, they may be less likely than others who are more advanced to arrive at a knowledge of the secondary conclusions of natural law. And conceivably, in some, or even many of these cases, they might as a group arrive at the use of reason at a later age than those who are growing up in a more advanced culture.

But as a rule, members of barbarous societies develop their powers of reason sufficiently to be responsible for observing primary conclusions of natural law. There may possibly be discovered some society in which the members are all imbeciles even apart from some intrinsic cause such as inbreeding (see above) but certainly this is not true of the primitive societies which have been studied up to the present time.[122]

Primitive peoples, in general, possess sufficiently developed powers of reason to enable them to perceive easily the malice of those customs of their society which are opposed to primary conclusions of natural law. If they perceive this malice, and still commit these sins, they are guilty of the sin itself. If they do not perceive the malice of one or more of these sins which they themselves fall into, and remain in for a long time, this failure is due to deliberate and culpable negligence.

There is, however, another possible type of mental retardation due to faulty education of a person with a normally functioning brain. This is the case of those rather rare individuals who apparently have been raised without any human companionship whatsoever. A recent instance was that of the so-called Gazelle Boy. Seemingly, he had grown up alone in the jungle with no companions except animals. At a chronologically advanced age he was found and captured by other human beings. He displayed the mannerisms of an animal, and seemingly had a completely undeveloped mind.

Are such persons to be considered imbeciles or is it possible that even they are adult in the moral sense? St. Thomas Aquinas deals explicitly with this question. He brings up the question of whether a person who grows up in the wilderness or is raised by wolves, or other brute animals, can make a minimal act of faith. And he says that if someone is brought up in such a fashion, and follows the directives of natural reason in pursuing the good and avoiding evil, it is certainly to be held that God will either reveal to him those things necessary for a minimal act of faith or will send some preacher of the faith to him in the way that He sent St. Peter to Cornelius (Acts 10).[123] St. Thomas, then, holds that even these people will reach moral adulthood. Catholic theologians have not discussed this matter to any great extent, however, and the lack of any exhaustive scientific studies on the subject makes it impossible as yet to settle in a definitive manner the theological question involved.

The question, in any case, has little practical importance. The number of Gazelle Boys is extremely small when compared with the total number of men on earth. Thus, regardless of the solution of this last question, the crucial conclusion remains: in almost all societies, the vast majority of human beings who have reached physical maturity qualify as moral adults. Therefore, the vast majority of men are personally accountable for at least the observance of primary conclusions of natural law.

But granting at least that most people, regardless of culture, will reach moral adulthood, and are therefore responsible for observing the primary conclusions of natural law,[124] the further question arises: At what chronological age will this occur? No set answer to this question is possible. Many will reach the knowledge of moral responsibility by the age of seven. Many others will reach it later, even much later.

We need not feel, however, that this age should be set

very high for many people. All that is required is a knowledge of personal moral responsibility. It is possible and even probable for a person to have this knowledge long before gaining a detailed knowledge of the precepts and customs of his own society. A child is responsible, in the context of the natural law, merely for avoiding pitfalls which he himself faces and which are easy to perceive (i.e., sins opposed to primary conclusions of natural law). That is, he is responsible for observing prohibitive precepts from the moment he meets a situation in which he has to make a choice. (As we have mentioned before, there could be invincible ignorance for a short period even after this but not indefinitely.)

With regard to positive precepts (v.g., the obligation to believe in God as Creator and Remunerator), God in His providence would at the least arrange it that anyone who reached the use of reason would not die without having been able to observe them.[125]

5. The Possibility of Serious Guilt

Having examined the meaning of the word adult as it is used here, we now turn to the last question relating to the fundamental postulate: No adult can remain for a long time in invincible ignorance of primary conclusions of natural law. Granting that this postulate is true, and knowing what we mean by each part of the proposition, what are its moral implications? Are adults who find themselves in vincible ignorance or in willful contempt of primary conclusions of natural law only guilty of peccadillos, or can they be guilty of serious and damning sins when they violate these primary conclusions. Do the words culpable and guilty as they have been used here imply that pagans can be seriously guilty and deserving of hell?

The question of the extent to which God will punish

violations of primary conclusions of natural law has been answered by God Himself in the pages of Sacred Scripture. In his Epistle to the Romans, St. Paul concludes his list of sins against primary conclusions of natural law for which he says pagans are inexcusable by saying: "Although they have known the ordinance of God they have not known that those who practice such things are deserving of death" (Rom. 1:32). "Tribulation and anguish shall be visited upon the soul of every man who works evil; of Jew first and then of Gentile" (Rom. 2:9).

This idea is repeated elsewhere in the New Testament (Cf. Acts 2:47; 13:48; and 2 Cor. 4:3). The waters of Baptism wash the sins of converts from paganism who otherwise would have lost heaven because of their sins.

Other lists of obvious violations of natural law are cited in the New Testament (Cf. 1 Cor. 6:9–11; Gal. 5:19–21; Eph. 5:5). Those who commit these sins, like those mentioned in Romans, are in each case cited as seriously culpable. They "cannot possess the kingdom of God."

These passages apply equally to all, Jew and Gentile. The sins of the pagans against primary conclusions of natural law, then, are not sins whose guilt is small and can be ignored. They are seriously culpable violations of the natural law of God, and as such are to be punished.

The Fathers of the Church reaffirmed the Biblical statements. St. Theophilus of Antioch wrote (c. 180) "Give reverential attention to the . . . Scriptures and they will make your way plainer for escaping the eternal punishments, and obtaining the eternal prizes of God."[126] Speaking of the depraved customs of the Romans, St. Clement of Alexandria wrote "Luxury has deranged all things. . . . no passage is closed against libidinousness; and their promiscuous lechery is a public institution. . . . Fathers, unmindful of the children of theirs that have been exposed, often without their knowledge, have intercourse with a son that has

debauched himself, and daughters that are prostitutes:
. . . These things your wise laws allow; people may sin
legally; and the execrable indulgence in pleasure they call a
thing indifferent. They who commit adultery against nature
think themselves free from adultery. Avenging justice follows their audacious deeds, and dragging upon themselves
inevitable calamity, they purchase death."[127]

St Irenaeus (c. 140–c. 202) said "All those are not partakers (of the means through which the Spirit works) who
do not join themselves to the Church, but defraud themselves of life through their evil opinions and infamous be-
havior."[128]

And it would seem that the words of Pope Benedict XIV
reiterated by Pius X are not irrelevant here: "The greater
part of those who are damned . . . have become so by ignorance of mysteries of faith which they should have known
and believed."[129] He refers this to souls in general and not to
any particular group. He seems to refer here to pagans as
well as to Christians or other groups.

Revelation and the teaching of the Church, then, indicate
that pagans are seriously guilty when they violate any of a
great number of primary conclusions of natural law; and
that when they violate these laws and remain in their serious
sin, they will be punished for it eternally in hell. At this
point we stop.

It must be remembered that the statements in the foregoing chapter on primary conclusions are all principles, not
judgments. They do not enable any human being to judge
the subjective guilt of any other human being. We can set
down a list of some of the primary conclusions of natural
law. We can say that all adults (who can distinguish good
from evil and recognize the moral imperative) will be guilty
if they violate these conclusions for a long time. We can
also say that this guilt will be serious in the violation of many
of these conclusions. But whether a given individual who is

apparently violating one of these conclusions is *de facto* seriously guilty is not for men to say. Too many factors are hidden from view. A man who apparently has been violating a primary conclusion of natural law may not, here and now, be seriously guilty: because he may not as yet have had time for sufficient reflection, and thus not have incurred grave guilt at all; or if he did once incur that guilt, he may have secretly obtained the forgiveness of God since that time by making a perfect act of contrition (*cum voto sacramenti*); or because of some other hidden factor which human observers are unable to perceive. For the same reasons, we must also reserve judgment on those who have already made their exit from this life while apparently complacent in a violation of some primary conclusion.

Decisions on guilt in practice belong to God alone.

"Judge not that you may not be judged" (Matt. 7:1). Human beings cannot go all the way in this matter. "Who will ever dare to claim to determine the limits of (invincible) ignorance?"[130]

On the other hand, the fact that we can make no final judgment on guilt does not permit us to develop an attitude of unqualified optimism with regard to the state of soul of one who apparently has been violating a primary conclusion of natural law for a long time. We should not in such cases presume that he is free of guilt and therefore neglect to make even prudent efforts to correct him. On the contrary, we should have grave fears that he may be in the state of sin, and on that basis, efforts should be made to correct him if those efforts can be made prudently.

Applying this whole discussion to a society: if the laws of a society tolerate the violation of a primary conclusion of natural law, and if a large number of the members of that society take advantage of this toleration and violate that primary conclusion, we have very grave motives for suspecting the state of formal and serious sin in the great majority of this number. And if, indeed, a society or religious group does tolerate the violation of a primary conclusion of natural law, we have a very strong motive for introducing the Catholic apostolate in that society. For there is a very real danger of damnation *en masse* for those violating the primary conclusions if they do not receive the Catholic evangelization.[131]

From the foregoing chapter, then, we have seen that many of the primary conclusions are reasonably detailed and are not mere platitudes; that the phrase "developed powers of reason" in our context does not by any means exclude the vast majority of those who have reached physical adulthood; and that there is a real possibility of serious guilt in lengthy violation of primary conclusions of natural law.

But before drawing conclusions on the significance of primary conclusions as criteria of probative holiness of religion, and as furnishing pressing motives for the Catholic apostolate, it is necessary to examine one more point: the extent to which the major non-Catholic religions tolerate the violation of these primary conclusions. This is the subject of our next chapter.

CHAPTER THREE

The Major Religions and the Primary Conclusions

1. *Introduction*

Having these things in mind, we shall now study the moral codes of the various religions of the world in the light of primary conclusions of natural law.

In aligning the religions of the world for study, there is one fact which can surprise even a person who already has a fairly extensive knowledge of comparative religion: the holiest religions tend to have the greatest membership. We often hear of Christianity, Buddhism, Islam, Confucianism,[1] etc., as being more elevated in their moral code than the more gross forms of paganism. We might tend to think of the former religions as small islands in a sea of sin. But in fact, the reverse is true. The total number of adherents of these few well-known religions is much greater than the number of adherents of the almost infinite number of more primitive religions.

The statistics[2] run approximately as follows:

Catholics	480 million
Protestants	210 "
Schismatics	130 "
Confucianists	300 "

Moslems	420	million
Hindus	320	"
Buddhists	150	"
Taoists-Shintoists	80	"
Jews	12	"
All others	530	"

These statistics are, indeed, only approximations, and intended chiefly to show the rough proportion of the members of each group in the total population of the world. The numbers given do not include only the devout adherents of each, nor only those who are at least lukewarm. They refer to all those who consider themselves members of these religions even if they make little or no attempt to observe their moral codes.

The statistics reveal, then, that the great majority of men do claim some sort of membership in one or other of a handful of religions. This makes our task simpler. There is no need to treat a vast number of religions in order to get a picture of the various beliefs of men on earth. The total membership of a few of the largest religions far exceeds that of all other religions combined. Thus, in order to obtain a sketch of the moral codes of most men on earth, we need only study these few major religions. By concentrating on them, we get a bird's-eye view of what most men accept, and of the extent to which the creeds of most men are in accord with primary conclusions of natural law.

The Minor Religions

Apart from the few major religions of the present and past, there have been thousands of pagan religions restricted in their membership to a relatively small group of men, a tribe, a nation, etc. For the most part, these religions were stagnant, restricted to the groups in which they found themselves, making no serious attempt to proselytize among other peoples. Even when one group conquered another, often no attempt was made to spread the conquerors' religion among the conquered.

But what about their moral codes? Are the differences between the moral codes of these religions and that of Christianity restricted to disagreements on minor liturgical points, or obscure ethical conclusions? To be sure, most of the fundamental virtues are observed in every society of human beings. But a study of these small pagan societies reveals that in every known instance, their ethical codes will oppose at least one primary conclusion of natural law. But this does not mean that they oppose natural law in the same way. One religion will ignore the primary conclusion that the others will accept. The ancient Persians allowed intermarriage of parents and children.[3] The Scythians put out their servants' eyes to prevent them from running away.[4] In some primitive societies, murder for slight reasons (v.g., satisfaction of sadism) has been ignored as a slight fault or even as licit.[5] In Babylon, among other places, sacred prostitution formed part of the temple service.[6]

One of the violations of a primary conclusion of natural law which has been tolerated by many pagan religions is that of human sacrifice. In fact, few races and few religions can show a history free from the stain of it. And in a great many of these cases of human sacrifice the victim is no criminal nor member of an enemy tribe. Rather he is an innocent member, whether child or adult, of the sacrificing tribe itself.[7] Westermarck gives us an idea of the scale on which human sacrifice has been carried on: "It took place at least on certain occasions in ancient India and many modern Hindu sects practiced it even up to the last century. Numerous citations prove it was known among the primitive Greeks. At certain epochs it was a part of the Hellenic cult of Zeus; even up to the second century after Christ men seem to have sacrificed in Arcadia to Zeus Lycaeus. And in historical times, Porphyry asks: 'Who does not know that up until this day, in the great city of Rome, they butcher a man at the feast of Jupiter Latiaris?' And Tertullian writes that in his own North Africa . . . small children were being publicly sacrificed to Saturn. The Celts, Teutons, and Slavs offered human sacrifices; so did the ancient Semites, the Egyptians, the primitive Japanese, and in the new world the Mayas and to a horrifying degree the Aztecs. . . . It also existed or still exists (1929) among the Caribe (Caraibes), among some North American tribes, and in various South Sea islands, especially at Tahiti and the Fiji Islands. And one finds it among certain tribes of the Malay Archipelago, . . . and very frequently in Africa."[8]

Many pagan societies allow killing of human beings for other obviously invalid reasons. Allowing infanticide for motives of shame, or in order to avoid difficulties of raising the children, is not uncommon.[9]

Some form or other of polytheism is tolerated "among practically all peoples who have lacked the guiding star of divine revelation."[10]

There are other examples of violations of primary conclusions of natural law (v.g., unlimited divorce, and abandonment of infants)[11] which are tolerated by a great many pagan religions. In fact, virtually all of the minor pagan religions tolerate the violation of at least several primary conclusions of natural law. The minor pagan religions, in general, then, are blatantly defective in leading their members to practice all of the most elementary and necessary virtues.

The Major Religions

But what about the major religions of the world? We have mentioned that the major religions are, in general, holier than the others. But is this superiority so great that none of the major religions tolerates the violation of any primary conclusion? And if not, which ones fail, and to what extent?

In the list of major religions which we shall treat, we shall include both those religions which have numerically the greatest memberships and those religions and philosophies which have contributed to pre-Christian Western thought.

The numerically largest religions are all included for two reasons: a choice on the basis of numbers avoids the objection that those chosen were selected for proximity to Christianity for the purpose of giving a false impression of the similarity between religions; secondly, such a choice also avoids the charge that those chosen were selected for divergency from Christianity for the purpose of giving a false impression of the supereminent holiness of Christianity. In studying all the numerically greatest religions, we avoid a charge of ethical bias in selection.

The pre-Christian Western religions and philosophies have been added in spite of their numerically small following (at least in our own day) because of the fact that they are well known among us, and for that reason are of interest.

Many of the religions and philosophies treated below are not ideologically united or organizationally well-knit. In fact, most of them are merely conglomerations of people holding a few basic ideas in common and often disagreeing among themselves even on many fundamental questions of ethics.

The ethical systems which will be treated in detail here are: Hinduism, Buddhism, Confucianism, the systems of Plato and Aristotle, Stoicism, Islam, Judaism, heretical and schismatical systems, and Catholicism.

2. Hinduism

Unlike most of the great religions and philosophies of the world, Hinduism cannot be traced to any single founder.

As much as or more than any of the others, Hinduism is the result of a slow process of amalgamation of different and often even contradictory philosophical ideas. The study of Hinduism is the study of this amalgamation.

Hinduism can be said to have passed through three primary phases. The first or Vedic phase covered the period from c. 1000 to c. 800 B.C. The emphasis in the *Vedas,* the sacred literature of this period, is on prayer and sacrifice. A life of virtue is primarily a life of worship. The objects of this worship are many. Polytheism is rampant. The forces of nature are deified. But there are traces, too, of monotheism.[12] One of the gods, Varuna, is sometimes referred to as supreme over all men and all other gods. After death God will punish the sinner, and reward the virtuous. This reward and punishment will be personal. There is no reincarnation.

The second or Brahmanic period (c. 800–c. 650 B.C.) is one of formalization. In the *Atharva Veda,* the *Brahmanas* and the *Aranyakasa,* the sacred books of this period, the heritage of the Vedic period is excessively ceremonialized. The power of sacrifice is exaggerated. Sacrificial rites are considered to force the gods to do what is asked. Monotheism, however, grows. Nature-gods fade before the emerging figure of an Absolute. Asceticism and the eremitical life develop. The flexible class system of the Vedic period gives way to a rigid caste system.

The third or Upanishadic period covers roughly the years 650 to 500 B.C. Here the doctrine of reincarnation is fully developed. Those who are good on earth are reborn in a higher form of life; the evil, reborn in a lower. A man in a low caste, if evil, will be reborn after death as an animal; if good, he will be reborn in a higher or even in the highest caste as a human. Those who achieve the highest perfection on earth will be rewarded by escaping this tedious series of future rebirths through having their individual personalities absorbed into the absolute. God is often described not as a personal provider, but as an impersonal thing or being. Pantheism begins to be advocated. The writings of this period, the *Upanishads*, render token homage to all the writings that precede them, although in fact they often contradict or implicitly refute earlier teaching.

After the *Upanishads*, many other philosophies and religions arose in India, but most of the later ideas are based on the *Upanishads*. Later teachers either discovered their teachings originally in the *Upanishads*, or, *post factum*, found something in the *Upanishads* to support teachings which they had already formulated themselves.[13] The *Upanishads* contained such a variety of ideas that this latter task was not difficult.

Doctrinally, there is very little common ground among Hindus. On the moral law there is. Hindus agree on many moral questions. Of the sacred books dealing with Hindu law, by far the first in importance as well as the first in date is the one which is called the *Laws of Manu*.

Geographically, Hinduism, as such, has been restricted almost entirely to India. Heretical offshoots of it, however, such as Buddhism, have spread through other parts of Asia.

Hindu ethics are like our own to a surprising extent. "Truthfulness, honesty, self-control, obedience to parents and superiors, the moderate use of food and drink, chastity, and almsgiving are strongly inculcated."[14] Many other natural virtues are encouraged, and vices against nature forbidden.

Religious Assent

Sometimes we find Hindu literature even in the earliest times, as we have noted, expressing acceptance of one supreme God.[15] On the other hand, sometimes polytheism is taught. Texts like the following have been understood by some Hindus in a polytheistic sense. "Even an infant king must not be despised (from an idea) that he is a (mere) mortal; for he is a great deity in human form."[16] And at the same time, we have in other Hindu scriptures (at least in the absolute of the *Upanishads*) the seeds of pantheism and also of a reduction of God to nothing more than an impersonal and indifferent fate. On the other hand, no Hindu scripture is brought forward by Hindus to support strict atheism or agnosticism. Atheism is abhorred.[17]

On the question of the next life, Hinduism provides a variety of answers. The *Rig-Veda*[18] and the *Laws of Manu* teach a personal reward and punishment after death. The exact nature of future life is not clear. But the *Laws of Manu* do specify that the reward for virtue in this life is to be "eternal bliss" after death.

Some aspects of the Hindu doctrine of reincarnation do not exclude completely all idea of personal consciousness of the reward or punishment in the next life. "In consequence of a remnant of the guilt of former crimes, are born idiots, dumb, blind, deaf, and deformed men who are all despised by the virtuous. Penances, therefore, must always be performed for the sake of the purification, because those whose sins have not been expiated are born (again) with disgraceful marks."[19] "Some wicked men suffer a change of their appearance in consequence of crimes committed in this life, and some in consequence of those committed in a former (existence)."[20] If the next rebirth is conceived of as human, then, reflexively, by seeing one's station in life, one is in a sense made conscious of having previously been a sinner or a man of virtue.

But this reflexive awareness of sin is not a complete personal consciousness of reward and punishment. There is no memory of what specific crimes were committed or of what virtuous acts were performed. And there is no continuity of consciousness. One cannot know who or what one was in any previous life. Even Hindus make no claim that all men have an awareness of having existed previously. At best, only a few can gain this awareness. "By daily reciting the Veda, by (the observance of the rules of) purification, by (practicing) austerities, and by doing no injury to created beings, one (obtains the faculty of) remembering former births."[21]

And if in the Hindu system there is only a remnant of consciousness when a man is reborn as a human, what is to be said if, because of his sins, he is reborn as an animal? The failure of the Hindu teaching on reincarnation to include a real idea of personal future sanction is especially evident when the future existence is thought of as that of a brute animal. St. Justin expresses this in his *Dialogue with Trypho*. Speaking of the opinion that sinners after death pass into wild beasts as a punishment, he asks: "Do they know, then, that it is for this reason that they are in such forms, and that they have committed some sin?" Receiving the reply, "I do not think so," he continues: "Then these reap no advantage from their punishment; . . . moreover, I would say that they are not punished unless they are conscious of their punishment."[22]

The Hindu belief in reincarnation, then, cannot logically include a belief in a personal sanction. But what people believe and what is logical do not always coincide. It is possible that a Hindu, in the concrete, could believe in reincarnation, and by a series of misapprehensions also believe that his future sanction will be personal.

Whatever its shortcomings, the Hindu doctrine of reincarnation does represent an attempt to arrive at a concept of future retribution, and it also tries to explain how there can be consciousness of reward or punishment. But what is to be said of the Hindu doctrine of absorption after death of those who have become perfect in this life? How can a person who is absorbed into the absolute be conceived of as retaining any semblance of personal consciousness of reward whatsoever?

Paradoxically, even the doctrine of absorption does not

necessarily imply that the soul completely loses individuality and personal consciousness. Not all Hindu thinkers express the idea of absorption in terms of complete negation of individual consciousness. Many hold that there is a persistence of the conscious self in absorption just as there was in the previous series of rebirths.

At times, it seems that the Hindu concept of absorption can be likened to an expression in negative terms of the Christian idea of heaven. The Christian heaven can, to be sure, be described in negative terms, but the emphasis in Christianity is on the positive aspect of the perfect happiness which will be found there. The Hindu emphasis in absorption is on the complete absence of unhappiness. In describing this, Hindus often seem to destroy so much that nothing is left of the individual. But at times there is a glimmer of personality left even after absorption. Radhakrishnan speaks of an "eternal self" and says absorption "is neither waking nor dreaming nor sleep, but a fourth witnessing to as well as transcending the three." It is not waking, because this consciousness of internal and external objects implies change, and there can be no change. It is not dreaming or sleep since there is a likelihood that these can be confused with sheer unconsciousness. "It is not the absence of unhappiness. It is positive bliss." "It is a pure intuitional consciousness." The *Upanishads* did not intend to "make of the deeper self an abstract nothingness . . . . or a mere blank. It is the fullest reality, the completest consciousness, . . . untroubled by any unrest and unpolluted by any spot or blemish."[23] "Nothing of value is lost. Whatever spiritual values we seek after on earth and find imperfectly, we possess in the highest condition absolutely."[24] "The true eternal self . . . is not a bundle of qualities called the me, but the I which remains beyond and behind inspecting all these qualities. . . . The self . . . is free from sin, free from old age, from death and grief, from hunger and thirst, which desires nothing but what it ought to desire and imagines nothing but what it ought to imagine."[25]

In this last sentence especially, we see an expression admirably suited to describe the Christian heaven.

The discourse as a whole, however, seems to a Christian to be full of contradictions. How, for example, can there be any kind of consciousness without any consciousness of internal or external objects? Radhakrishnan sees these difficulties and at the end wisely adds that, in this whole question, the *Upanishads* are forced to use "inadequate concepts." "Strictly speaking," he says, "we cannot say anything of it. Yet for purposes of discussion we are obliged to use intellectual concepts with their limited validity."[26]

Perhaps the whole reason for the Christian misunderstanding of Hindu thought is that Hinduism tries to go too deeply into the exact nature of perfect bliss. In doing so it goes beyond the power of language and mundane thought and becomes involved in contradictions. Christians are accustomed to hearing the entire discussion end where the Hindus begin: The greatest reward in the next life is perfect bliss.

Every type of future existence, according to Hindu teaching, then, can be understood in either of two ways: as annihilation of personal consciousness, or as true personal retribution. If a Hindu accepts these doctrines in the sense of annihilation or essential destruction of the person after death, he does not make a minimal act of religious assent. If, on the other hand, he understands them as promising him a future personal reward or punishment, he can have this minimal assent.

Moral Effort

Hinduism inculcates a strong sense of fatalism. Wilkins has set forth the traditional Hindu attitude on this subject.

In his chapter on "Religious Notions Common to Hindus Generally," he lists Fate as sixth, and says: "No doctrine is more commonly and implicitly believed than this, that all man's life is arranged by the deity, and that it is useless for him to attempt to go against the Divine decrees; all that man can do is submit"; "This bowing to Fate paralyzes effort, and multitudes die year by year through its baneful influence. In times of sickness remedial measures will not be tried, because if it is written that the patient must die, he will die, whatever trouble be taken or expense incurred"; "No doctrine seems to be more necessary to India than this: that it is not enough to say, 'God mend all.' "[27]

Benevolence

Love of God presupposes that God is thought of as a person. Thus, for the Hindu thinkers who deny that God is a person, there can be no true love of God.

But some of the Hindus who conceive of God as a person also encourage a love for Him. The great Hindu scripture, the *Bhagavadgita* (date uncertain: estimates range from the fifth century B.C. to 200 A.D.), teaches that salvation is attained by love of God and devotion to Him. And Rabia, a Hindu woman mystic, says: "O my Lord, if I worship Thee from fear of hell, burn me in hell; and if I worship Thee from hope of paradise, exclude me thence; but if I worship Thee for Thine own sake, then withhold not from me Thine eternal beauty."[28] Whether the Hindu concept of love of God is native to India or borrowed, the fact remains that this concept can be found in Hinduism.

Love of neighbor can be discussed from two points of view: externally (the expression of that esteem in concrete acts of charity) and internally (the esteem which men have for their fellow men considered as human beings).

In the first of these, love of neighbor considered externally, Hinduism differs from Christianity. In the teaching of Christianity, there is great emphasis on the necessity of performing corporal works of mercy: feeding and clothing and providing shelter for all those in need, visiting and caring for the sick, etc. Christianity teaches that charity should be universal, that all who are in need should be assisted. Hinduism qualifies this.

Hinduism does encourage generosity toward friends and toward those who are deserving of gifts.[29] "Both he who respectfully receives [a gift] and he who respectfully bestows it, to go to heaven."[30] "When he has bestowed [a gift] let him not boast of it."[31] On religious grounds, Hinduism also demands that all be ready to provide for the needs of wandering ascetics and all those whose lives are devoted to the service of religion.

But disinterested giving to others simply because they are in need, regardless of personal friendship for the recipient, and regardless of merit in the recipient is not encouraged in the Hindu scriptures.[32] On the contrary, we read, "Let him be liberal . . . and charitable . . . if he finds a worthy recipient [for his gifts]."[33]

Internal love of neighbor among Hindus is qualified greatly by the ideas prevalent throughout the East and also particularly by the Hindu caste system and the doctrine of reincarnation. In Hinduism, not all human beings are considered as equals before God.

Hinduism, like the other great religions of the East, teaches that women are unclean and inferior beings.[34] "Though destitute of virtue, or seeking pleasure [elsewhere], or devoid of good qualities [yet] a husband must be constantly worshipped as a god by a faithful wife."[35] "Women universally, and not just certain individuals, are depraved." "Women do not care for beauty, nor is their attention fixed on age; [thinking], '[It is enough that] he is a man,' they give themselves to the handsome and the ugly. Through their passion for men, through their mutable temper, through their natural heartlessness, they become disloyal towards their husbands, however carefully they may be guarded in this [world]. Knowing their disposition which the Lord of creatures laid in them at the creation, to be such, [every] man should most strenuously exert himself to [protect them from sin]. [When creating them] Manu allotted to women [a love of their] bed, [of their] seat and [of] ornament, impure desires, wrath, dishonesty, malice, and bad conduct. For women no [sacramental] rite [is performed] with sacred texts."[36] Women can be saved, but only with great difficulty.

Hindu internal love of neighbor is also restricted by the caste system. The caste system is not simply an external grouping of men into social classes. Members of different castes are regarded as essentially different as human beings. "One-fourth [of the penance] for the murder of a Brahmana is prescribed [as expiation] for [intentionally] killing a Kshatriya [member of the second highest caste], one-eighth for killing a Vaisya [third highest caste]; know that it is one-sixteenth for killing a virtuous Sudra [lowest caste]."[37] "Let [the Brahman householder] not give to a Sudra advice, nor the remnants [of his meal], nor food offered to the gods; nor let him explain the sacred law [to such a man], nor impose [upon him] a penance."[38] Wilkins says, "It is among the Hindus . . . that the imagination of natural and positive distinction of humanity has been brought to the most fearful . . . development ever exhibited on the face of the globe." . . . The upper class has ruled "often without the sympathies of a recognized common humanity."[39]

There are some teachings in the Hindu scriptures which, when developed, would lead to the disintegration of the caste system. But in strict Hinduism, the idea of division of men into castes is very strong.

The doctrine of reincarnation also has serious implications in the matter of fraternal charity. In the *Laws of Manu,* we read, "In consequence of a remnant of [the guilt of] former crimes, are born idiots, dumb, blind, deaf, and deformed men, who are [all] despised by the virtuous. Penances, therefore, must always be performed for the sake of purification, because those whose sins have not been expiated, are born [again] with disgraceful marks."[40] This idea that those who are born with physical defects are to be despised because these defects are due to sins in a former birth is not illogical once the doctrine of reincarnation is accepted.

Paradoxically, however, the *Laws of Manu* also contain this passage: "Let him not insult those who have redundant limbs, or are deficient in limbs, nor those destitute of knowledge, nor very aged men, nor those who have no beauty or wealth, nor those who are of low birth."[41]

If Hindus wish to equal Christian charity, they must ignore much of the teaching of their own scriptures and pick out only those parts of them which are in accord with correct ideas of fraternal charity. And in order to discover and practice some types of charity, notably the corporal works of mercy in their fullness, they must go completely beyond the restrictions set down by their own scriptures.

First Commandment

On the first of the ten commandments, Hinduism encourages acts of worship of one supreme God. But we also find toleration and even encouragement of polytheistic worship. "Teaching [and studying] is the sacrifice offered to Brahman, the [offerings of water and food called] Tarpana the sacrifice to the manes, the burnt oblation the sacrifice offered to the gods, the Bali offering that offered to the Bhutas, and the hospitable reception of guests the offering to men. . . . He who does not feed these five . . . lives not, though he breathes."[42] "A Brahmana shall offer . . . a portion of the cooked food . . . in the sacred domestic fire to the following deities: First to Agni, and [next] to Soma, then to both these gods conjointly, further to all the gods [Visve Devah], and [then] to Dhanvantari: Further to Kuhû [the goddess of the new-moon day], to Anumati [the goddess of the full-moon day], to Pragapati [the lord of creatures], to heaven and earth conjointly, and finally to Agni Svishtakrit [the fire which performs the sacrifice well]. . . . Let him throw Bali offerings in all directions . . . saying '[Adoration] to the Maruts,' . . . to the waters . . . to the trees."[43]

And in practice, there seem to be clear instances of worship which is strictly idolatrous. In the temples where Gopal is worshipped, for instance, the idol is treated as if it were itself alive. At certain times of day it is washed, anointed, given food and drink; and at the close of the day, placed in bed.[44]

Second Commandment

Apart from disrespect for God arising indirectly from sins against the virtue of faith, Hindus are strict in their observance of the second commandment. There may be disagreement on the forms of religious observance which should be followed, but any thought of deliberate blasphemy or contempt of God is far from the Hindu mind.

On oaths, the *Laws of Manu* say "Let no wise man swear an oath falsely, even in a trifling matter; for he who swears an oath falsely is lost in this [world] and after death."[45] A series of penalties is listed for those who commit perjury from motives of covetousness, distraction, fear, friendship, lust, anger, ignorance, or childishness.[46]

But perjury is not wrong in all circumstances. "In [some] cases a man who, though knowing [the facts to be] different, gives [false evidence] from a pious motive, does not lose heaven; such [evidence] they call the speech of the gods. Whenever the death of a Sudra, of a Vaisya, of a Kshatriya, or of a Brahmana would be [caused] by a declaration of the truth, a falsehood may be spoken; for such [falsehood] is preferable to the truth."[47] In other special cases the guilt of perjury is at least mitigated. "No crime, causing loss of caste, is committed by swearing [falsely] to women, the objects of one's desire, at marriages, for the sake of fodder for a cow, or of fuel, and in [order to show] favor to a Brahmana."[48]

Whether or not these exceptions would be opposed to primary conclusions of natural law would depend on the extent to which a liberal interpretation were given them.

Third Commandment

Hinduism, generally, cannot be accused of violating the third commandment by defect. The worship may frequently be misdirected, but at least its frequent performance is encouraged. "When he has risen . . . let him stand during the morning twilight, muttering for a long time [the Gayatri], and at the proper time [he must similarly perform] the evening devotion."[49]

Hinduism can, however, be accused of having too many liturgical rules, especially for the Brahmans. The list of foods that a Brahman "must never eat" makes the Jewish and Moslem lists seem quite moderate. Even foods which in themselves are not objectionable, can become so when they are received from any of a multitude of objectionable donors. "Let him never eat [food given] by intoxicated, angry, or sick [men], . . . nor that at which the slayer of a learned Brahmana has looked . . . nor the food [given] by a thief, a musician, a carpenter, a usurer, . . . a miser, . . . by one accused of mortal sin, . . . by a physician, . . . a cruel man, . . . an actor, a tailor, . . . a blacksmith, . . . a basketmaker," etc.[50] (A starving man, however, may eat any food.)

The Brahmans were oppressed by a maddening number of regulations which covered virtually every move they could make.[51] The penances for the violation of some of these laws were severe, even when the violation was inadvertent. "But if a Brahmana unintentionally kills a Kshatriya, he shall give, in order to purify himself, one thousand cows and a bull; or he may perform the penance prescribed for the murderer of a Brahmana during three years, controlling himself, wearing his hair in braids, staying far away from the village, and dwelling at the root of a tree. A Brahmana who has slain a virtuous Vaisya, shall perform the same penance during one year, or he may give one hundred cows and one [bull]. He who has slain a Sudra, shall perform that whole penance during six months, or he may also give ten white cows and one bull to a Brahmana."[52]

At the other extreme, if he performed a certain difficult liturgical act, that of memorizing the Rig-Veda, he was excused not only from all other liturgical laws, but from the natural moral law as well. A Brahman who "retains in his memory the Rig-Veda" is thereby excused in committing any sin. He "is not stained by guilt, though he may have destroyed these three worlds, though he may eat the food of anybody."[53]

But "the Brahmans were under so many restrictions that did not bind other castes that the more scrupulous felt life to be a burden and became imbued with the spirit of pessimism."[54]

Fourth Commandment

Under the fourth commandment, Hinduism strongly inculcates respect and obedience for parents, teachers, and for those with civil authority. And those in authority, in turn must protect and provide for the needs of their subjects. The king must "behave like father to all men."[55]

Fifth Commandment

Under the fifth commandment, Hinduism forbids murder but allows killing in self-defense and in the defense of others. "In their own defense, . . . and in order to protect women and Brahmanas; he who [under such circumstances] kills in the cause of right commits no sin. One may slay without hesitation an assassin who approaches [with murderous intent], whether [he be one's] teacher, a child or an aged man, or a Brahmana deeply versed in the Vedas."[56] And on a wider scale—war is allowed if there is a just cause.

Euthanasia, suicide and certain other methods of killing innocent adults are, at least under most circumstances, forbidden. On the other hand, with regard to the killing of infants, although abortion is forbidden,[57] abandonment of newly-born infants is allowed by some of the scriptures and is practiced on a wide scale. "The father and mother have power to give, to sell, and to abandon their children."[58] This toleration usually applies only to infants and not to older children. Once the support of a child has been taken on, it is considered wrong to abandon it later. But up to modern times, the abandoning of infants, especially female infants, has been allowed on a wide scale among Hindu peoples,[59] even though there is strong evidence that those who resort to it experience a sense of guilt.[60]

To a lesser extent, the notorious Hindu practice of immolating the widow on her husband's funeral pyre has received official approval. This practice, however, is not common to all Hindu peoples, and it is not sanctioned by the Hindu scriptures, but only by later writings.[61]

In one way, the Hindus carry the fifth commandment too

far. As a consequence of their doctrine of reincarnation, they have strict laws prohibiting the killing of all animals. The killing of any animal or insect, however small, is to be avoided even at the cost of great inconvenience. The ascetics, in walking, have to scan the ground carefully before them in order to avoid crushing any living creature. "In order to preserve living creatures, let him always by day and by night, even with pain to his body, walk carefully scanning the ground."[62] It is forbidden them to tread on a ploughed field. During the rainy season when insects swarm on the ground in greatest numbers, they move about as little as possible. We read "[Some] declare that agriculture is something excellent, [but] that means of subsistence is blamed by the virtuous; for the wooden [implement] with the iron point injures the earth and the [beings] living in the earth."[63] Insects, however noxious, cannot be killed. This whole system of laws is impossible to observe and leads to discouragement and despair. More of this later, however, in the treatment of Buddhism.

Hindus also teach that anger is to be avoided: "Let him avoid . . . hatred, . . . anger, and harshness. Let him when angry not raise a stick against another man, nor strike [anybody] except a son or a pupil; those two he may beat in order to correct them."[64]

And damage inflicted upon oneself even short of suicide is also to be guarded against. Drunkenness is forbidden. However, "to drink is no sin, although it is better to abstain."[65] Gluttony is sinful.[66]

Sixth Commandment

Under the sixth commandment, Hinduism forbids fornication, adultery, incest, contraception, and sodomy.[67]

On the positive side, the attitude of Hinduism on celibacy resembles that of Christianity. "There is no sin . . .

in marital relations for that is the natural way of created beings, but abstention brings great rewards."[68] For the Hindu, however, the life of renunciation of the rights of marriage is to be initiated only after one has been married. For widows, celibacy is compulsory. Widows must not remarry.[69] Widowers are given a choice. They may remarry,[70] but they are encouraged to take up the celibate life of a hermit or of a monk.

Hinduism allows polygamy, divorce, and, in some places, polyandry. Monogamy is encouraged and praised. But polygamy has been allowed from the earliest times[71] to the present. No limit has been set on the number of wives. The husband may take an additional wife without any need for justification or consent on the part of his present wives.

Hinduism certainly does not actively encourage divorce. "Learned Brahmanas propound this [maxim], 'The husband is declared to be one with the wife.'" "Once is the partition [of the inheritance] made, [once is] a maiden given in marriage, [and] once does [a man] say, 'I will give [a maiden in marriage]'; each of those three [acts is done] once only."[72] Nevertheless, divorce is allowed. "A barren wife may be superseded in the eighth year, she whose children [all] die in the tenth, she who bears only daughters in the eleventh, but she who is quarrelsome without delay."[73] Hindu divorce is not without restrictions. A wife may be repudiated but she may not remarry. "Neither by sale nor by repudiation is a wife released from her husband; such we know the law to be, which the Lord of creatures made of old."[74] Only men may remarry. By the fact that men are prevented from marrying anyone who has herself been married before, the number of women available as second wives is sharply reduced. "The nuptial texts are applied solely to virgins, [and] nowhere among men to females who have lost their virginity, for such [females] are excluded from religious ceremonies."[75]

But in many areas the various restrictions on divorce have been thrown off. The "orthodox Hindu law of divorce is more or less disregarded in certain low castes in the north of India and by many castes both high and low in the south, among whom usage has superseded texts. . . . In some cases the mere will of either party or of both parties suffices. . . . Where it is allowed by custom, a divorce by mutual agreement is also recognized by law."[76]

Seventh Commandment

With few exceptions, the teachings of Hinduism relating to matters covered by the seventh commandment are remarkably like those of Christianity. Honesty is appreciated; stealing forbidden. Contracts are binding. But when a contract is made by an "intoxicated or insane man, or by an infant or a very aged man," it is invalid.[77]

The concept of a just price (i.e., that above which no one should be forced to pay) is set forth. "Let [the king] fix [the rates for] the purchase and sale of all marketable goods, having [duly] considered whence they come, whither they go, how long they have been kept, the [probable] profit and the [probable] outlay."[78]

One can gain ownership by prescription. "[In general] whatever [chattel] an owner [has] seen enjoyed by others during ten years, while, though present, he says nothing, that [chattel] he shall not recover. If [the owner is] neither an idiot nor a minor and if [his chattel] is enjoyed [by another] before his eyes, it is lost to him by law; the adverse possessor shall retain that property." But "a pledge, a boundary, the property of infants, . . . the property of the king . . . are not lost in consequence of [adverse] enjoyment."[79]

Moderate interest may be taken on a loan; usury may

not. "A moneylender may stipulate as an increase of his capital, for the interest, . . . and take monthly the eightieth part of a hundred,"[80] when the debt is secured by a pledge. If there is no security, according to many commentators, a Brahman is to pay two per cent per month; a Kshatriya, three; a Vaisya, four; and a Sudra, five.[81] "In money transactions, interest paid at one time [not by installments] shall never exceed the double [of the principal]."[82]

The *Laws of Manu* forbid all gambling and betting. "Gambling and betting, let the king exclude from his realm. . . . They amount to open theft."[83] "Gambling has been seen to cause great enmity; a wise man, therefore, should not practice it even for amusement."[84] But other Hindu literature tolerates gambling in a public gambling house where the king may have it supervised and collect taxes from it.[85]

Eighth Commandment

Under the eighth commandment, the *Laws of Manu* say "Contumely, calumny, detraction, and gossip shall be the four kinds of [evil] verbal action."[86]

Lying in general is forbidden. But in certain special cases, it is licit. (Cf. what has been said above on the subject of perjury under the second commandment.)

Ninth and Tenth Commandments

Hinduism also recognizes the possibility of sins of thought. "Let him abstain . . . from looking at . . . women." "Coveting the property of others, thinking in one's heart of what is undesirable, and adherence to false [doctrines] are the three kinds of [sinful] mental action."[87]

Conclusions on Hinduism

Beyond precepts, Hinduism especially praises the ascetical life. There are among the adherents of Brahmanism many, especially among the old, who become hermits. They are encouraged to practice austerities. Sometimes this encouragement is very enthusiastic. "In summer, let him [the hermit] expose himself to the heat of five fires, during the rainy season live under the open sky, and in winter be dressed in wet clothes, [thus] gradually increasing [the rigour of] his austerities."[88]

The teaching of Hinduism is far superior in many particulars to the teaching of most pagan religions. On certain points of natural law it even equals Christianity. But on the other hand, Hinduism does tolerate some practices which are obviously evil. Among the evil practices officially[89] tolerated by Hinduism which are also opposed to primary conclusions of natural law can be numbered at least: lack of faith in God as Creator and Remunerator, idolatry, the abandoning of infants, and divorce for an insufficient reason.

3. Buddhism

The founder of Buddhism, called Buddha, was born in about the year 563 B.C. in the northeastern part of India. Reared by wealthy parents, he married and lived in the midst of worldly enjoyments until the age of 29. At this time he fled luxury and took up a life of asceticism. He mortified himself severely for six years. At the end of this period, he received an "enlightenment" and began to teach and win disciples. He taught for 45 years up and down the Ganges Valley, founding monastic orders. He died, many think, at the age of 80 in about the year 483 B.C.

The origin of the Buddhist "scriptures" is uncertain. Originally, and for a long time, the words of Buddha were preserved only by memory.[90] The time and circumstances of their transcription into a written text and of the collection of these texts are unknown. "To speak without qualification of the final revision of the Scriptures is perhaps to take too much for granted, but it is usually held that the general arrangement was fixed at the third Council, 247 B.C. . . . It is from this period, more than two centuries after Buddha's death, that we must start in an inquiry about the age of the canonical texts. In the present state of our knowledge we cannot in any instance declare that Buddha said so and so. The fact that we start from is that we have a collection of documents, which were held some two centuries after Buddha to contain his utterances.

"The texts do not profess to form a uniform whole, every word of which is revealed, as in the case of the Vedas, the Bible or the Koran. That which is revealed is the word of Buddha. . . . But in the texts there is much which does not claim to be in any sense Buddha's utterance. This is recognized by the Buddhist commentators themselves, as when they explain that certain sentences or whole verses have been added by the revisers at one of the Councils. This is also recognized or implied in the considerable number of discourses which are attributed to various disciples, and this not merely in the commentaries, but in the text itself. In some cases these discourses are said to have been given after the death of Buddha. . . . The verses of one monk who lived . . . nearly two centuries after Buddha's death, are said to have been added at the third Council." Doctrinally these facts are not important, as all the teachings of the disciples found in the canon are held to have been first expounded by Buddha.[91]

Historically, Buddhism has been called a "Hindu heresy." Buddha's doctrinal and moral ideas were taken, or rather selected, from the Hindu scriptures.[92] Early Buddhism, we venture to hazard a conjecture, is only a restatement of the thought of the *Upanishads* from a new standpoint. Buddha's originality lay in the way in which he adopted, enlarged, ennobled, and systematized that which had already been said by others, and in the way in which he carried out to their logical conclusion principles of equity and justice already acknowledged.[93]

Buddha, then, was selective. His teaching did not contain the multitude of contradictions found in Hinduism. From Hinduism, he chose those elements which he thought were best and formed them into a fairly consistent philosophy.

Buddha improved on Hinduism, among other things, in his teachings on charity and monasticism. He was inferior, if anything, in his teaching on God, but this inferiority would seem to have been caused rather by simple default than by malice.

There have been many offshoots from Buddhism. Some of these differ so radically that they can be classified in turn as "Buddhist heresies." Among the latter are Zen, Lamaism, Tantrism, Amidism, etc. Some (v.g., Amidism)[94] are lofty and even an improvement on Buddhism in general, others (v.g., Tantrism)[95] are sunk in vice.

Here, however, we shall treat of Buddhism in its more conservative forms, as it is understood by the vast majority of its adherents. The spread of Buddhism has been restricted almost entirely to Asia. In its historical development, the religion has been roughly divided into two segments, Northern and Southern, called the Mahayana and Hinayana, respectively. The Mahayana is found chiefly in the more northern section of Asia (China, Tibet, Japan, etc.). The Hinayana is found chiefly in the south (Ceylon, Burma, Siam, Java, etc.). There are far more Mahayana Buddhists than Hinayana. Theologically, the Hinayana tries to adhere much more strictly to the original ideals set forth by Buddha than does the Mahayana.

Religious Assent

In strict Buddhism, there is neither polytheism nor monotheism. Buddhism is essentially agnostic. According to its founder, the world is uncreated and is self-regulating. There is no concept of an intelligent first cause. The word "God" is understood as "Godhead" or "Fate" and not as "God" in our sense. There is no concept of God as the necessary object of the adoration of men.[96] "We cannot deny . . . that even the absolutely fundamental and indispensable idea of the one and personal God is lacking in pantheistic Buddhism, which yet commands the religious loyalty of hundreds of millions of people."[97]

Buddhist teaching on the next life is similar to that of the *Upanishads*. Reincarnation brings a lower existence to sinners and a higher to the virtuous. The perfect attain *nirvana*, a state of absorption. There is some idea of personal remuneration here, even in nirvana. Buddhists, like the Hindus, do not go so far as to teach that nirvana is annihilation. The difficulties, however, in reconciling Buddhist ideas on reincarnation with a personal future sanction are the same as found in Hindu reincarnation.

A second point in which Buddhist teaching on the future life is opposed to the natural law is a consequence of the Buddhist concept of God. Future retribution is not thought of as administered by God, but by blind Fate. This idea of a future sanction without a concurrent idea of an intelligent Lawmaker or Judge is one of the incongruities of theoretical Buddhism.

It is only the Buddhist ascetics and scholars, however, who accept this theoretical Buddhist teaching on the nature of God. In practice, most Buddhists tend to the opposite extreme from agnosticism, that of polytheism.

Both in theory and practice, then, Buddhism presents obstacles to the making of a minimal act of religious assent.

By following the theoretical teachings, a Buddhist is led toward agnosticism; by following popular Buddhism, he is led toward polytheism. "Nevertheless even in [Buddhism there is] a ray of hope piercing the gloomy shadows. It [would not seem] unlikely that the worship so surprisingly prescribed for the Buddhists, in spite of their ill-concealed [agnosticism], may lead simple untaught people to transform the vague object of their worship into a personal God." Specialists in the history of religions "find it difficult to understand . . . how simple people, incapable of abstract speculations, form for themselves a [concept of a] personal all-powerful God, even when their philosophers pronounce in favor of pantheism or dualism." May we not hope in such a case that a well-disposed soul may be able to make an unconscious but wise correction?[98]

Moral Effort

Buddha emphasized, more than did Hinduism, the power of free will. No man is doomed to punishment nor impelled toward reward apart from personal effort. Neither despair nor presumption (as defined above) is natural to Buddhism. Men are exhorted to make personal effort to gain virtue.

No external force makes of man a helpless victim. He chooses his own destiny. A man's fate in the next life is self-caused. His life proceeds, not on lines determined by another, but on those marked out by himself.[99]

Benevolence

Buddhist love for neighbor is a decided advance on that of Hinduism. In fact, it is the beauty of her teaching on fraternal charity more than anything else that makes Buddhism one of the greatest of world religions. Fraternal charity is the essence of Buddha's religion. "None of the means employed to acquire religious merit, O monks, has a sixteenth part of the value of loving-kindness."[100]

"It is the kindness of everyone which strikes observers in countries saturated with Buddhism, such as Burma."[101] This kindness is planted in their hearts and encouraged by many striking texts in the Buddhist scriptures. "He who by causing pain to others, wishes to obtain pleasure for himself, he entangled in the bonds of hatred, will never be free from hatred."[102] "Let a man overcome anger by love, let him overcome evil by good."[103] "O monks, that man would not be fulfilling my commands who even whilst ruffians were cutting him limb from limb with a saw, allowed hatred to fill his heart."[104]

Buddhist love of neighbor is looked upon as founded upon love of self. Love for neighbor is an imitation of love for self. And this love of neighbor is to be universal. The concept of neighbor is not restricted on the basis of nationality, race, or religion. All men are to be loved. "Just as a mother at the risk of her life protects her son, her only son, so should a man develop benevolence without measure toward all beings—a love and a friendship without limits toward the entire world; above, below, and all around him."[105]

Sometimes it is said that Buddhism "does not command its followers to love their enemies, but merely to refrain from hating them."[106] But Buddhist charity is not purely negative; it has a positive element.[107]

The elevation and universality of Buddhist charity was achieved by destroying the idea of caste. Buddha did this not so much directly by denouncing the caste system as indirectly by proclaiming a doctrine which pulled out the supports from under the caste system. "A man does not become a Brahmana by his plaited hair, by his family or by birth; in whom there is truth and righteousness, he is a Brahmana."[108] "The man who is not hostile among the hostile, who is peaceful among the violent . . . him I call a Brahmana."[109]

Buddhist charity is extraordinary, especially considering its exclusively pagan origin. Probably the most striking and appealing characteristic of Buddhist charity is that, like Christian charity, it is extended to all men. So many pagan religions begin and end charity with fellow citizens or co-religionists, that the universality of Buddhist charity is doubly impressive. Some students of religion, however, have become over-enthusiastic on this matter and have asserted that Buddhist charity is entirely on a par with or even superior to Christian charity.

A close study of Buddhist and Christian charity will enable us to distinguish between the two.

Buddhist charity, according to De Lubac, is more properly described as pity or compassion. This pity extends to all animals and men. It is not directed toward the individual himself, but only to his moral or physical sufferings. It cannot be directed to the individual because, for the Buddhists, the ego is not something permanent but is entirely illusory. The individual exists only to be destroyed.

Christian charity includes pity, but it is more than that. Human beings themselves are not entirely without nobility. They have been created "in the image and likeness of God" (Gen. 1:26). Just as "the insignificance of the individual is for the Buddhist a fundamental axiom, [so too] . . . the infinite value of the human soul [is] for the Christian."[110]

The Buddhist and Christian concepts of charity, then, are founded on two widely different concepts of the nature of man. "Buddhist tenderness, even when manifested in action, never rises above pity. And if it often appears as true human tenderness, this is in spite of its doctrine. For the individual counts for little in Buddhism."[111]

Practical charity, when it is considered from a purely internal point of view, can be very difficult to evaluate. It is easier to evaluate it by its external manifestations in the virtues of politeness (Buddhism strongly inculates this virtue) and generosity, and in the performing of the spiritual and corporal works of mercy in general. There is an interesting discrepancy between Buddhist and Christian ideas on helping those in need.

Buddhism does inculcate generosity. Generosity "means this: helping men and animals with acts of loving kindness; having compassion on the multitude who are in error; rejoicing that the wise have achieved salvation; protecting and helping all living beings; transcending the boundaries of heaven and earth with a charity as wide as a river and as large as the sea; performing acts of generosity to all living beings; feeding the hungry; giving drink to the thirsty; clothing those who are cold; refreshing those overcome by the heat; being ready to help the sick; whether it be carriages, horses, boats, equipment, or any kind of precious material or famous jewel, or beloved son or kingdom—whatever it may be that you are asked to give, it means giving it at once."[112]

But Buddhism teaches that generosity should fade out as one advances in perfection. Love of neighbor should gradually give way to indifference to all the creatures of this earth. The scriptures say, "Generosity is preached to beginners, vows to the semi-advanced, and the void to the advanced."[113] In Christianity, love of and generosity to neighbor are characteristic of all stages in the spiritual life. At no point in his progress is the Christian free to abandon, either internally or externally, all acts of charity toward his neighbor.

Over all, Buddhist social work does not compare with Christian achievements in this field. The Hinayana for the most part have neglected active charity. For Southern Bud-

dhist monks, the practice of medicine is even forbidden. The
Mahayana encourage works of charity, but have not as yet
developed them on the scale of Christianity.[114]

Another difference between Buddhist and Christian charity is in the attitude toward women. Buddhism shook off
the caste system, but did not free itself from the parallel
Eastern doctrine on the nature of women. Buddhism, like
the other Oriental religions, considered women to have a
natural moral inferiority to man.[115] They were not complete
human beings in the sense that men were. Salvation was far
more difficult for them. The number of women in religious
or monastic life never compared to the number of men.[116]
"Femininity was on the whole a bar to the highest spiritual
attainment, and on approaching [nirvana] the Bodhisattva
ceased to be reborn as a woman."[117]

First Commandment

On the matter of worship, Buddhism follows Hinduism.
She has accommodated herself to a wide variety of forms of
worship.[118] Polytheistic worship of all kinds has been sanctioned. The cult of Buddha himself has sprung up.[119] Idols
are abundant, and even if the idols themselves are not worshipped as gods, the beings that they represent or symbolize
frequently are.

Second Commandment

Positive acts of contempt for the Supreme Being are condemned in Buddhism.

Third Commandment

On matters pertaining to the third commandment, Buddhism broke with Hinduism by repudiating all Vedic cere-

monial. The rites of the Vedas were no longer necessary. Contrary to what some have said, however, primitive Buddhism did not do away with all liturgical forms. Some religious services remained. But it was only later that elaborate ceremonial regulations were adopted in Buddhism. Lamaism developed a complicated ritual. And Buddhists in general, after the death of their founder, came to venerate images and relics of Buddha himself and places associated with him. But the original Buddhist scriptures certainly did cut away much of the Hindu ceremonial.

Apart from ceremonial precepts, Buddhism differed in other ways from Hindu positive law. The rigid Brahmanical precepts covering every aspect of daily life were repudiated. Emphasis was placed on the natural virtues; special man-made positive laws were kept to a minimum.

Fourth Commandment

In Buddhism, as in virtually all the religions of the Far East, there is great emphasis on respect for authority, that of parents and of the local ruler. The same can be said of the correlative obligations of those who exercise authority.

Fifth Commandment

The killing of innocent human beings is forbidden by Buddhism as it is by other religions. Murder and suicide are both forbidden. Suicide is not a legitimate avenue for escape from every evil in this world. Buddha rebuked the custom which had sprung up among his monks of committing suicide as a means of showing their freedom from the desires of this world.[120] On the other hand, one text allows suicide in the special case where the motive is to escape disease or old age.[121]

Abortion[122] and, surprisingly, euthanasia[123] are also forbidden. Even when the motive for killing another innocent person is ostensibly good, killing such a person is wrong. An adulteress may not have an abortion as a means of concealing her unfaithfulness to her husband. A man whose hands and feet have been cut off may not be put to death by his relatives.

Infanticide and abandonment of infants have been condemned in the Buddhist sacred literature. However, in areas of extreme poverty, parents, impelled by lack of means to feed another child, "often kill it." Reproved by the *Chinois cultivés,* this practice meets indulgence or indifference from the mass of the people and the acquiescence of the mandarins. But it is not overtly approved by the civil government, nor is it conformed to the general spirit of the laws and institutions of China.[124]

Because of their belief in the doctrine of reincarnation, Buddhists hold that the malice of killing an animal is comparable to that of killing a human being. If anything, the Buddhists adhere more firmly to this principle than do the Hindus. Westermarck says that a disciple of Buddha may not knowingly take the life of an animal, even that of a worm or an ant. And this doctrine which prohibits the killing of all animals is not only professed, but also observed in large measure by the great majority of the inhabitants of Buddhist countries. "In Siam, it is remarkable to see the extent to which those animals which would run from man in Europe, are tamed." Rich Siamese buy live fish in order to gain the merit of returning them to the sea. In Burma, although fish is one of the principal foods, they despise the fisherman. He is not abhorred as much as if he had killed other animals, but he is always excluded from good society, and he will have to undergo a terrible punishment before being purified of the sins that he commits daily. In Tibet, because of the cold climate, meat is an essential part of the diet, but butchers are regarded as professional sinners, and form the most despised class in the country. And the necessary occupations of butcher and fisherman are condemned even by the Buddhist sacred writings themselves.[125]

Rarely, if ever, are wild animals killed.[126] And Buddhists are counseled, when attacked by an animal, not to kill it in self-defense.[127]

Not all Buddhists are equally strict in discouraging the killing of all animals. But as a group, they are far more strict on the point than the vast majority of other religious groups.

At first glance, the Buddhist teaching on respect for all animal life is attractive. It even seems like an improvement on Christian charity. But an absolute prohibition of the killing of animals leads to certain conflicts. Firstly, Buddhists condemn as sinful occupations such as those mentioned above, which can be necessary for the sustaining of a given society. And a compulsory sin is an ethical monstrosity. Secondly, on a broader scale, Buddhism demands from all something which is impossible to fulfill. All Buddhists are commanded to refrain from killing knowingly any form of animal life. But in many of our daily activities, we are forced to kill great numbers of living beings. "By merely washing our hands, we kill as many living creatures as there are human beings in the whole of Spain."[128] Every Buddhist, then, logically, is a murderer many times over each day. He is left simply with the goal of trying to reduce the infinite number of murders he will commit in the future. Such a dilemma leads either to scrupulousness (tending toward a complete cessation of all activity) or to a lowering of respect for religious law. In either case, it would not be difficult to fall into despair.

Christianity teaches that we must indeed respect animal life. It is one of the most extraordinary creations of God. But brute animals are not made in the image of God, as man is. Animals are subordinate to man and are intended by God to serve his needs.

As well as murder, Buddhism forbids that which sometimes leads up to murder, the sin of anger. "Beware of anger of the body, . . . of the tongue, . . . of the mind."[129]

Sixth Commandment

Buddhist ideas as to the relation of the sexes can best be treated under two heads: as they apply to members of the Buddhist monastic order, and as they apply to Buddhist laymen. For the advanced soul, Buddhism encourages a life of celibacy. It developed the Hindu ideal of the ascetic, and also advised, far more than Hinduism did, that this withdrawal from the world be accomplished as a monk in community life and not as a hermit.

For the layman, Buddhism is less definite. Her sacred books encourage purity but seldom define it. Buddhism does not, for example, condemn either polygamy or divorce.[130]

When Buddhism spread to a new area, for the most part she accommodated herself to the practices already existing there. "Neither at the beginning, in the precepts put into the mouth of Buddha in our earliest documents, was any attempt made to interfere in any way with those [family] customs; nor afterwards, as the influence of the new teaching spread, do we find any decree of a Buddhist Council, or any ordinance of a Buddhist king, prescribing a change there in family relations. When Buddhism was subsequently introduced and more or less widely or completely adopted in other countries, the Buddhists evinced no desire . . . to reconstitute the family according to any views of their own on the subject."[131]

Seventh Commandment

On matters of justice between individuals, Buddhism is very similar to most other religions, even in details. The taking of another person's property by mistake, thinking it to be one's own, is no sin.[132] Those who command or who cooperate in an act of theft are just as guilty as the thief himself.[133]

Though Buddhism does agree with other religions on most points connected with justice between individuals, she differs on the matter of social justice. Buddhist morality is more individual than social.[134] The idea of the existence of duties toward society in general as well as toward other individuals within society is alien to Buddhist minds. This has weakened Buddhism in modern times. An industrial society cannot function properly without an awareness of the obligations of social justice among its members. Accordingly, most strictly Buddhist groups have failed to adapt themselves to the new form of society.[135]

Eighth Commandment

Buddhism "improved on Hinduism" in the matter of telling the truth. A man who seeks nirvana must "never lie under the influence of any desire, or passion, or any advantage, material or otherwise."[136]

On the sin of detraction, the Buddhist scriptures say "If a man looks after the faults of others, and is always inclined to be offended, his own passions will grow."[137]

Anything even approximating the sin of contumely is seldom found in a Buddhist. Politeness is very strongly inculcated.[138]

Ninth and Tenth Commandments

Buddhism is aware of the malice of sinful desires. Efficacious desires for sin which are frustrated are still sins.[139]

Conclusions on Buddhism

In general, then, Buddhism is an improvement on Hinduism. Many aspects of Buddhist charity, in particular, reach the level of Christian charity and are outstanding when compared to what other pagan religions teach on charity.

Four major weaknesses exist in Buddhist ethics. Firstly, between the theoretic atheism or at least agnosticism and the polytheism actually practiced, it is very difficult for a Buddhist to steer a middle course toward worship of one God. Secondly, Buddhism's lack of central authority and its collective tolerance of even the wildest aberrations from ethical teachings make it possible for various Buddhist groups to plunge into violations of primary conclusions of natural law without receiving any warning from an outside source. Thirdly, no adequate distinction is made between what is counseled and what is commanded. And fourthly, most of the laws are directed only toward those who are striving for the highest goal, nirvana. There are a great many rules for monks. But not much of the moral legislation is directed toward the layman. A man who chooses a life short of the very highest ideals can find no complete set of standards for a normal "good" life in theoretical Buddhism. The layman cannot obtain a complete rule of life from the Buddhist scriptures; he is forced to seek it either in the local customs or in his own conscience.

4. Confucianism

The man known in the Western world as Confucius was born about 550 B.C. He was a contemporary of Buddha, but the two never met. Buddha remained in India, and Confucius spent his life in northeastern China. He was born of a noble family, but in his early years he was reduced to poverty by the death of his father. At the age of fifteen, he decided to devote his life to learning. He was married at nineteen and had a son and two daughters by the union. He spent much of his time teaching, traveling through the eastern part of China, and gathering disciples. He accepted public offices in some of the states which he visited.

All during his life, he was fascinated by Chinese antiquity. He felt that his task in life was to preserve and transmit a love for the traditions of China. Contemporary morality, he believed, was to be improved only by returning to that of the ancients. He presented nothing as new, nor did he attempt to develop and improve upon what had been handed down, as did Buddha. He was more a spokesman for the ancient morality than a founder of a new one.

He did not put any of his own thoughts in writing, but edited many Chinese classics that were in danger of perishing from neglect. These included some annals covering the years 2357 to 627 B.C., a collection of poems, and books treating magic, rites, and etiquette.

His writings and sayings on ethical matters centered around principles of good government and the proper regulation of the family. He himself had no lasting success in winning any civil rulers over to the observance of his teachings. He became discouraged in his last years, returned to his home province, and died there in about 478 B.C.

His disciples and followers did succeed later in winning influential positions in China. And gradually Confucius' teachings were accepted as the ideal for all Chinese government. Disciples compiled sayings of Confucius in the *Analects*. Later followers in the fourth and third centuries B.C. composed three other books, *The Great Learning, The Doctrine of the Mean,* and *The Book of Mencius*. These "four books" contained substantially the teaching of the master.

Confucianism is not a religion like Buddhism or Christianity. It does not attempt to deal with all the major problems connected with man's purpose and duties in life. Some of man's relationships are covered in detail; others are virtually ignored.

Confucianism is completely cut off from the Hindu-Buddhist tradition, and was not influenced in its origins by either of these two.

One general way in which the approach of Confucianism differs from that of Hinduism and Buddhism is in its emphasis on the positive nature of virtue. More than the Indian religions, Confucianism teaches that virtue requires the pursuit of good as well as retreat from evil.

Religious Assent

Confucius apparently acknowledged a supreme God, Tien, who was a personal intelligent Power who ruled the universe.[140] The literature which preceded him as well as that which followed him frequently spoke of this God. Confucius himself, however, seems to have kept these beliefs to himself. In his writings, the vague, impersonal term, Heaven, took the place of the divine name. Over a century later, his great follower Mencius was more open in acknowledging a supreme God than was his master.

It is on the question of the future life, however, that Confucianism is radically different from the Hindu-Buddhist tradition. Confucius prescinded almost entirely from any discussion of a future life. Doubts as to the continued existence of the departed were manifested by many leading men in China before the era of Confucius. In the pages of Tso ch'iu-ming, when men are swearing in the heat of passion, they sometimes pause and rest the validity of their oaths on the proviso that the dead to whom they appeal really exist. The "expressive silence" of Confucius himself has gone to confirm this scepticism.

"His teaching was thus hardly more than a pure secularism. He had faith in man, man made for society, but he did not care to follow him out of society, nor to present to him motives of conduct derived from the consideration of a future state. Good and evil would be recompensed by the natural issues of conduct within the sphere of time—if not in the person of the actor, yet in the person of his descendants. If there were any joys of heaven to reward virtue, or terrors of future retribution to punish vice, the sage took no heed of the one or the other."[141] "Blessedness in the flesh was purely human, and spiritual blessedness in the past or future was—and this only doubtfully or agnostically—supposed to be the same thing."[142]

Confucianism emphasizes very strongly veneration of ancestors. Accordingly, it might be thought that this would necessarily imply a belief in a future life. This, surprisingly, is not so. "It should be remembered that there is, and long has been a very large number of people in China who have been more or less sceptical on the question of the continued existence of human individuals after death, and who have nevertheless been among the most zealous supporters of the ancestral cult. . . . The practical if not the theoretical basis of the cult is social and moral rather than religious." It has been preserved among many because it fosters among living men feelings of love, respect, reverence, and duty toward family and state.[143]

Moral Effort

Moral effort is encouraged in Confucianism. However, hope of reward in a future life as a motive for moral effort is absent.

Benevolence

Confucian fraternal charity, in broad outline, is more like Christian charity than that of the Hindus or Buddhists. Benevolence is inculcated toward all men without regard for distinctions of nationality,[144] and at the same time there is no attempt to place all animals on the same level with men.

"In regard to inferior creatures [i.e., animals; see footnote], the superior man is kind to them but not loving. In regard to people generally, he is loving to them but not affectionate. He is affectionate to his parents, and lovingly disposed to people generally."[145]

Of the particular obligation of charity toward enemies, Confucius laid down several principles which, depending on the interpretation, can be the same as those of Christianity or not: "Benevolence subdues its opposite just as water subdues fire. Those, however, who nowadays practice benevolence [do it] as if with one cup of water they could save a whole wagonload of fuel which was on fire, and when the flames were not extinguished, were to say that water cannot subdue fire. This conduct, moreover, greatly encourages those who are not benevolent."[146]

On the other hand, we read, "Someone said, 'What do you say concerning the principle that injury should be recompensed with kindness?' The master said, 'With what then will you recompense kindness? Recompense injury with justice, and recompense kindness with kindness.' "[147]

Confucianism encourages the practice of corporal works of mercy. Men who aid those in need, feed the hungry, clothe the naked, help the sick, and save those in danger, will be rewarded by the invisible powers which watch the conduct of men, while chastisements wait upon those who neglect this duty. This principle is to be applied to the needy both inside and outside the family.[148]

Here again, though, the corporal works of mercy are not carried to the extent that they are in Christianity. Confucianists are not encouraged to give all their possessions to the needy, nor to contribute to such a variety of persons and needs as Christianity counsels.

First Commandment

Just as its teaching on belief in a personal and just God is uncertain, so too is Confucianism's idea of the worship of God. Confucianism has "no idea of collective worship . . . and no need for praise [of God] . . . ever even remotely entered the Chinese mind."[149] "In regard to the relative importance of serving God and serving man Confucius has often been blamed for setting man before God; but it should be remembered that his interpretation of true service to God was embodied in right and proper performance of duty to one's neighbor. The idea of direct personal service to God Himself, as understood by the Jewish patriarchs, is entirely foreign to the Chinese conception of a Supreme Being."[150] Legge observes of Confucius himself that there is "no glow of piety in any of his sentiments."[151] When someone asked Confucius what constituted wisdom, he replied, "To give one's self earnestly to the duties due to men, and while respecting spiritual beings, to keep aloof from them."[152]

In practice, however, Confucianists, like the Buddhists, often ignore the advice of their founder on this point; they frequently do carry on some forms of religious worship. But it cannot be doubted that a great deal of this worship, as it is actually carried on and sanctioned, is idolatry. "It is a mixture of nature-worship and worship of the dead. . . . Images as well as tablets are inhabited by spirits. . . . Confucian worship and sacrifice, then, being actually addressed to animate images, is idolatry. Certainly it is quite inconsistent with the Chinese spirit to think of such tablets and images as mere wood and paint."[153] "The popular worship of Confucian divinities [was] practiced all through the Empire, the images of gods [existed] by tens of thousands, the temples by thousands. Almost every temple [had] its idol gods which [were] coordinate or subordinate in rank to the chief god, so that [pre-Communist] China fully [deserved] to be called the most idolatrous country in the world."[154]

Second Commandment

Confucianism does not inculcate a contempt for God. Theoretical Confucianism's neglect of worship of God is not due to contempt for Him, but to the conviction that by serving man one fulfills all one's obligations toward God.

Third Commandment

Chinese ritual centers on the cult of ancestors. This cult serves several functions: to honor the ancestors, to ask their intercession, to solidify family and social ties by this common activity.

There is a great deal of outright idolatry in this ritual. But on the other hand, many elements of the Confucian cult could be fitted into a framework of monotheistic worship, simple veneration of ancestors, and prayer for the dead.

Confucian ritual does not extend to all the activities of daily life. Confucianists are in no sense bound by an impossible load of external rules, as are the Hindu Brahmans.

Fourth Commandment

Just as Buddhism can be said to center its teachings around the virtue of charity, so Confucianism centers its teaching around matters pertaining to the fourth commandment. The most important of virtues is respect for parents. The greatest of sins is disrespect for elders. "A man can have no greater [crimes] than to disown his parents and relatives, and the relations of sovereign and minister, superiors and inferiors."[155] If the fourth commandment is observed, all the other virtues will follow. "If each man would show the due respect to his elders, the whole empire would enjoy tranquillity."[156]

A great part of the Chinese scriptures is devoted to advice for rulers. This is motivated by a principle repeated often in these books: "If the sovereign be benevolent, all will be benevolent. If the sovereign be righteous, all will be righteous."[157]

Fifth Commandment

The general principle of natural law forbidding the killing of innocent persons is by no means unknown to Confucianism. "To put a single innocent person to death is contrary to benevolence."[158] On the other hand, the execution of the guilty is licit in some cases.[159]

Two violations of the fifth commandment, however, have been tolerated on a wide scale in China. The abandoning or killing of infants by parents impelled by poverty, among Confucianists as well as Buddhists, is common. The practice (as noted above in the treatment of Buddhism) has met indifference or indulgence from the mass of the people and the acquiescence of the mandarins. It has never been sanctioned by law, however.[160] It is not impossible that in some exceptional cases parents could abandon their children in good faith. On the other hand, good faith in such matters presupposes first, extreme need, and second, that every means of saving the child (v.g., seeking other families to adopt the child) has been tried. In any case, Chinese law has not adequately warned parents of their obligations in this matter.

Suicide has not been regarded by Confucianists as an absolutely indifferent act. If it is committed for an ignoble reason, it is wrong. An ignoble reason would be a fit of rage, fear of the consequences of a crime punishable with death, the hope of causing undeserved harm to another person. On the other hand, suicide is licit and even virtuous when committed by officials who do not wish to survive a defeat or an outrage inflicted on their sovereign; by young men incapable of avenging an insult suffered by their parents; by women out of grief over the death of their husbands or fiancés; by one who wishes to avenge himself on one who is otherwise out of reach; or in general, by anyone motivated by loyalty to the sovereign, or by filial piety, chastity, or friendship. In practice, "suicide is very common in China among all classes and ages."[161] Here again, some of these reasons can be given a rather broad interpretation. Confucian law does not adequately safeguard the primary conclusion of natural law on this matter. Even within the law, the killing of one's self is allowed for a slight cause.

Drinking is allowed, but not if it is done to excess.[162]

Sixth Commandment

The ideal Chinese family is monogamous. Widowers usually remarry; widows may remarry, but are encouraged to remain faithful to the memory of their first husband.

Incest, especially that prohibited by a primary conclusion of natural law, is forbidden. "Concubinage is legal"; "and there is no legal limit to the number of concubines that may be taken." "Concubinage is common among the wealthy classes; among the poorer it is less common, and usually is practiced only for the purpose of securing a male succession."

"According to law there are seven reasons for which a husband may divorce his wife; but the law recognizes no right of the wife to divorce her husband. The seven legal reasons for divorce are: unfilial conduct (toward the husband's parents), adultery, jealousy, loquacity, theft, grievous disease (e.g., leprosy), and barrenness. But some of these reasons, e.g., barrenness, are not recognized by custom. To these legal reasons must be added poverty, which is the commonest cause of all. It is difficult to estimate the percentage of divorces, but divorce is not supposed to be frequent. . . . No legal process is necessary, though a writing of divorcement should be given, and is usually demanded by the second husband of the repudiated woman as a precaution. . . . Remarriage even for the wife is not too difficult."[163] In any case, legally it is possible to violate the primary conclusion of natural law prohibiting divorce at least apart from a serious reason.

The two great religions of China, Confucianism and Buddhism, take opposite views on the matter of celibacy. Confucianism in no way encourages a life of celibacy. It is necessary to carry on the succession of generations in each family. "There are three things which are unfilial, and to have no posterity is the greatest of them."[164]

Seventh Commandment

The Chinese agree with most other religions in the world in their ideas of private property, honesty, theft, the guilt of cooperation, the right of children to inherit, prescription, etc.

Eighth Commandment

Lying, especially in the form of calumny, is sinful. "Words which are not true are inauspicious, and the words which are most truly . . . inauspicious, are those which throw into the shade men of talents and virtue."[165] Detraction, too, is wrong. "What future misery have they and ought they to endure, who talk of what is not good in others."[166]

Truth, however, may be abandoned in the case of a father hiding the misconduct of a son, or vice versa.

In practice, Westermarck seems to imply that Chinese respect for truth is not so great as among the Biblical religious groups in the world.

Ninth and Tenth Commandments

Emphasis on control of desires is not so great in Confucianism as in Buddhism or Christianity. But we do find remarks like the following: "He who seeks to be rich will not be benevolent."[167]

Conclusions on Confucianism

Confucianism, then, has high standards for many of the virtues, especially those of fraternal charity and respect for authority. She tolerates, however, violations of some primary conclusions of natural law, particularly in the matters of unbelief, idolatry, and murder (abandoning infants and suicide).

5. The Systems of Plato and Aristotle

Turning toward the West, the Athenian philosophers, Plato (c. 427–347 B.C.) and Aristotle (384–322 B.C.) merit special consideration as great teachers of ethical principles. Plato and his pupil, Aristotle, did not found or preserve systems which would, in themselves, direct the lives of hundreds of millions of human beings as was true of the Hindu, Buddhist, and Confucian teachings.[168] Ethically, their importance lies in the fact that, of all the ancient Western thinkers, their philosophy was best suited as a foundation for later development of Western religious thought. In the midst of pagan idolatry and depravity they were able to re-establish the concept of the existence of a universal moral law discoverable by reason, and to reassert explicitly, among other things, many of the primary conclusions of natural law which had almost fallen into oblivion in some circles.

On the other hand, these great thinkers were not without egregious errors. In some instances they contradict even primary conclusions of natural law. Along with monotheism, pantheism can be found in Plato. Along with a prohibition of murder in general can be found a statement that in the ideal state, deformed children or children of inferior parents should be exposed, and another statement that children born of women under 20 or over 40, or of men beyond the range of 25 to 55 should be aborted.[169]

In the *Laws*, Plato does state that a marriage bond is necessary. He condemns sexual intercourse outside marriage, whatever the circumstances.[170] But on other matters, he is not so strict. In the *Republic*, he speaks without disapproval of unnatural physical love. And in his ideal state, he advocates the abolition of the family and the establishment of community of women among the guardian class, i.e., among the rulers and soldiers.[171] To be sure, it would seem that, apart from the ideal, and for conditions as they really were, Plato advocated a strict code of chastity. But the fact that he allowed license in his utopia (although the possibility of attaining this utopia was admittedly doubtful) certainly permits room for error on the part of his disciples.

Aristotle criticized Plato for advocating a community of wives. But Aristotle himself foundered on other questions. In particular, he erred seriously in his teaching on the next life. He had nothing to say "on the lot of man after death. . . . Personal immortality has no room in his system; the rational soul is eternal but not as an individual soul."[172]

And, like Plato, he encouraged frequent abortions provided certain conditions were verified. "Aristotle, not content with posing a law relative to the exposition or education of children which required that nothing imperfect or mutilated be brought up, proposed also that the number of children permitted to each marriage be regulated by the state, and that if a woman is pregnant after she has borne the number [of children] prescribed [by law], the fetus must be aborted."[173]

On several points, then, both Plato and Aristotle fail to safeguard adequately primary conclusions of natural law.

6. Stoicism (Seneca)

Stoicism is a philosophy which flourished especially among the upper classes in ancient Greece and Rome. Some of its leading exponents were Zeno (late 4th and early 3rd centuries B.C.), Cleanthes (3rd century B.C.), Chrysippus (3rd century B.C.), Cicero[174] (106–43 B.C.), Seneca (3 B.C.–65 A.D.), Epictetus (c. 60–120 A.D.), and Marcus Aurelius (121–180 A.D.).

The Stoics had quite a high standard of morality. In many respects it equals Christian ethics—so much so that some have thought of its ethical code as a source from which Christian ethics were formulated.[175] Stoic morality centers on the eradication of the emotions. The emotions—perturbationes as Cicero calls them—are movements of the mind contrary to reason. Now, there is a "desire" which is according to law and reason, and this is the natural impulse toward what is good. The desire, on the other hand, which is according to emotion is intrinsically unreasonable and therefore bad; for all emotions are contrary to reason. It follows that the wise man should aim at eradicating all his emotions; he should strive to become absolutely emotionless. This "apathy" is one of the most characteristic doctrines of the Stoics.[176]

The Stoics did not all agree with one another. And even on many basic questions they held widely divergent views. On certain points, however, they did concur. In general, they tended toward monotheism, but they denied that God is a person, and immortality of the soul was either denied or doubted by many of them. Rewards and punishments came entirely in this life. Stoicism taught indifference to wealth and the conveniences of life, and contempt for suffering. Manual labor and poverty were despised, or, at best, pitied.[177] The philosophy appealed to the upper classes, those who already possessed wealth. On chastity the Stoics were weak. Epictetus contented himself with advising moderation in immorality.[178]

Stoicism in some ways is a philosophy of despair. Against the evils of life, the Stoics had only one antidote—self-respect; and only one sovereign remedy—suicide. There is, however, something noble and touching in this effort to preserve human dignity, and in this philanthropy which was conformable to reason but foreign to the feeling of true sympathy, which was regarded as a weakness.[179]

Various reasons have been given as to why Stoicism never gathered a very large number of adherents and eventually died out. One of the reasons often given is that, by despising suffering, the Stoics despised the very thing of which most men's lives are made up. Another reason is the fact that one of their central doctrines (that the wise man is a law unto himself and exempt from all moral laws and restraints) is both debilitating and untenable.

Seneca is not the least worthy among the Stoics, and for several reasons he is deserving of special study. From his earliest years, he tried to follow the highest ideals. In youth he was a vegetarian and drank no wine. Upon reaching adulthood, he entered public life. He achieved some success, but this was interrupted for eight years by the Emperor Claudius who had him exiled. He was recalled by the next empress, Agrippina. In the year 48, she entrusted Seneca with the education of her son Nero, then eleven years old. When Nero succeeded to the throne in 54, Seneca shared the administration of affairs, and while he was in power the government was wise and humane. But Nero tired of him, and eventually ordered him to commit suicide.

The brilliance of Seneca's mind on ethical matters is evident, not only when seen against a background of Stoicism, but also against the background of the other great ethical systems of history. Seneca concentrated on ethics more than did most of the other great philosophers. He did not deal to any great extent with religions or with virtues in the abstract. He was more concerned with virtue in practice; his work is to a great extent hortatory. He does not seek intellectual knowledge for its own sake, but pursues philosophy as a means to the acquirement of virtue.[180]

In his "Moral Letters" and "Moral Essays," he shows great insight into the workings of human nature. "No man is born rich. Every man when he first sees light is commanded to be content with milk and rags. Such is our beginning and yet kingdoms are all too small for us."[181] In a striking fashion, he demonstrated the evils involved even in simple attendance at the gladiatorial combats.[182]

He also had great ability in solving moral problems which, in his day, were especially difficult. He, a Roman, living at the height of Roman power, was able to perceive that wars of aggression, and in particular Roman wars of aggression, were wrong.[183]

Seneca recognized a supreme "God, who is the Father of us all."[184] But, like the other Stoics, he had difficulties on the question of God as Remunerator. At times, he seems to believe in some sort of immortality.[185] But, for the most part, he seems to doubt or even deny personal immortality. A passage in his 54th letter is not atypical of such a denial: "Death is non-existence, and I know already what that means. What was before me will happen again after me. . . . We mortals . . . are lighted and extinguished; the period of suffering comes in between, but on either side there is a deep peace. For unless I am very much mistaken, . . . we go astray in thinking that death only follows, when in reality it has both preceded us and will in turn follow us. Whatever condition existed before our birth, is death. For what does it matter whether you do not begin at all, or whether you leave off, inasmuch as the result of both these states is non-existence?" Whether or not Seneca is evincing here belief in some kind of immortality, it certainly is not personal.

Seneca improves somewhat on the general Stoic teaching on charity. He "lays emphasis on the Stoic doctrine of the relationship that exists among all human beings, and instead of the self-sufficiency of the wise man—a self-sufficiency tinged with contempt for others—he calls on us to help our fellow men and to forgive those who have injured us. . . . He stresses the necessity of active benevolence: 'Nature bids me to be of use to men whether they are slave or free, freedmen or freeborn. Wherever there is a human being there is room for benevolence.' 'See that you are beloved by all while you live and regretted when you die.' "[186]

On the giving of benefits, we should give not only to those who will return our gift, but also to those who cannot. "If we give only when we may expect some return, we ought to die intestate."[187] But Seneca's charity is not unconditional. We should give only to the virtuous. "It is not gain that I try to get from a benefit, nor pleasure, nor glory; content with giving pleasure to one human being, I shall give with the single purpose of doing what I ought. But I am not without discrimination in doing what I ought. Do you ask what the nature of this choice will be? I shall choose a man who is upright, sincere, mindful, grateful, who keeps his hands from another man's property, who is not greedily attached to his own, who is kind to others; although fortune may bestow upon him nothing with which he may repay my favor, I shall have accomplished my purpose when I have made choice of such a man."[188]

Suicide, which Seneca advocates so frequently, is not to

be committed except under very restricted conditions: i.e., v.g., when one is incurably ill, or when one reaches such an advanced age that he can no longer be of service to anyone.

Seneca's chief weakness, that in which he differs most radically from primary conclusions of natural law, then, would seem to be in the matter of religious assent. At least in his writings, he displays a lack of minimal assent to one personal God who is both Creator and Remunerator.

7. *Islam*

Mohammed, the founder of Islam or Mohammedanism, was born in about the year 570 A.D. When he was 25, he married a rich widow. At the age of 40, he claimed that he had received revelations from God and began his active career as a preacher of a new religion. By his preaching against Arab paganism, Mohammed provoked a persecution which drove him from his home city of Mecca to Medina in 622. This year, 622, has been called the year of the Hejira (Flight) and the beginning of the Mohammedan Era. At Medina, his followers increased, and by 632, the year of his death, he had won over or conquered a large part of Arabia, including Mecca. After his death his religion spread through the Near East, to North Africa and through Southern Asia.

The Koran, which contains the revelations which Mohammed said he received from God, is the great scripture for the Moslems. Of less authority than the Koran are the *hadith,* collections of sayings of Mohammed or of one of his early disciples, which are not considered as inspired or revealed by God.

Islam is a combination of three religions which pre-existed Mohammed in Arabia: Judaism, Christianity, and the pagan Arab religion. The religion of Mohammed differs radically from those of the Far East. One of the chief differences lies in the unity of Islam: Two persons could be members in good standing of one of the religions of the Far East, while they could disagree with each other on many fundamental points of morality. In Islam, this is not so. Moslem teaching is uniform and well defined on a great many points, both moral and dogmatic. Accept them all and you can be a Moslem; reject one basic point and you are on the outside.

Religious Assent

Of the non-Biblical religions, certainly one of the most acceptable from the point of view of religious assent is Mohammedanism. In the Koran, we read, "Say [unto them, O Mohammed]: I am only a warner, and there is no God save Allah, the One, the Absolute, Lord of the heavens and the earth and all that is between them, the mighty, the pardoning. Say: It is tremendous tidings" (sura 38:65-7). Islam is in full agreement with the primary conclusion of natural law that God is One and that He is Creator and Remunerator. Neither a polytheist nor an atheist can find acceptance in Islam. For the Moslems, God is the Creator and Sustainer of all things. In the next life, He will reward the good in heaven, and punish the wicked in hell. And this sanction will be personal. "Then one blast is sounded on the Trumpet, and the earth is moved and its mountains and they are crushed to powder at one stroke. On that Day, shall the [great] event come to pass, and the sky will be rent asunder, for it will that Day be flimsy, and the angels will be on its sides, and eight will, that Day, bear the throne of thy Lord above them. That Day shall ye be brought to judgment: not an act of yours that will lie hidden. Then he that will be given his record in his right hand will say: . . . 'I did really understand that my account would [one day] reach me!' And he will be in a life of bliss in a garden on high. . . . And he that will be given his record in his left hand will say: 'Ah! would . . . that I had never realized how my account [stood]! . . . [The stern command will say]: 'Seize ye him, and bind ye him, and burn ye him in the blazing fire'" (sura 69:13–31). The exact nature and duration of these personal rewards and punishments as taught by Islam differ from Christian teaching. But it would be difficult to prove that these discrepancies pertain to the primary conclusion of natural law on religious assent, and not to secondary conclusions.

Moral Effort

Islam emphasizes God's foreknowledge far more than Christianity does. Free will is not denied outright, but for a Moslem its role is far less important than it is for a Christian. The Koran and Islam stress the idea of the omnipotence of God and there is a tendency to forget, weaken, and almost to deny human liberty and to teach fatalism.[189] The primary cause of the relatively mild attitude of orthodox Islam toward sin has been traced to the Moslem emphasis on predestination.[190]

Islam, however, has had its defenders of free will. And it cannot be said, at least in its teachings, to deny free will outright and thus to provide only two alternatives for its members: despair or presumption.

Islam teaches that all believers, regardless of their other sins, will eventually reach paradise. It might seem that this teaching is an outright encouragement of presumption. But it would not be presumption in the sense used here. Sinful Moslem believers know that they will be punished at least temporarily in hell. Sin will not go completely unpunished. That presumption which is opposed to the primary conclusion of natural law on hope, defined previously, would deny all future punishment for sin.

Benevolence

Islam is not without a concept of love for God (cf. suras 2:177 and 3:31). Emphasis on it, however, is far weaker than in Christianity.

Moslems are encouraged to love their neighbor. In a *hadith*, we read, "a man called on his brother in a different village. Then Allah sent for him an angel who was waiting on his way. He asked: Where do you intend [to go]? He said: I intend to go to my brother in his village. He asked: Have you got any gift for him to offer? He said, no, but I love him for cause of Allah. He said: Verily I am a messenger of Allah to you [to tell you] that Allah loves you as you love him for His cause."[191] Moslems also have a concept of spiritual and corporal works of mercy. "Each Moslem must encourage his brother in Islam to observe the religious Law and to intervene in case of scandal."[192] Almsgiving is a religious duty in Islam, and, in practice, the obligation is taken very seriously. Islam, however, is far less ardent than Christianity in the matter of caring for the sick. In many areas this office is entirely avoided, and no one is available to fulfil it. Even on religious grounds, the Mohammedan has little desire to care for the sick, because wounds are unclean ceremonially.[193]

In Islam, there is no monasticism, and there are very few groups or individuals who devote their entire lives either to the spiritual or corporal works of mercy.

Another major difference between Moslem charity and that of Christianity is in the object of one's charity. For a Moslem, the obligation of charity extends only to co-religionists. There is no strict obligation to love or to practice active charity toward non-Moslems. In fact, though Moslems are not forbidden to be just and kind toward non-Moslems under all circumstances, love for non-Moslems is positively discouraged.[194]

First Commandment

Islam prohibits the worship of idols. In his account of the story of the worship of the golden calf by the chosen people, Mohammed says, "Then he brought forth for them a calf, a body, which had a hollow sound, so they said: This is your god. . . . Could they not see that it returned no reply to them, nor controlled any harm or benefit for them?" (sura 20:88-9). Islam, from the very beginning, made tremendous progress in its suppression of idolatry in Arabia. Before Islam, idolatry was rampant; after it, virtually nonexistent. Its elimination of idolatry among the peoples with which it has come in contact is one of the great contributions of this religion to the world.

Second Commandment

Reverence for God is another outstanding virtue of the Moslems. Blasphemy is one of the worst of sins. So too is perjury and temptation of God. Oaths are to be respected: "And break not your oaths after the asseveration of them, and after ye have made Allah surety over you" (sura 16:91).

Third Commandment

Islam cannot be accused of failing to encourage frequent worship of God. Five times a day, Moslems are required to stop secular activities for a moment and recite certain brief prayers. Once a week, on Friday, the men are to gather for a communal service consisting of prayer and sermons. Once a year, during one of the Moslem months, all the faithful are required to fast from food and drink every day from sunrise to sunset. And at least once in his lifetime, a Moslem is bound to make a pilgrimage to Mecca if he is physically and financially able to do so.

Fourth Commandment

Nor does Islam ignore the virtue of reverence for parental and civil authority. Parents must be cared for in their need. "Thy Lord hath decreed . . . [that ye show] kindness to parents. If one of them or both of them attain old age with thee, say not 'Fie' unto them nor repulse them, but speak unto them a gracious word" (sura 17:23). Those who have civil authority should be obeyed. "O ye who believe! Obey God and obey the messenger [Mohammed] and those of you who are in authority" (sura 4:59). Though Islam does not place the tremendous emphasis on the virtue of filial piety that is placed on it by the religions of the Far East, the basic obligations of subjects and those in authority are set forth quite clearly.

Fifth Commandment

Islam condemns murder and suicide.[195] Mohammed moved well ahead of the religions of the Far East by correcting the practice of abandoning infants. He was incisive in his remarks on the subject: "Slay not your children, fearing a fall to poverty. God shall provide for them and for you. Lo! The slaying of them is a great sin" (sura 17:31). His command was obeyed, and the practice of abandoning infants (which had been fairly common among the Arabs before the time of Mohammed) was suppressed.

Although Islam was firm in decrying all kinds of murder, she advocated one method of halting murders, which itself bred more homicides than it stamped out—that of private revenge. In cases where an innocent person, whether child or adult, has been killed, the nearest relative of the murder victim is allowed by Islam to take revenge. This relative is given power to decide the identity and subjective guilt of the murderer and to hunt out and kill him. "Whoso is slain wrongfully, we have given power to his heir, but let him not commit excess in slaying" (sura 17:33). Christianity teaches that in order to safeguard the innocent, suspected murderers should be tried in court.

Islam also disagrees with Christianity on religious wars of aggression. In Islam, there is a large number of theologians who hold that it is permissible for Moslems to initiate a war against non-Moslems specifically for the purpose of converting them to Islam.[196] Christian theologians unanimously oppose any war initiated simply for the purpose of spreading Christianity.

Sixth Commandment

Islam forbids fornication, adultery, polyandry, incest, and, with one exception (marital onanism), the unnatural sins against the sixth commandment.

She does, however, allow polygamy. "Marry of the women who seem good to you, two or three or four; and if ye fear that ye cannot do justice (to so many), then only one, or [the captives] that your right hands possess" (sura 4:3). A Moslem may have as many as four wives, and in addition as many concubines as he wishes.

On the matter of divorce, Islam can only be described as one of the most liberal religions on earth. Islam allows the husband to repudiate his wife on his own authority (without court, arbiters, or witnesses) at any moment without any misbehavior on her part and without assigning any cause for his action.[197] This indulgence of Islamic teaching on divorce is not purely theoretical. Divorce is extremely common in Moslem countries, far more so generally than in the territory of any other major religious group. Twenty-five or more successive divorces and remarriages by one man is not at all outlandish in some areas. But even with all this, it is interesting to note that Islam does give her adherents some warnings about divorce. Mohammed himself is reported to have made the following rather paradoxical remark: "The most detestable of lawful things near Allah is divorce."[198]

In defense of Mohammed, it can be said that this system of divorce did not originate with him. He incorporated it into Islam from the pagan Arab religion. The pagan Arab system was even more lax. Mohammed eliminated certain abuses, one by which unscrupulous husbands were using divorce as a tool to fleece wives of their dowries. He also introduced a period of waiting. No woman could remarry until three months after her husband had divorced her.

Seventh Commandment

Islam prohibits theft unequivocally. "Woe unto the defrauders: Those who, when they take the measure from mankind demand it full, but if they measure unto them or weigh for them, they cause them loss. Do such [men] not consider that they will be raised again unto an awful day, the day when [all] mankind stand before the Lord of the worlds?" (sura 83:1–6).

Islam forbids the taking of usury from Moslems but not from non-Moslems.

Gambling, however, is sinful under all circumstances.

Eighth Commandment

Lying, slander, contumely, and unjustified detraction are wrong, at least in general. "Lies are allowed in certain exceptional cases: in war, in restoring peace between two contending parties, and in conversations between husband and wife."[199]

Ninth and Tenth Commandments

Islam, like the other major religions of the world, teaches that efficacious desires to commit sin are themselves sinful.

Conclusions on Islam

Islam, then, is superior to the religions of the Far East in some ways, especially in her teaching on the obligations of men toward God. But even Islam finds in her teachings at least one instance of toleration of the violation of a primary conclusion of natural law: unlimited intrinsic dissolution of marriage.

8. Judaism

Judaism in its origins is the religion of the descendants of the Old Testament patriarch Jacob. Before Christ, the religion of the Jews was the religion of God, and its original formulation is found in the inspired words of the Old Testament. God protected His "chosen people" in a special way from the time of His first promise to Abraham (c. 200 B.C.) until the time of Christ. Through the mouths of Moses and the other inspired authors of the books of the Old Testament, He gave them a strictly monotheistic moral code which was far superior to the codes of the pagan nations which surrounded them. Their worship centered at the Temple in Jerusalem. God promised to send a Savior to the Jews, and He repeated this promise many times through the mouths of the Biblical prophets.

In the fullness of time, when He felt that the Jews and mankind in general were ready to receive a perfection and completion of the law of the Old Testament, God sent that Savior, Jesus of Nazareth. Christ clarified and developed certain parts of the Old Law (v.g., the teaching on the future life); corrected certain distortions of it which had been made by certain groups of Jewish lawmakers (v.g., the excessive sabbatical restrictions); and revoked certain concessions which God had temporarily granted the Jews (v.g., permission to give a bill of divorce).

Many Jews were converted to Christianity. For those who were not, Judaism, as it had existed up to that time, was totally destroyed. In the year 70 A.D., a pagan Roman army destroyed the Temple. With the Temple fell the priesthood and sacrifices. Judaism assumed an entirely new aspect. The Temple was supplanted by the Synagogues; prayer and sacrifices, by prayer alone; the priest, by any layman who was able to read, teach, and interpret both the written and the oral law. This new system, treated at first as provisional, became definitive after attempts to restore the nation and Temple failed. The expansion of Biblical teaching found in the Talmuds was accepted as the supreme law.

The most important religious division of Judaism at the present day is that between "Orthodox" and "Reform" groups. Orthodox Judaism holds quite strictly to the "written and oral" Law. Reform Judaism has lax views of Biblical inspiration and, on faith and morals, does not adhere strictly to theoretical Jewish law.[200] We shall center our attention on Orthodox Judaism, both because it is ethically more strict, and because it has the greater number of adherents. Unless the contrary is stated, the word Judaism, here, will refer to its Orthodox form.

Most of the moral laws of Judaism can be found in the Old Testament. The nineteenth chapter of Leviticus has been said to contain the major ethical principles of this religion.

Religious Assent

Judaism is monotheistic. God is one, omniscient, omnipotent, eternal, invisible and the source of all perfection. He is the creator of the universe; He sustains all creatures in being; and He will reward the good and punish the evil in the next life. This reward and punishment is definitely personal, but its exact nature is uncertain.[201]

Moral Effort

Judaism holds a middle course between presumption and despair. She accepts unqualifiedly the existence of free will and that man, by the use of free will, is able to overcome temptations to sin.

Benevolence

Judaism does not emphasize love for God as much as Christianity, but love for God is by no means alien to it. "Thou shalt love the Lord thy God with thy whole heart, with thy whole soul, and with thy whole strength" (Deut. 6:5).

One must love fellow human beings. "Love thy neighbor as thyself" (Lev. 19:18). But this love need not extend to all human beings. "As a matter of fact, for the Jew the neighbor was a friend or relative, someone close to him, a compatriot, but not a stranger nor an enemy, much less a heretic or an idolater. It is certain that the Talmud applies the divine command of love of neighbor only to Israelites. As late as the twelfth century, Maimonides makes bold to affirm that the Sanhedrin may not condemn to death the murderer of a pagan, because the Mosaic law which punishes murder takes into consideration only the murderer of one's neighbor, that is to say, the Jew."[202]

The Old Testament was comparatively[203] silent about the matter of benevolence toward enemies; but many teachers in later Judaism held that it was permissible to hate them.[204]

On benevolence toward the poor, Judaism is roughly the same. The duty of giving to the poor is a serious one, but charity is not to be unlimited. First of all, Judaism ordains that "no one should give away more than a fifth of his fortune, lest from independence, he may lapse into a state of dependence."[205] The idea of renouncing everything for the service of God, and of entering the religious life with no possessions of one's own, is as completely foreign to Judaism as it is to Islam.

Then, too, Judaism holds that charity toward the poor should not depend on need alone, but also should depend on the personal merit of the needy person.[206]

The one to whom aid is given should be a co-religionist. The Jewish poor are scrupulously cared for. With regard to non-Jews, one text is usually cited recommending gifts to the non-Jewish poor,[207] but the tendency of Jewish alms-giving is to restrict the recipients to fellow-Jews.[208]

Edersheim says that regardless of what modern Judaism may say to the contrary, Judaism has a certain hostility toward the outside world. The text in Exodus, "If thou see the ass of him that hateth thee lie underneath his burden, thou shalt not pass by, but shall lift it up with him" (Ex. 23:5), is interpreted: "Except to avoid hostility, a burden is only to be unloaded if the beast that lies under it belongs to an Israelite, not if it belong to a Gentile; and so the expression, 'the ass of him that hateth thee,' must be understood of a Jewish, and not of a Gentile enemy."[209]

First Commandment

Even since the time of Christ, orthodox Judaism has conscientiously taught that the worship of idols or of false gods must be avoided.

Second Commandment

Reverence for God is so great among the Jews that today they do not pronounce at all in their daily speech the word that they consider to be the proper name of God. Instead, in referring to this name for God, they use substitute words.

Christ denounced a practice among the Jews of His day,

that of the over-frequent and casual use of the oath. Conversation was so coated with oaths that they were introduced almost unconsciously. (Due to the Semitic fondness for emphatic speech, this practice is firmly rooted in Judaism even today.)[210] But in its theoretical teaching, Judaism cannot be accused of laxity in the matter of oaths. There are many texts in Rabbinic literature which express abhorrence of false or vain oaths. Such falsehood is one of the seven capital sins which provoke God's severest judgment on the world.[211]

Promissory oaths, or vows, are to be carefully observed. Even the silent determination of the heart is considered as the spoken word which must not be changed.[212] But such oaths do not bind under all conditions. A vow is valid only if made voluntarily, and not under duress. The votary must be conscious of the scope or character of his vow. The age of discretion with reference to promises is for men the beginning of the thirteenth year, for women the beginning of the twelfth, at which age the votaries are presumed to understand the importance of a vow. A father may annul the vows made by his daughter, and a husband may annul those of his wife, if they be of such a nature that the keeping of them would cause distress to the daughter or wife. The father or the husband may, however, annul such vows only on the very day when he is informed of their having been made.[213]

Any vow, be it a dedication, a promise, a prohibition, or a deprivation, can, in case the promisor regrets it, be declared void by an ordained teacher, or by three unordained teachers.[214]

Third Commandment

Modern Jewish worship does not include sacrifices; it consists in the reading of the scriptures and in prayer. While

Jews do not insist on attendance at the synagogue, they do enjoin all to say their prayers at home or in any place they chance to be, three times a day, and also to repeat certain blessings and particular praises to God at meals and on other special occasions.[215]

During the year, certain festivals are celebrated, and fasts observed. The Jewish fast is a strict one lasting twenty-four hours, and is observed on specified days of the year. Over and above the fasts, the Jews are bound to abstain from certain "unclean" foods at all times.

The Sabbath, Saturday, is a prescribed day of rest, but most modern Jews cannot be accused of attempting to be as over-scrupulous as the Pharisees on the Sabbath observances. "Nominally, for all, the Sabbath is the day of rest; but only a small number even of the Orthodox Jews keep their places of business closed on that day."[216]

Fourth Commandment

Judaism has never denied the existence of any basic precept connected with the relation of those in authority to their subjects. Parents must care for their children. Children must obey and love those who raise them and must provide for their needs in old age. "Among all the commandments the weightiest of the weighty is filial piety."[217] Citizens must observe the laws of the state, and the state, for its part, must protect the rights of its citizens.

The Pharisees, in the time of Christ, used reverence for God as a pretext for dishonoring father and mother. In some cases, they made a vow dedicating all their goods to God. When the parents asked for help, the Pharisees pleaded that they were prevented by their vow from assisting them. Christ denounced this practice. "For God said 'Honor thy father and thy mother' . . . But you say, 'Whoever shall say to his father or mother, "Any support thou mightest have had from me is dedicated to God," does not have to honor his father or his mother.' So you have made void the commandment of God by your tradition" (Matt. 15:3–6).

It might seem that the Pharisees could have been in good faith in dedicating all their possessions to God in this way. But, as a matter of fact, the unnatural son did not offer to God anything at all. He kept his property and used it for his own purposes, and used the vow as a pretext for not giving it to others, even to his parents.

Rabbinic law still holds that such an oath is valid. Most Rabbinic authorities hold that it is, however, subject to dispensation. But the existence of this power of dispensation has been disputed by some Judaic teachers. "It is expressly declared . . . by R. Eliezer that if a vow infringes upon the honor due to father or mother, the right procedure is to endeavor to convince him who made it that he failed to consider the consequences sufficiently, and then to dissolve the vow; others, however, dissented, holding that God's honor ought to be considered first."[218] The dispute over the point was not confined to the time of Christ. It has continued long after.

It would seem that the practice which was denounced by Christ was opposed to a primary conclusion of natural law. Here, as noted above, the motive of the vow was not really devotion to God but avarice.

Fifth Commandment

Judaism has a high regard for the life of an innocent person. Murder in any form is forbidden. Suicide is wrong.

Even those violations of the fifth commandment which are common among other Semitic peoples or in the religions of the Far East are rare among the Jews. The abandoning of infants is not only theoretically forbidden, but has seldom been practiced.[219] So, too, with abortion.[220] Blood revenge under certain conditions was allowed when the civil authority was incapable of restraining murder by itself (cf. Num. 35:19). But in later times, when society was better organized and regulated, the punishment of murderers was reserved to civil authority.[221]

Capital punishment of the guilty is allowed, and under certain conditions, war is permissible.

Sixth Commandment

Judaism prohibits all fornication and adultery. Polyandry was never allowed; polygamy was tolerated in certain cases before the coming of Christ; and even since Christ, Judaism has been slow in condemning it. Judaism did not explicitly forbid polygamy until the eleventh century of the Christian era. "This prohibition was originally made for the Jews living in Germany and Northern France, but it was successively adopted in all European countries." "Among European Jews polygamy was still practiced during the Middle Ages, and among Jews living in Mohammedan countries it occurs even to this day."[222]

Judaism perceives the evil of incest. In particular, the marriage of a father with his own daughter (and of a son with his mother) has been forbidden at all times as incestuous.[223] And, in general, there is a fairly large area of blood relationships within which intermarriage is forbidden by Jewish law. One of the notable differences between Judaism and Christianity on this point is that Judaism allows first cousins to marry.[224]

The possibility of entering marriage with the previous intention of dissolving it at some future date is completely excluded in Judaism. At the time of the marriage ceremony, there must be an agreement to enter a permanent union.

But after the ceremony this agreement may be broken. From the time of Moses, divorce has been tolerated. According to Mosaic law, a husband was allowed to put away his wife if "she find not favor in his eyes, for some uncleanness" (Deut. 24:1). There was a great dispute as to the meaning of the word uncleanness. Some interpreted it to refer to nothing less than adultery. Others, more liberal, applied it to anything which became offensive to the husband (even spoiling his food). In legal respects the more liberal opinion prevailed.

But at the same time, divorce was not allowed for any reason whatsoever. Divorce without good cause was morally disapproved of by the rabbis in general.[225] The rabbis set down certain restrictions on the husband's power of divorce. If his wife had become insane, he was forbidden to divorce her. Above all, certain formalities were prescribed which made the divorce procedure extremely tedious. The husband was compelled to seek the help of one learned in the law to assist him in divorcing his wife, and this person was expected to use every effort to reconcile the parties, unless sufficient reason appeared for the divorce. The husband also was required to pay the divorced wife the dowry. And after the divorce, he was prevented from annulling the divorce decree. The theoretical right of the husband to divorce his wife whenever it pleased him to do so ceased to exist in practice, and was at last, in the earlier part of the eleventh century, formally abolished.[226]

The Jewish wife was never allowed to dissolve her marriage at will. But she was allowed, for certain causes, to sue for divorce in court.

Divorce was regarded by the rabbis as a privilege accorded only to Israel, not to the Gentiles.[227] Pagans who divorced each other were considered to be sinning against a commandment of God.

The various laws and restrictions regarding Jewish divorce were formulated to make it at least very difficult in theory to obtain one without a serious reason. With regard to practice, it is very difficult, because of the dispersion, among other things, to get an accurate estimate of the frequency of divorce among the Orthodox Jews.[228] But, on the basis of what we do know, it does not seem that divorce is very frequent among them.[229]

All perversions of the marital act are condemned by Orthodox Judaism. In particular, like Catholicism, Orthodox Judaism denounces every form of contraception. (On the other hand, both Conservative and Reformed Judaism allow the use of contraception in some instances.) The Orthodox Jewish attitude is based on the command of God to the first parents: Be fruitful and multiply. The Book of Codes states that it is wrong to use the sexual faculty for no good. It is also generally agreed by teachers of Orthodox Judaism, firstly, that Onan (Gen. 38:6–10) was slain for a wasteful discharge of seed, and secondly, that the generation of Noah was destroyed principally for the same reason. The Orthodox Jewish position on the necessity of parenthood in the married state is that, except for unusual conditions, parents should have at least two children before they are entitled to practice even natural methods of birth control, such as rhythm or complete abstention.[230]

Modern Orthodox Judaism, as well as its ancient form, certainly discourages voluntary celibacy. All men must marry and raise a family. Women who did not marry were a cause of shame to their parents. Orthodox Judaism would have no part of the Christian or Essene ideal of celibacy. The only instance of celibacy among the Orthodox Jews of the pre-Christian era was the prophet Jeremias who remained single in order to dedicate himself completely to the mission of prophet (Jer. 16:2).

Seventh Commandment

The general teaching of Judaism on property, contracts and commercial dealings in general is similar to that of other religions.

On the matter of taking interest on loans, however, Judaism differs from Christianity. Christianity allows the taking of moderate interest on all loans, to compensate for risk and the loss of profit that might have been gained if the money had been invested in other ways. Judaism takes either of two extremes, depending on the religion of the recipient of the loan. If the borrower is a Jew, no interest at all may be charged. If he is a non-Jew, the lender may charge any interest he can get, however high the interest rate may be.[231]

Judaism bases its toleration of usury taken from Gentiles on an elaboration of some texts in the Old Testament. Not atypical of these texts is Deut. 23:19–20, "Thou shalt not lend upon interest to thy brother; interest of money, interest of victuals, interest of any thing that is lent upon interest. Unto a foreigner thou mayest lend upon interest; but unto thy brother thou shalt not lend upon interest; that the Lord thy God may bless thee in all that thou puttest thy hand unto, in the land whither thou goest in to possess it." As it stands in the original language, the word which is translated "interest" above does not refer to excessive interest, nor usury in its modern sense.[232] It means interest generally. The same is true of the other Old Testament passages where the subject is mentioned, so that the Old Testament admits of several interpretations on this point. Judaism has selected one of the possible interpretations: that interest of any amount, whether moderate or excessive, may be taken from non-Jews.

Eighth Commandment

Lying in general has been repeatedly and firmly denounced in Judaism. But lying is not forbidden under all conceivable circumstances. Some types of *Falsi-loquia* (*negationes veritatis indebitae*) are allowed in case a life depends on the telling of a falsehood, as, for instance, when a robber or murderer inquires after one he pursues, the law permits lying.[233] And when one is motivated by love of peace, and especially of domestic peace, one can lie without sin.[234]

Calumny, detraction, contumely, and rash judgment are forbidden.

Ninth and Tenth Commandments

Judaism is conscious of the necessity of avoiding efficacious intentions to commit sin. "Evil thoughts are an abomination to the Lord" (Prov. 15:26).

But on the question of inefficacious desires to commit sin, the Old Testament is silent. And later Judaism had nothing to add as to whether such desires were or were not evil themselves. Christ did develop the teaching of the Old Testament on this point, and stated that all such desires are sinful.

Conclusions on Judaism

From the foregoing, it would seem that Orthodox Judaism, even in its modern form, is superior to the other major non-Christian religions from the point of view of natural law. Other non-Christian religions tolerate violations of at least one primary conclusion of natural law. But in none of the instances cited above, at least, does Judaism open the doors to the violation on a broad scale of any such primary conclusion. In some cases, violations of secondary conclusions of natural law may be tolerated, such as polygamy, or lies for grave reason. Then too, Judaism has not completely closed off all avenues to the violation of some primary conclusions. The Jewish systems of corban and divorce, for instance, allow individuals within the law to violate primary conclusions. But if these loopholes are present, at least it is difficult to use them. And, unlike the other non-Christian religions, Judaism does not let hordes of members violate these conclusions without any reprimand or warning whatsoever.

9. Heretical Systems

Ever since the earliest times, as well as in our own, many attempts have been made to establish that the only essential difference between Catholic and heretical Christianity is one of doctrine. It has often been said that the difference between Catholicism and heresy lies chiefly in whether or not one accepts certain doctrines or dogmas, and that therefore this difference between the two types of Christianity is largely a theoretical one with little practical bearing on everyday ethical conduct. And, in some cases, those who embrace heresy and refuse to accept the Catholic Church feel that they are rejecting only Catholic dogmatic teaching.

Historically, heresy has inevitably rejected Catholic morality as well as her doctrine. Heresy frequently begins by trying to differ only on doctrinal points. But as Christian doctrine is discarded, morality disintegrates. For, as Van Noort has put it, "There is an indissoluble connection between the theoretical dogmas and moral precepts. The latter either arise from the former, or are strengthened by them, or receive their sanction from them."[235]

Belief in God as a Remunerator helps men to serve Him. Belief in Him as a Personal Creator and Sustainer helps men to love Him. Belief that man has been created in the image of God helps men to love one another. And, on even a higher plane, "the moral precepts receive new and extremely valid motives of obligation from the mysteries [of Catholic faith]. What could more stir a man to love God above all things than the dogma of the Incarnation and [the dogma that men by] adoption [can become sons of God]? What could more strongly urge a man to love his neighbor than the common redemption of all men through Jesus Christ? What could more powerfully move a man to sobriety and chastity than a reflection on the Eucharist . . . received into our very bodies, and on the Holy Spirit dwelling within us? With good reason then, can one compare Christian ethics without Christian dogma to a house without a foundation."[236]

Abandon Christian doctrine, and moral code inevitably will begin to slide as well. In some cases, those who have discarded large segments of Christian doctrine, retaining little more than the name Christian, have, almost without noticing it, plunged to a moral level lower than Buddhism, Stoicism, or any one of the other pagan religions mentioned above. These "liberal" heresies are not restricted to the liberal Protestant sects of modern times, but can often be found in history long before the advent of Protestantism. Some of the liberals who preceded their Protestant counterparts were Gnostics, Donatists, and Albigensians.

Some Gnostics of the second and third centuries of the Christian era, for instance, had some hair-raising ideas on the nature of morality. They considered themselves completely different from all other men. They were "spiritual and perfect" men who by that very fact were exempt from the need which other men had for practicing continence and good works. Good works were beneath them and unnecessary.[237] They gave "themselves up to the lusts of the flesh with the utmost greediness, maintaining that carnal things should be allowed the carnal nature. . . ."[238]

Modern liberal Protestantism, too, does more than simply reject doctrinal Christianity. Its moral code, as a code, has shrunk almost to the vanishing point. For the most part, each man is allowed to decide for himself what is right and wrong. The ministers, fearing controversy of any kind, prescind from discussing a great many moral questions, even fundamental ones pertaining to primary conclusions of natural law. Their adherents are left without external direction, advice or encouragement, and on those questions upon which custom does not agree with the primary conclusions of natural law, with only their consciences to guide them in selecting the proper course of moral life.

In this way, then, some liberal Christian heresies, even today, exist on a lower theoretical moral level than that of some of the major pagan religions. Where the pagans tolerate the violation of one or two primary conclusions of natural law, the liberal "Christians" tolerate many.

But what of the "fundamentalist" heresies, those which reject only a selected few of the Christian doctrines and retain the rest, and which do not, in fact, ignore or deny any primary conclusion of natural law?

The basic answer to this question was given by St. Ignatius of Antioch in the beginning of the second century: "Flee from all . . . heresies . . . as the beginning of evils."[240] At the beginning, such heresies look very much like Christianity, but in time both their dogmatic and moral teachings begin to collapse.

Pius XI has traced the process of disintegration of doctrine which inevitably occurs even in the "fundamental" heresies: "We regret that, whenever anyone separates himself obstinately from the infallible teaching of the Church, he loses gradually the certain and true doctrine about Jesus Christ. If we should ask the many different sects, those especially dating from the sixteenth and seventeenth centuries and still bearing the honored name Christian, all of which at the time they broke away professed firm belief in Christ as God and man, what they now think of Him, we would receive various and often conflicting answers. Indeed, few of them have kept the right doctrine and full faith concerning the person of our Redeemer."[241]

And as the doctrine crumbles, so does the moral code. Eventually, robbed of a dogmatic foundation, the moral code comes to have no reason for existence. And what began as a relatively strict moral code, in the course of the centuries becomes more and more tolerant of sin and eventually comes to ignore or tolerate even violations of the obvious conclusions of natural law. In fact, even those heresies which begin in an apparent blaze of glory by adding superfluous precepts to the moral code of Christ overtax their members and in the long run, as St. Paul says, "lead to the full gratification of the flesh" (Col. 2:23).

In this way, even "fundamentalist" heresy can be criticized from the point of view of primary conclusions of natural law. At the beginning, to be sure, some conservative heresies cannot be distinguished from the Church from the point of view of these primary conclusions. But gradually, even these heresies will draw away. And thus, later generations, innocent of the original break from the Church, will find themselves being indoctrinated in an increasingly inadequate moral code, and eventually being left to discover for themselves many of the primary conclusions of natural law.

10. Schismatical Systems

A schismatic is one who separates himself from the Catholic Church to form another sect independent of the jurisdiction of the Church. Schism is distinct from heresy in that heresy breaks the doctrinal unity of Christians while schism breaks the disciplinary or social unity. Heresy breaks away by explicitly denying some part of the deposit of faith. Schism makes no such denial, but does refuse obedience to the legitimate pastors of the Christian flock. But in the long run, schism descends frequently into heresy.

The chief schisms in the history of Christianity have been the following: that of the Novatians in the third century, that of the Donatists in the fourth and fifth centuries, and that of the Greek or Eastern Church attempted by Photius in the ninth century and consummated by Michael Caerularius in the eleventh. The first two have not continued down to our own day. The third has. Known as the Greek Orthodox Church, the Greek Schism is found chiefly in those areas which composed the Byzantine Empire at the time of the split. Since then, it has not spread to a great many other parts of the world but has been largely confined to the Eastern European countries.

It is not unified within itself, but is split up into as many autonomous segments as there are nations which profess it, each Eastern nation having its own Church. By far the largest of these Churches numerically, at least before the advent of the Communists, was the Russian Orthodox Church. Of the hundred million Schismatics before 1917, about three-quarters were in Russia.[242]

The history of the Greek Schism has not been one of continuous flight from Catholicism. Short-lived reunions of the Eastern Church, including the Russians, with Rome were effected by the Second Council of Lyons (1274) and the Council of Florence (1439). And at these times there was real hope that the union might be permanent.

If we prescind from the primacy of the Pope, the Greek Schismatical Church does not differ from the Catholic Church on fundamental doctrine. At various times, however, certain minor doctrinal or liturgical disagreements have been stressed, or even created, by reaction against the definitions of the Popes or the general councils. Disagreements such as those on the "filioque" or on purgatory have frequently been more on the choice of the manner of expression of the doctrines than on the ideas contained. But the true and fundamental reason of the Eastern Schism is the negation of the primacy of jurisdiction of the Roman pontiff as successor of St. Peter.[243]

Ethically, there are very few differences between the

teaching of the Eastern Schismatics and the Catholic Church. Perhaps the major difference from a strictly ethical point of view is on the matter of divorce.

The Oriental Churches[244] all agree that one of the properties of Christian marriage is indissolubility. This is taught both in their theological treatises and in their catechisms. But they disagree on their definition of indissolubility. A few of them teach, like the Catholics, that this indissolubility is absolute, and that the marriage bond cannot be broken for any cause while both parties live. Many others acknowledge one cause for divorce (adultery), but no others. And still others permit divorce and remarriage "for grave causes."[245] Of the three opinions, the second, that allowing divorce only on grounds of adultery, is the most common.[246]

But the dispute of the theologians is not reflected in the laws of the Oriental Church. The canonists, legislating for everyday practice, make the indissolubility of marriage lose its significance almost entirely. They admit a wide variety of grounds for divorce. Nor is this variety a recent innovation. Since the ninth century, the nine causes for divorce listed by the emperor Justinian I have been accepted in law and in practice. Although these first causes were grave (v.g., adultery, attempted murder, absence in captivity for a long time [five years], false accusation of adultery), others were added in the course of time which opened the way to greater abuses (v.g., hatred of the wife toward the husband because of injuries and indignities recieved, mutual implacable enmity, etc.).[247]

The Russian Church until the time of Peter the Great (1672–1725) generally followed the rules of the other Eastern Churches. There were some exceptions. They offered as further grounds such things as the squandering of the wife's fortune by the husband, shrewishness in the wife. But, unlike the others, they did not consider an illness contracted subsequent to the marriage sufficient grounds. But other, even more serious abuses were tolerated in Russia. Any priest could give a bill of divorce to a spouse who asked for it. And, in southern Russia, divorce by mutual consent accompanied by certain formalities was rampant.[248]

From the time of Peter the Great onward, however, these abuses were suppressed and the number of grounds for divorce considerably reduced. From his time up to World War I, the Russian Church accepted only three causes for divorce unless the spouse was willing to appeal to the czar himself: 1, juridically proved adultery of one of the parties; 2, absence of a spouse without report for over five years (the most commonly invoked of the three); and 3, exile of a spouse to any one of three more permanent types of punishment in Siberia.[249]

Thus, over the last two centuries, the Russian Church has been more strict on divorce than the other Oriental Churches in general. Over this same period, one cannot unhesitatingly accuse the Russian Church of tolerating violations of the primary conclusion of natural law pertaining to divorce.[250]

11. Summary and Conclusion

From the point of view of the primary conclusions of natural law, the major religions and ethical systems of the world which we have treated can be divided into two groups. In doing this we are, as before, taking these religions as they have been traditionally understood. We are prescinding from relatively recent changes which have occurred in some of them (v.g., the attempts to abolish the caste system in India). The first group includes Hinduism, Buddhism, Confucianism, Stoicism, Islam, liberal heresy and the teachings of Plato and Aristotle. All in this first group tolerate the violation of at least one primary conclusion of natural law. The second group includes Catholicism, ancient

Hebraism, and perhaps also both modern Orthodox Judaism and the pre-Communist Russian Orthodox Church. Those in this second group tolerate no such violation.

It will be noticed that the classification above also coincides with a classification of the same religions on the basis of acceptance of the Bible as inspired. The religions in the first group all fail to accept the Bible as the revealed word of God. They may, in some cases, be acquainted with it and even have a great deal of respect for it. But this respect does not include acceptance of the Bible as the inspired and infallible word of God. The religions of the second group, on the other hand, all accept the revealed nature of the Bible. The Bible of the Orthodox Jews, of course, is much smaller than that of the Christians, and there are other important differences between the various religions of the second group in their attitude toward the Bible. But they all do, at least, accept its inerrancy.

The division of the major religions and philosophies into two groups does not imply that each religion has the same essential degree of holiness as the others in the same group. There are wide discrepancies in holiness within each group.

The members of the first group all ignore at least one necessary virtue, but some of them ignore more than others. Buddhism, for example, from the point of view of these necessary virtues, is superior to Hinduism. Having abolished the caste system, she lifted her members up from the dangers inherent in the traditional Hindu restrictions on fraternal charity, without at the same time sagging below Hinduism in her teaching on any of the other necessary virtues.

In the second group, Orthodox Judaism and Russian Orthodoxy are at a lower level than Catholicism. Ultimately, both the former will permit a member to violate a primary conclusion of natural law if that member desires to do so badly enough. Each, for example, in the last analysis, will allow its members to obtain a divorce for a slight cause if they are willing to overcome the legal obstacles involved (i.e., the complicated legal process for the Jews, and appeal to the supreme civil authority for the Russians).

The religions within each of the two groups are still further differentiated from others in the same group by their varying attitudes toward merely secondary conclusions of natural law. These attitudes, too, serve to raise or lower the standing of each religion within the confines of its own group.

The Catholic Church, then, is the only one of the major religions which does not bend an inch on the primary conclusions. She is the only major religion which does not, either as a general rule or even in certain special cases for certain individuals, fail to try to dissuade her members from violating these obvious precepts.

This fact has two implications: one indicative, and the other missiological.

First, it demonstrates the holiness of the Church. The primary conclusions are obvious to all men and, as such, constitute a standard of judging holiness which will be acceptable to all. And by this same standard, the Church is seen to be holier than all other major religions.

Secondly, the unique identity of the moral teachings of the Church with the primary conclusions of natural law has a missiological implication. One of the clearest explanations as to how and why the Christian apostolate is necessary is given by the study of these primary conclusions. A study of the attitudes of the non-Catholic religious groups toward the primary conclusions shows why we cannot presume that the members of these religions are, for the most part, in good faith. They are not warned about all of the necessary virtues. And, on a wide scale, they stray from these necessary virtues in practice. Catholic evangelization is needed among these people to call them back at least to the observance of these virtues. As Lombardi says, although "all adults, considered individually, can be saved without that apostolate, nevertheless, there is a very real danger of damnation, and it is very probable that *en masse,* many indeed will be damned if they do not receive Catholic evangelization. When dealing with the individual unbeliever, it is well to bear in mind the possibilities, however slight these may be, of his justification, but we must not forget the very grave motives we have for suspecting a state of sin in the great majority."[251] Lombardi was speaking only in the context of religious assent, but what he says is doubly true when we consider the dangers not only in the matter of religious assent, but in the other primary conclusions as well.

Moreover, what he says applies not only to "many pagans" within a few selected pagan religions, but to many within all of the non-Biblical religions (at least). For we have seen that all of these religions ignore some necessary virtue, and that in all of these religions many people stray from one or more of these necessary virtues in practice. Thus Catholic evangelization is necessary among all of the non-Biblical religious groups (at least) to call them back to the observance of these virtues.

12. *The Constancy of the Church*

Through over nineteen centuries, the Church has constantly sought to dissuade men from violating both primary and secondary conclusions of natural law. Her perfect agreement with natural law has been preserved in the face of tremendous obstacles.

In evangelizing a new country, instead of compromising even a few of her moral principles, she has insisted that the new converts accept all of her strict code. Having received a great many disparate peoples into her ranks, she has continually been subjected to pressure to ease or change her teaching on this or that moral point. But she has worked to bring each of these peoples to a gradual abandonment of immemorial customs of vice and corruption.

Abolishing these crimes, she has also introduced other changes, and, given time and the opportunity, she has civilized those barbaric cultures which she evangelized. The German barbarians (who except for the Church would have made the Dark Ages the Black Ages and buried all knowledge of previous cultural advances) glorified war as a vocation higher than peace. They held that a child who reached adulthood was still bound by engagements which his parents had entered into in his name during his infancy.[252] The Church gradually changed these ideas, holding that peace was more noble than war and that an adult was bound only by those contracts which he himself had agreed to. These Christian ideas are taken for granted today as self-evident, but at one time there were many who opposed them as impracticable.

As time went on, and more and more nations became Catholic, pressures became stronger from within Christendom. Rulers who granted special favors to the Church sometimes asked a special favor in return: a relaxation of some point in the moral code. Immoral rulers frequently tried to soothe their consciences and to win back the esteem of their subjects by seeking or demanding official approval by the Church of bigamy. Yet "ecclesiastical history does not show a single example of bigamy officially tolerated."[253] The Church stands alone among all the great religions of the world in never having granted special exemptions from moral law to any person or any group.

When these exemptions were not granted, whole nations sometimes threatened to leave the Church, and at times these threats were carried out. Henry VIII took away with him a large section of the Catholic Church of the 16th century because the Church would not grant him an annulment or a divorce. Notwithstanding, the Church remained firm on moral principle, and saw England depart.

The Church is no less outspoken and courageous in our own day. With many pleading the radical social changes as reason for making relaxations in moral codes, the Church still holds fast to the same code she held in the time of Christ. The fact that she still stands and lives today in all nations and after so many centuries of change, but with the same code with which she started, is not the least of reasons for perceiving in her a divine guidance in selection of her moral principles.

To the danger of schism is added a physical danger in her open denunciation of evil. In our own day, the Church has been in the forefront in denouncing Nazism and Communism. She spoke out against these systems, not when they were in their last agonies or dead, but when they were at the height of their power and able to inflict staggering damage on the physical structure of the Church. Pius XI, for one, condemned Nazism in an encyclical in 1937.[254] The Popes and hierarchy have denounced Communism from the time of its inception until now.

When this whole question is studied from the point of view of the human nature of the successors of St. Peter, it becomes all the more remarkable. All of them were human beings, and, as such, naturally responsive to appeals on the part of others to mollify somewhat the strictness of the Catholic moral code. Yet not one of them through so many centuries ever gave in. No one of the successors of St. Peter has ever officially condoned violations of moral law in any form, in any person or group whatsoever. Without God's special guidance, this would have been impossible. The historical fact that the Supreme Pontiffs were so preserved from relaxing, even temporarily, Catholic doctrine is one of the greatest Catholic miracles of all.

CHAPTER FOUR

Further Manifestations of the Holiness of Catholic Teaching

1. *Higher Concepts of Virtue Introduced by Christianity*

When we go beyond an exclusive consideration of primary and secondary conclusions of natural law, we still see that the holiness of the Church surpasses that of the pagans. "The virtues which in the Christian ideal are the most fundamental of all, lie altogether outside the scope of the highest pagan ethics. Christian humility [and] charity . . . are instances in point.

"Humility which in the Christian scheme is the necessary groundwork of all sanctity (Matt. 18:3), was previous to Christ an unknown virtue. The sense of personal unworthiness in which it consists, is repugnant to all the impulses of unregenerate nature."[1]

And Christian charity is worthy of detailed study from this same point of view. "The charity which Christ sets forth in the Sermon on the Mount and in the parable of the Good Samaritan—a charity which knows no limits (and is unconditioned even by merit or gratitude in the recipient), and which embraces enemies as well as friends—exceeds all that moralists had deemed possible for men. And this charity Christ requires not of a chosen few, but of all His followers."[2]

The unique elevation of Christian charity is shown also by a comparison of devotional works. Cardinal Gibbons has said, "Our books of piety are adapted to every want of the human soul, and are a fruitful source of sanctification. Who can read without spiritual profit such works as the . . . *Imitation of Christ* by Thomas à Kempis; the *Christian Perfection* by Rodriguez; the *Spiritual Combat* of Scupoli; the writings of St. Francis de Sales, and a countless host of other ascetical authors? . . . You will search in vain outside the Catholic Church for writers comparable in . . . healthy piety to such as I have mentioned. Compare, for instance, Kempis with Bunyan's *Pilgrim's Progress,* or Butler's *Lives of the Saints* with Foxe's *Book of Martyrs.* You lay down Butler with a sweet and tranquil devotion and with a profound admiration for the Christian heroes whose lives he records; while you put aside Foxe with a troubled mind and a sense of vindicative bitterness."[3]

And what Cardinal Gibbons said chiefly in relation to Protestants, can, in truth, be applied to all non-Christian religions as well. There is a certain serenity and spirit of love for all men in Catholic devotional works which is absent in those of all the other major religions. Even Buddhism, which is not impeded by any ideas of intolerance, does not reach the Christian level of love and respect for one's fellow men.

With regard to the corporal and spiritual works of mercy, no non-Catholic religion even approaches the teaching and achievements of the Church. Christian efforts in the development of hospitals, in care for the lepers and for the poor, in the instruction of the ignorant and illiterate, and in many other such works of active charity, have through the ages dwarfed the attempts of other religions along the same lines.

One reason why so many religions fall short of Catholicism in trying to alleviate physical and moral suffering is doctrinal. Some religions, especially those originating in the East, are somewhat sluggish in this matter because of a fatalistic creed. Suffering for them is caused either by the unalterable intention and decree of God or of the gods, or by the victim's own sins either in this life or in a previous existence. In either case, to attempt to alleviate it would be to attempt to upset the order of the universe. In other parts of the world (v.g., ancient Greece and Rome),[4] disease was regarded as a curse inflicted by supernatural powers, and it was to be cured more by trying to propitiate the malevolent deity than by trying to organize the work of relief. Christianity, on the other hand, teaches that it is in no sense a sin to try to cure a disease, and that the cure should be sought by the use of both prayer and physical medicine.

On many other virtues besides humility and charity, the Church goes far beyond the pagans. Thus, there is a tremendous gap between Christian and pagan holiness considered at a natural level. Christianity transcends non-Christian religions both in that she alone teaches her members all the primary and secondary conclusions of natural law, and also in that she encourages still other virtues which transcend natural religion.

2. Correlation of Holiness with Catholicity[5]

The Church provides her members with instruction in all the natural laws of God. Her holiness is truly catholic or universal. But this note of catholicity or universality in the holiness of the Church is not restricted only to the scope of the doctrines themselves. Her holiness can be described as universal for two other reasons:

First, her holiness is universal in the motives she offers for the practice of virtue. The other major religions present a certain number of motives for virtue, but omit others. Stoicism presents earthly motives: virtue should be sought because of its intrinsic goodness, or because it gains for us the esteem of other reasonable men, or because virtue brings health to the body, and vice leads to disease, corruption, and an early death. Stoicism almost entirely neglects motives connected with God or a future life. Islam inculcates the motives of hope of reward and fear of punishment in the next life, but almost entirely neglects love of God. The Church offers all of these: love of God, hope of future reward, fear of future punishment, and earthly motives. Not that every Catholic must be conscious of each of these motives at all times. Rather, the motive to be emphasized varies with the state of soul (fear of hell for the beginner, love of God for the advanced).

In addition to these four basic motives, she provides others, such as those which arise from the sacraments: Penance holds off despair at past sins and buoys us up with hope for the future. The Eucharist instills a greater desire to improve in order to become more worthy of receiving it. All the sacraments encourage us with the knowledge that God is giving us His special assistance. As Pius X said, in her moral discipline, the Church "gives a mighty impulse to the more perfect observance of the natural law inscribed in our hearts."[6]

The second additional reason why the holiness of the Church can be called universal is that she, as St. Cyril of Jerusalem says, "brings into subjection to godliness the whole race of mankind, governors and governed, learned and unlearned."[7] Van Noort says, "The Church is catholic . . . in personnel because she welcomes people of every sort of temperament and condition in life and erects no racial, national or social barriers."[8] In other words, the Church's holiness is universal not only in the extent to which her doctrines correspond with natural law, or in the extent to which she offers valid motives for virtue, but also in reference to personnel. This particular aspect of catholicity is not usually associated with the note of holiness. But this association can logically be made, since that religion which can appeal to and elevate the moral standards of a greater variety of human beings deserves to be called more holy (all other things being equal) than another religion which appeals to a smaller range of people.

Non-Christian religions characteristically appeal either to the members of only one nation or race or to one segment of society, or of humanity.

Hinduism, Confucianism, and Judaism are admittedly restricted to one nation or race. There is no proselytizing in Hinduism because of a belief that the blessings of Hinduism are gained only by birth in a Hindu family.[9] Confucianism makes no serious attempt to spread far beyond its traditional territorial limits. Orthodox Judaism will admit converts; but these proselytes never will be accepted as having the same standing in Judaism as one who is born of Jewish parents.

Other religions restrict full membership to one segment of society. Hinduism, as well as being largely restricted to India, is not universal in its appeal even within this ambit. Traditional Hinduism excluded the members of the lowest caste, the Sudras, from taking an active part in religion. "Only the three upper castes, had the right . . . to take part in the sacrifices and to know the Vedas; for Brahmanism, far from being a religion open to all, was exclusively a privilege of birth."[10]

Somewhat similar to Hinduism, the religion of ancient Rome excluded the lowest social class, in this case, the slaves, from religious functions in many circumstances. It was felt that the presence of slaves defiled the ceremony.[11]

The ancient Greek and Roman philosophers, Plato, Aristotle, Seneca, etc., could not attract the masses. The theorizing, however brilliant, of Plato and Aristotle was too abstract and complex to be grasped by the man on the street. Their teachings, at least as they were originally presented, could be assimilated and put into practice only by a relatively limited group of students. Seneca's teaching was more concrete and easily understood than that of Plato and Aristotle but, as we have seen, not intended to be taken up by the lower classes of society. It was a philosophy for the wealthy and the influential. It had nothing for the poor and oppressed.

Buddhism avoids some of the foregoing self-imposed restrictions. Buddha abolished caste as a consideration in the pursuit of virtue. All could, if they desired, enter his order. His teaching could appeal not only to those brought up in the Indian social system, but to those who had never heard of caste. Nor was poverty in any form an obstacle to full participation in Buddhist life. In fact, as far as opportunity for membership goes, Buddhism is as universal as any non-Catholic religion. Essentially, there are no national or social restrictions on membership, but there remain at least two other major restrictions against full participation in Buddhism.

The first is one which has developed in practice rather than having resulted from application of theory. Buddhism does not look with favor upon women attempting to achieve perfection by joining a monastic order. "Apparently only with much reluctance did the Buddha consent to the establishment of an order of nuns. . . . The concession . . . would prove disastrous [so Buddha prophesied] to the prosperity and duration of the faith which he taught. . . . On the same occasion, [however], he prescribed the obligations and duties of the [nuns] contained in the 'Eight Chief Rules' to which they were bound in strict obedience. The regulations involved subservience to and dependence upon the order of monks in all respects. . . . It is probable that the . . . establishment of nunneries [is] in reality due to a later age than that of the founder of Buddhism. The institution has never become popular or gained a strong hold in any Buddhist country; and the number of the nuns has always been small relatively to the number of monks."[12]

The second limitation on participation in Buddhism is, perhaps, one which is a more direct result of Buddhist theoretical teaching than the first. Buddhism over-emphasizes the place of the monastic life. The only way in which one could gain salvation and attain Nirvana was to abandon the world and become a monk. The ideal of a perfect lay life remained undeveloped. No detailed and complete code was set down for the layman. As a result, if a man had no desire to take up the life of a monk, Buddhism, as such, had no substitute holy ideal to offer him. He was forced, to a great extent, to obtain his moral code, not from Buddhism itself, but from the social system in which he found himself. In Buddhism, then, though all men are invited to take up an ascetical life, no lofty moral ideal is offered to those who do not. A layman, then, can never be a Buddhist in the full sense of the term.

Islam has no social barriers. All classes of society, rich and poor, the noble and the lowly, are welcomed into its ranks. Having no monasticism at all, it could not fall into Buddhism's error; all Moslems are laymen and the moral law applies to all. And although it borrows heavily from Judaism in many ways, Islam is not a national religion in the same sense as Judaism. In Islam there is not the same consciousness of birth as the prime factor in the establishment of a man's religion. Non-Arabs are much more welcome in Islam than are non-Jews in Judaism.

But Islam is still to a great extent a national religion. It has been unable to shake off its many peculiarly Arabian characteristics, such as the strict use of Arabic in prayer and the liturgy, which have tended to destroy its appeal to many non-Arabs. Certain heretical Moslem groups have tried to adapt Islam to a wider audience, but, in doing so, have cut away at the supports of the religion: the Koran and the written traditions. Orthodox Islam remains, in many ways, a religion of Arabia and for those of Arabian origin. "The character of its teaching is too exact a reflection of the race, time, place and climate in which it arose, to admit of its becoming universal."[13]

Non-Christian religions, then, even the superior ones, are not catholic in personnel. They are restricted nationally, socially, financially, intellectually, or in other ways. This has its implications in holiness. We have previously seen that the introduction of these religions into a thoroughly Catholic environment would in no way elevate the moral level. But this lack of catholicity of personnel weakens their potentialities for good even in a non-Christian environment.

There are many pagan religions which are at a far lower level than the ones which we have studied above, and there are many adherents of these depraved religions who are ignorant of Christianity, and who would more easily move toward observance of all the primary conclusions of natural law (not to mention the secondary conclusions) and thus toward holiness, if they could be admitted to one of the superior pagan religions. To be sure, they still would not be taught all the primary conclusions in their new and superior pagan religion, but at least the number of false moral principles taught them would be reduced, and their task of sifting the good from the bad would be made easier.

Thus, if the superior pagan religions were capable of appealing to and reaching all these people, and if they could, in fact, spread to all pagan areas, the moral level of the world in general could be raised.

But the pagan religions cannot perform this task. There are many members of lower pagan religions who cannot be raised up by any neighboring superior pagan religion because of an essential incapacity of these superior religions to reach them.

The lack of catholicity of personnel in these superior non-Catholic religions, then, is a defect in holiness.

The Catholic Church, on the other hand, is not only geographically catholic, but she is catholic in personnel. She has been so at all times. And she was established with that purpose in mind: to appeal to, instruct, and elevate all nations and people. "Go therefore, and make disciples of all nations" (Matt. 28:19); "Go into the whole world and preach the gospel to every creature" (Mark 16:15).

The Church can grow in all nations. Membership in any nation or race is no bar to becoming a Christian in the full sense of the word. In fact, one's national identity can be perfectly preserved even while one enters completely into the life of the Church. Becoming a Catholic does not require destruction of all ties with one's national or familial heritage. "Where can anyone find a someone more Jewish than St. Paul, more Italian than St. Francis of Assisi, more Spanish than St. Ignatius of Loyola or St. Teresa, more French than St. Joan, or more English than St. Thomas More?"[14]

The Church's dogmatic and moral teachings are simple enough to be grasped and appreciated even by children, and yet are so profound and mutually consistent that they can and have satisfied the greatest intellects. Arnobius' words can be applied to all times: "Men endowed with great ability—orators, grammarians, rhetoricians, lawyers, and physicians, even those who explore the profundities of philosophy—eagerly seek instruction in these things."[15]

The Church can appeal to all degrees of age, social status and wealth; she can appeal to both sexes, to all temperaments, to all intellects, to all men of good will.

Christ was the first to establish a religion which avowedly was for all people in the world. And in all history, He was the only one who successfully accomplished this purpose.[16] "Hardly out of its cradle, Christianity broke down the barriers of race, language and culture; and right from the beginning recruited its disciples and its martyrs from all classes of society. This penetration of society by the Church was no less remarkable than its geographical expansion."[17]

PART II

Holiness of Founder

Holiness of Founder

1. The Contribution of the Various Founders of Religions

In our treatment of holiness of teaching we have considered the holiness of the religions considered absolutely, that is, independent of the time, place or other circumstances of their origin. Each moral code was studied and compared with other moral codes, but without considering its merit solely against the background of its place of origin, and without any study of the virtue of its human originator or founder.

In treating the holiness of founder, we consider both the character and virtues of the founders of these codes themselves, and the contribution of each of these moral codes to the specific society or milieu in which it originated.

When these philosophies are studied against the background from which they arose, some of them are seen to have made a startling contribution to the elevation of mankind. Some of them did not originate in a Catholic or in any superior moral environment, but were formulated as a step forward from a thoroughly pagan and depraved moral system. They raised rather than lowered the standard of morality.

On the other hand, some of these philosophies did the opposite.

Those heretical groups which have broken off directly from Catholicism (as opposed to those which have themselves split off from still another heresy) may make a pretense or show of raising moral standards, but historically, such heresies have always sooner or later cast off one or more Catholic moral principles. And they reject not just disciplinary decrees of the Church but some point or points of natural law. Heresy (as a break from the Church), then, is always a step backward, a step in the direction of moral disintegration.

But many of the major pagan religions were not begun as a relaxation but as a strengthening of moral law. And some of them, it would seem, in so far as they introduced changes, did so entirely for the better. That is, in no significant case, did they impose on the original society in which they existed a moral law which was more lax than the parallel law already existing in that society.

Two examples of this type of religion are Islam and Buddhism. It does not seem that either Mohammed or Buddha relaxed any essential point pertaining to natural law in their native societies. Mohammed entirely wiped out widespread polytheistic worship and abandonment of infants in Arabia. Other evils (v.g., easy divorce, blood revenge, polygamy), he did not abolish, but to each he added restrictions which somewhat cut down their frequency. In no case did Mohammed take a previously existing good custom and change it for the worse. Islam was not, in its origins, presented as a step downwards in any sense. Every major change was for the better.

It was only later, when Islam spread to non-Arab countries, that it found itself presenting moral teachings which were more lax than those already existing in the area. In some of these areas, divorce was by no means so easily obtained as in Islam. In these areas, Islam might have appealed to some because of its more lenient moral code. But during the lifetime of Mohammed, and while Islam was confined to Arabia, its moral laws either corresponded with or were superior to the already existing customs of the country.

The same is true of Buddha. His major innovations, from the point of view of the essentials of natural law, were in no instance inferior to the parallel customs in Hinduism.

Mohammed and Buddha were not strict innovators, but promulgators of moral points already known by some people in their native society. They took what was previously a little-known moral law and made it well-known. Their greatness lies in that those customs which they did change, they changed for the better.

Because of the fact that so many of the moral laws introduced by the great non-Christian religions and philosophies have been improvements over existing laws, attempts have frequently been made to prove that the founders of these systems thought they had developed a perfect moral code. Not atypical of such attempts is that by Lane-Poole who, in effect, denies that Mohammed had any insight into the defects in Islam.

"The fatal blot in Islam is the degradation of women. . . . Yet it would be hard to lay the blame altogether on Mohammed. The real roots of the degradation of women lie much deeper. When Islam was instituted, polygamy was almost necessitated by the number of women and their need of support; and the facility of divorce was quite necessitated by the separation of the sexes, and the consequence that a man could not know or even see the woman he was about to marry before the ceremony was accomplished. It is not Mohammed whom we must blame for these great evils, polygamy and divorce; it is the state of society which demanded the separation of the sexes, and in which it was not safe to allow men and women freely to associate. . . . Mohammed might have done better. He might boldly have swept away the traditions of Arab society, unveiled the women, intermingled the sexes, and punished with the most severe measures any license which such association might at first encourage. With his boundless influence, it is possible that he might have done this, and, the new system once fairly settled, and the people accustomed to it, the good effects of the change would have begun to show themselves. But such an idea could never have occurred to him. . . . Mohammed's ideas about women were like those of the rest of his contemporaries . . . [and the idea that] a woman should be the counsellor and companion of a man does not seem to have occurred to him."[1]

Humanly speaking, the greatest of the non-Christian religious leaders (Buddha, Mohammed, etc.) are not entirely without a plausible rebuttal for failing to correct certain serious defects in their native culture. They did correct many things, and very possibly felt that if they tried to correct every major defect, they would succeed in nothing. They corrected as much as they could, and left the rest as beyond their powers to remedy.

A further hypothesis, however, that these great men were in complete and invincible ignorance of the existence of any evils in their systems, is untenable. Not that Mohammed and the others necessarily saw every defect in their systems, but they must have perceived at least the major ones, those which tolerated violations of primary conclusions of natural law.

On the other hand, granting that they perceived the major defects, they may very well have been ignorant of the way in which they could successfully have been corrected: for Mohammed: how to legislate so that the pagan Arab system of divorce would eventually be wiped out; for Buddha: how to develop an adequate code for those who did not enter monastic life; etc. In view of the great difficulty involved and also of the fact that these men were working without the help of revelation, it is small wonder that they, great as they were, failed in eliminating all the major defects which they found in their native culture.

The net contribution of the founders of the non-Catholic religions varied. The work of some was partly negative, relaxing an already existing and beneficial moral law, or adding some unnecessary laws binding on all, yet impossible for all to observe (v.g., the Pharisees). That of some others was largely positive, and the only criticism that can be leveled against them is that they did not go far enough.

2. *Personal Holiness of These Founders*

In considering the personal holiness of the founders of religions, we prescind, for the moment, from the holiness of their teachings as such and from the specific contributions which their teachings made to the societies in which they were first spread. Here we consider the lives of the founders themselves. In their personal lives, did these men surpass, equal, or fall short of the moral level of their own teachings? And did any or all of them deny the existence of any defects in their own conduct, and claim to be perfect?

In this sense, then, the concept of holiness of founder refers to the extent to which the founder himself is a model of virtue. As such, this concept can be extended to include, besides the founders of the religions, the God, or in the case of polytheistic creeds, the gods who are held up as objects of worship, and who in many cases are credited with having had a part in the founding of their own religion.

A. HOLINESS OF GOD

We take it for granted that the God of the Bible is perfectly holy. God the Father is perfect. All His actions and instructions are in accord with right reason. All His dealings with man have been in full accord with the virtues of truth, prudence, justice, mercy, charity, etc. But this is not necessarily so with the gods of the pagans.

The gods of the ancient Greeks were notoriously deficient in this respect. The ancient Greeks "proclaim that their gods took the lead in committing unutterable acts of adultery, and in monstrous banquets. For who does not sing of Saturn devouring his own children and of Jove, his son, gulping down Metis?"[2] As Justin Martyr said to the pagans in the second century, "The poets who have flourished among you raise a laugh out of the uncleanness of Jupiter with his own children. And those who now adopt such instruction are not restrained by you; but, on the contrary, you bestow prizes and honors upon those who euphoniously insult the gods."[3] Nor are the abominations confined to the actions of the chief gods. Lesser gods, Apollo,[4] Mercury, Esculapius, etc.[5] imitated their superiors. The pagans "composed fables and foolish stories about their gods and did not exhibit them as gods, but as men, and men of whom some were drunken, and others fornicators and murderers."[6] Clement of Alexandria refers to the "troops of damsels deflowered" by Poseidon and Apollo.[7]

And to compound their crimes, the gods were not even considered exempt from moral law; but rather they committed these crimes knowing full well that they were doing evil.[8]

Some of the gods were not only presented as being immoral in their own actions, but also as presiding over immorality among humans. Laverna was the Roman goddess of thieves and the patroness of dishonesty in general: "Grant me, sweet Laverna, to be thought just and upright" is the hypocrite's prayer in Horace.[9]

Other pagan gods besides those of the ancient Greeks and Romans have been thought of as lacking in holiness by their own worshippers. The ancient Babylonian, Egyptian, and Sumerian gods and goddesses were guilty of adultery, murder, incest, drunkenness, sadism, etc.[10] "Canaanite theology presented the gods as relishing sexual and sensual excesses."[11]

Not all pagans, however, ascribe immorality to their gods. For one thing, "not all nations were equally interested in their gods to develop a mythology about them. Of the Chinese deities, Moore says: 'These powers have no plastic, dramatic individuality, like the gods of Greece; no mythology recites their exploits. They have definite functions, and by these alone they themselves are defined.' On the other hand, in Japan, Shinto has an abundant and even grotesque genealogy of its many gods."[12]

The existence of immorality among some of the gods of the pagans had its effect on the morality of the pagans themselves. Sin among the gods weakened the motivation of those who worshipped these gods. If the gods may sin, so may men. The Roman playwright, Terence, has one of his characters set up Jove as his example of lewdness. After describing a sin of Jove with Danaë, the actor, in St. Augustine's words, "excites himself to lust, as if by celestial authority, when he says: 'Great Jove, who shakes the highest heavens with his thunder, and I, poor mortal man, not do the same! I did it, and with all my heart I did it.'"[13] Nor did the pagans themselves fail to see the force of this argument. Seneca confessed: "Since we have such gods the horror of vice should disappear from among men. . . . To attribute vices to the gods—what is it but to inflame passion in the hearts of men, at the same time legalizing all the disorders through the example of the divinity?" Hence, as we read in the works of the same Seneca, a pagan could logically say: "Why should that be forbidden to me what the gods have the right to do."[14]

Nor are these objections restricted to the gods of the

ancient Greeks and Romans. They can be leveled against Hinduism, among the other major religions, as well. Wilkins says that "in Hinduism almost any vice can be committed under the impression that it is pleasing to some deity or other."[15]

The concept of God as holy, then, is not universal and inevitable. Not a few pagan religions, while correctly admitting personality in their divinities, go too far and ascribe moral defects to them.

But a discussion of holiness of founders from the point of view of the gods in various religions can include only those religions which do have a concept of a personal divinity. If a religion has no god with an intellect and will, then there can be neither virtue nor a lack of it in its gods.

B. HOLINESS OF THE HUMAN FOUNDERS

A study of the human founder (i.e., the man who originated or who gave the greatest impetus to a given religion or philosophy), then, will enable us to study a greater variety of religions and philosophies from this point of view.

In studying these founders, we shall not examine their conduct against the background of Christian morality. Since their teachings do not reach the level of Christian teachings, we take it for granted that their lives, too, will not measure up in all respects to the heights of Christian spirituality. Each of these founders will be studied in the light of his own teachings and by his own standards. To what extent did the founders of the various religions claim to live up to their own code of morality? And in each case, was this claim accurate, or was it exaggeration or self-depreciation?

Christ Himself was certainly unambiguous in His statements on this matter. He not only claimed to be without sin, but put this claim in the form of a challenge to His enemies: "Which of you can convict me of sin" (John 8:46).

And He said, "He who sent me is with me; he has not left me alone, because I do always the things that are pleasing to him" (John 8:29); "I know him and I keep his word" (John 8:55); "The prince of the world is coming, and in me he has nothing" (John 14:30).

Christ did not claim to have achieved perfection only after a struggle of many years. He had possessed perfect virtue "always" and during His entire life. He challenged His enemies to find any sin in Him, present or past. They remained silent.

Christians have been completely unanimous in declaring that Christ was, indeed, free from all sin. The Apostles who had lived familiarly with Him for a long time, and had Him continually under their observation, openly testified to His perfect sinlessness. St. Peter told the early Christians: "You know that you were redeemed . . . with the precious blood of Christ, as of a lamb without blemish and without spot"; "Christ . . . who did no sin, neither was deceit found in his mouth" (1 Pet. 1:18–19; 2:21–2). And St. Paul said, "For it was fitting that we should have such a high priest, holy, innocent, undefiled, apart from sinners" (Heb. 7:26). Since the time of the Apostles, all Catholics have been of one mind, reaffirming their belief in the perfect holiness of Christ.

And this estimate of the virtue of Christ is by no means monopolized by Catholics. The vast majority of non-Catholics and non-Christians do not question the pre-eminent sanctity of Christ. Those non-Christians who have heard of Him, v.g., the Jews, Moslems,[16] admit His holiness.

But what about sin in other men? According to the Bible, all human beings, apart from Christ and His mother, are sinners. "For in many things we all offend" (James 3:2). Even the greatest of saints offend in many things with regard to venial sins which result from the weakness of the present life.[17]

And even apart from those who accept the New Testament, there have been others who have held that sin is universal. Philo said, "The best man is he who has committed the fewest faults, for no one is without some blemish." Libanius said, "Not to sin is divine and peculiar to God alone." Coates felt that "it is impossible to find a human being who has not fallen. Rather it is true that in every man . . . there is hidden a foul core." The Stoic Epictetus agreed: "Can it be possible to be free from sin? The only thing possible is that we should continually strive not to sin."[18] Buddha says: "It is a serious sin to think oneself perfect."[19] And Mohammed says: "If Allah should punish men according to what they deserve, He would not leave on the back of the earth so much as a beast" (sura 35:45).

Many pagans and non-Christians, then, agree with Christian teaching at least to the extent that for ordinary men, complete freedom from sin is impossible.

Frequently, however, pagans will glorify their special heroes and spiritual leaders, saying that these men were not like the rest of men and were both free of all sin and models of perfect holiness. But it is interesting to see what these spiritual leaders said of themselves. Did the giants of pagan spirituality claim perfect holiness, or did they admit that they were imperfect?

In studying what these men claimed for themselves, it is necessary to keep in mind that perfect holiness is not equivalent to mere freedom from sin. Perfect holiness includes two things: freedom from sin and the observance of all the counsels. Every society has a certain number of ideals which are not strictly commanded for all but are only recommended. He who wishes to advance in holiness is encouraged to follow these ideals, but failure to do so does not imply sin. Failure to follow these ideals is not blamable or reprehensible, but is a mere lack of something better. And each society also has a certain number of precepts, rules which everyone must observe. Failure to observe these precepts is blameworthy and is a positive revolt against the moral laws of the society. Such failures are sins.

Of course, this distinction between precepts and counsels is not made by the pagans so clearly or in such detail as it is in Christianity, as we have seen. Often, pagan religions will not specify whether a particular ideal is commanded or only recommended. Thus the number of moral points to be considered as strict precepts and counsels is far less in most pagan religions than in Christianity. Nevertheless, every society or religion does have at least a certain number of ideals which must be sought and a certain number of other ideals which are only recommended.

This distinction is important in discussing the holiness of the founders of the great religions. If one of these men lacks or admits he lacks perfect holiness even in the light of his own code of morality, he is not necessarily admitting that he is guilty of sin. He may be observing all the precepts of his code, but may not as yet have come to follow all the counsels.

It is impossible to study all the great founders of religion as to whether or not they claimed perfect sanctity, because some of them, as far as we know, did not make any clear or direct statement on this point.

The Socratic tradition was not one in which claims of perfect virtue would be likely to be found. For Plato, ignorance at least of some kind (i.e., v.g., of the malice itself of a sin, or of the way to avoid it) is the source of all sin or evil. And the best man is the one who most readily admits his ignorance or inability to avoid imperfections. Socrates says, "But having become good, to remain in a good state and be good, as you, Pittacus, affirm, is not possible, and is not granted to man; God only has this blessing."[20]

The teachings of the Stoics tended to lead to complacency and pride in one's own ethical achievements. The virtue of humility was certainly not greatly emphasized. Accordingly, we would not be too surprised if Seneca had claimed for himself the absolute heights of perfection. But he did not. He admitted, "We have all sinned, some more, some less grievously, and we have not only committed faults in the past but we shall go on committing faults to the end of time."[21] "What, then, am I myself doing with my leisure? I am trying to cure my own sores. If I were to show you a swollen foot, or an inflamed hand, or some shrivelled sinews in a withered leg, you would permit me to lie in quiet in one place and to apply lotions to the diseased member. But my trouble is greater than any of these, and I cannot show it to you. The abscess, or ulcer, is deep within my breast. Pray, pray, do not commend me, do not say: 'What a great man! He had learned to despise all things; condemning the madnesses of man's life, he has made his escape!' I have condemned nothing except myself. There is no reason why you should desire to come to me for the sake of making progress. You are mistaken if you think that you will get any assistance from this quarter; it is not a physician that dwells here, but a sick man."[22]

On the other hand, the Moslems, at least at first glance, do seem to claim perfection for certain men. In one of the creeds of the Moslems, we read: "All the Prophets are exempt from sins, both light and grave, from unbelief and sordid deeds. Yet stumbling and mistakes may happen on their part. Mohammed is His beloved, His servant, His Apostle, His Prophet, His chosen and elect. He did not serve idols, nor was he at any time a polytheist, even for a single moment. And he never committed a light or a grave sin."[23] Among the "Prophets exempt from sin," Moslems also include Moses, David, and Christ.

The above statements, however, in spite of the fact that they are found in a Moslem creed, do not represent a uni-

versal and constant opinion of Moslems. This creed was
composed in about the tenth century of the Christian era,
the fourth or fifth century of the Moslem system of dating.
Orthodox Moslems today, to be sure, generally agree that
Mohammed was entirely without sin. But, for the first few
centuries, there is no trace in Islam of belief in the impeccability of Mohammed. Wensinck is of the opinion that
the "doctrine of the impeccability of Mohammed was perhaps formulated for the first time" in this tenth century
creed. He adds, "We must suppose that it arose out of the
growing [veneration for] . . . Mohammed. . . . In the present article [of the creed] this tendency finds dogmatic
expression for the first time. . . . At any rate from [this
creed] onwards the impeccability of the Prophets in general
and of Mohammed in particular belongs to the accepted
dogmas of Islam, though there are differences as to the
precise extent of the idea."[24]

This doctrine is not found at all in the canonical literature
of Islam. "In the canonical traditions (i.e., the 'six books')
there is no trace of the impeccability of the Prophets; on the
contrary, several of them are connected with grave sins:
Adam is the father of all murder, Abraham did not shun
lying, Moses committed manslaughter, and so on. Mohammed, it is true, is opposed to them in this respect, and this
distinction is the ground of his privilege of intercession. Yet
the dogma of Mohammed's impeccability is never mentioned
explicitly in the canonical hadith."[25]

And in the earliest of the canonical literature of Islam,
the Koran itself, the contrary seems to be stated quite
clearly. In the Koran, Mohammed speaks quite frankly of
his faults. "Then have patience [O Mohammed]. Lo!
The promise of Allah is true. And ask forgiveness of thy
sin, and hymn the praise of thy Lord at fall of night and
in the early hours" (sura 40:55); "We have given thee

[O Mohammed] a signal victory, that Allah may forgive thee of thy sin, that which is past and that which is to come, and may perfect His favor unto thee, and may guide thee on a right path" (sura 48:2); "If I err, I err only to my own loss, and if I am rightly guided it is because of that which my Lord hath revealed unto me" (sura 34:50); In one sura, Mohammed criticizes himself for his rebuff of a blind man who came to him seeking knowledge of Islam. "He [Mohammed] frowned and turned away because the blind man came unto him. What could inform thee but that he might grow [in grace] or take heed and so the reminder might avail him? As for him who thinketh himself independent, unto him thou payest regard. Yet it is not thy concern that he grow not [in grace]. But as for him who cometh unto thee with earnest purpose and hath fear, from him thou art distracted" (sura 80:1-10). He thus criticizes himself for having, on one occasion, concentrated so much on trying to convert the leaders of the people to Islam that he neglected to help this lowly blind man, who perhaps was more deserving of his help. Pickthall, an orthodox Moslem, explaining the passage, says: "One day when the Prophet was in conversation with one of the great men [of his own tribe] . . . seeking to persuade him of the truth of [Islam], a blind man came and asked a question concerning the faith. The Prophet was annoyed at the interruption, frowned and turned away from the blind man. In this sura, he is told that a man's importance is not to be judged from his appearance or worldly station."[26]

The discrepancy in the Islamic teaching on the holiness of Mohammed between the later Moslem belief and the earlier canonical literature[27] would seem, as Wensinck says, to be the result of a growing tendency in Islam to venerate Mohammed. The evidence shows that Mohammed, in reality, saw his own failings and admitted them freely.

Confucius is unambiguous in his answer to the question of whether he considers himself a perfect man. "A sage it is not mine to see; could I see a man of real talent and virtue, that would satisfy me."[28] "In letters I am perhaps equal to other men, but the character of the superior man, carrying out in his conduct what he professes, is what I have not yet attained to. . . . The sage and the man of perfect virtue— how dare I [rank myself with them?] It may simply be said of me, that I strive to become such without satiety, and teach others without weariness."[29] "The things that trouble or concern me are the following: lest I should neglect to improve my character, lest I should . . . fail to move forward when I see the right course, or fail to correct myself when I see my mistake."[30] "There are four things in the moral life of a man, not one of which I have been able to carry out in my life. To serve my father as I would expect my son to serve me: that I have not been able to do. To serve my sovereign as I would expect a minister under me to serve me: that I have not been able to do. To act toward my elder brothers as I would expect my younger brother to act toward me: that I have not been able to do. To be the first to behave toward friends as I would expect them to behave toward me: that I have not been able to do."[31] "If some years were added to my life, I would give fifty to the study of the Yi, and then I might come to be without great faults."[32]

The followers of Confucius claim that he was a perfect man. But these texts and others indicate that he himself knew and admitted his failings and imperfections.

The question of Buddha's claims to holiness presents special problems. The greatest of these problems is the fact that the Buddhist scriptures, from which we must gain the pertinent testimony, originated no earlier than three centuries after the death of Buddha. For about four hundred years the Buddhist teachings, including the Buddhist version of the character and life of Gotama, were transmitted only orally.[33] All that we know of Buddha, then, is based on legend, and not on contemporary historical sources. Unlike the other great religions of the world, Buddhism can produce no documents or literature whatsoever which date back even approximately to the time of its origin.

But the Buddhist legends, such as they are, have not left the question of Buddha's holiness unanswered. In fact, the honors bestowed on him by these later writings outstrip the utmost extravagances of any Western legends. The tales of the prowess of Gotama, as Hardy says, "may be regarded as the prime effort of the mind of heathendom to present a faultless and perfect character. It is the eastern beau ideal of that which is the most beautiful, and praiseworthy, and great." "It is said of Buddha, that he is . . . the helper of the helpless; a mine of mercy . . . stronger than the strongest, more merciful than the most merciful; more beautiful than the most beautiful; having more merit than the most meritorious; more powerful than the most powerful; he who enables the being who only softly pronounces his name, or who gives in his name only a small portion of rice, to attain nirvana. The eye cannot see anything; nor the ear hear anything, more excellent, or more worthy of regard than Buddha."

"The following declaration . . . was made by Buddha (in one of the scriptures) . . . 'No one has been my teacher; there is none like me; there is no one who resembles me, whether among dewas or men . . .'"

Another Buddhist description of Gotama reads, " . . . a mustard seed may be used to declare the size of a great ocean; the eye of a needle may be used as a comparison for the whole sky; even so may the words of a stanza be used to declare the excellence of Buddha, but their power is utterly

inadequate to accomplish this purpose in a right manner. . . . "

"The rishis may tell the number of inches in the sky, the
number of drops in the ocean, and the number of atoms in
Maha Meru (a mountain in the center of the earth); they
may hide the earth by the tip of the finger; and they may
shake the forest of Himala, with all its high mountains, as
by a cotton thread; but there is no being in the wide universe
who has the hand of energy by which he can swim to the
opposite side of the ocean of excellence possessed by
Buddha."[34]

As noted above, there are no Buddhist documents dating
from the early period of Buddhism, and thus no early statements on the subject of Buddha's holiness. But the later
period certainly tries to compensate for this lack by providing
us with an abundance of assertions that Buddha was perfectly
holy.

But even taking these later assertions about Buddha at
their face value, they still, surprisingly enough, fall short of
what we know about the holiness of Christ in one important
respect. They lavish upon Buddha every conceivable form of
praise, but only as a Buddha, that is, only after his "enlightenment." Buddha became perfect; but he was not always so.
At the age of twenty-nine, "after a life spent in worldly enjoyments, [he] was startled out of his ease at the first sight
of old age, sickness, and death, and fleeing secretly at night
from his home became an ascetic."[35] The Buddhist legends
attribute perfection to Buddha after he became an ascetic.
But even Buddhists would not claim that he reached the
heights of perfection as a layman; that, he only achieved
later.

During the first twenty-nine years of his life, the legends
do not picture Buddha as a libertine by any means. For his
state in life, and according to contemporary ideas of morality,

he was a good man. He was raised in luxury. He married and had a son. During these twenty-nine years, he was, in Buddhist terminology, a Bodhisattva, i.e., "one who is on the way to the attainment of perfect knowledge,"[36] but he was not a Buddha, i.e., one who is perfectly enlightened. The Bodhisattva will certainly achieve Buddhahood; he will not turn back. He has conquered the sinful passions; his spiritual effort now is directed positively toward an increase in virtue, not the eradication of vice. But he is not yet perfect. Gotama had been born of a wealthy family; he had been living in luxury. Buddhist perfection requires poverty, the abandonment of all the goods of this world. At the age of twenty-nine Gotama took this step forward in the spiritual life, and renounced all his worldly goods. He spent six years in working for improvement until he achieved Buddhahood or perfection at the age of thirty-five. Even in the legendary account of his existence on earth, then, Gotama is not described as always perfect; rather, he worked for this as a goal and achieved it only after many years. In this way, then, even the Buddha as described in legends falls short of Christ, who was a model of the highest perfection at all times during His life.

But, again taking the Buddhist legends at their face value, there is a second and far greater discrepancy between the Buddhists' notion of the character of their founder and the Christian concept of Christ. Here we take the Buddhist doctrine on reincarnation (which can look quite ridiculous to a Christian), and try to understand it, and Gotama's personal relation to it, in the way that a Buddhist would understand it.

For the Buddhists, taking their teaching at face value, there is a kind of survival from rebirth to rebirth, at least to the extent that every one on earth participates in the guilt and merit of his previous existences. His present ego, in a real sense, is held responsible for actions which it performed in those previous births. Thus a Buddhist views a person, not as a man living one life, but a series of lives. And Buddha himself is considered (however illogically) as a person who lived not just one life on earth, but many different lives.

The pattern of the previous lives of Gotama was like that of his last life but at a lower level. His previous lives were periods of trial and self-improvement. The Mahayana and Hinayana agree in accepting this idea of his progress through rebirth culminating in Buddhahood. The Mahayana developed the idea more than the Hinayana. The works of the Mahayana described certain stages of progress in detail, but in doing this they did not present anything which was opposed to the ancient ideas.[37]

The spiritual level of the future Buddha during the later and higher stages of these preliminary births is described as follows. "The future Bodhisat . . . possesses a certain 'disposition' which predisposes him to the vow of Bodhi. He possesses certain innate [i.e., acquired during the process of former existences] qualities which incline him to compassion. . . . He is kind and good. Incapable of committing a mortal sin [for these are, above all, sins of hatred] [sic], he avoids also the heresies which would condemn him for eternity; but he commits sins of love. Everyday experience, in fact, shows innumerable examples of good and generous men forgetting themselves, e.g., in passion. These men, although ignorant and guilty, belong to the race of Bodhisats."[38] "The future Bodhisat . . . possesses the privilege that his sins are punished only during seven births, pain in the end being reduced to headache. . . . The first [stage] is produced by the thought . . . 'May we become perfect Buddhas.' This thought immediately destroys previous sins, literally, 'covers' them. Nevertheless, the Bodhisat of this stage and of the six following is an 'ordinary man' . . . His works are mixed with good and evil. In theory, he does not encounter evil destinies; murder, theft, etc., do not lead him to hell. . . . But if he commits a mortal sin, the murder of a Bodhisat, of a Sravaka, of a Srotaapanna, or of a Pratyekabuddha, he will go to hell."[39]

From this description, it is apparent that even in the later stages of his preliminary births, the future Buddha is not thought of as completely free from sin and perfect. He may have advanced a great deal, and be far ahead of most of his contemporaries, but he still is subject to occasional lapses.

And going back further, into still earlier births, legend tells us that Gotama had been born many times as an animal. He had been reborn as a monkey, a lion, a bull,[40] a dice-player, a jackal.[41] And also according to the "[Buddhist scriptures] . . . [Gotama] was in many of his existences reborn as . . . a god, a king, a Brahmana, a minister, an ascetic, a merchant, but he was also a gardener, a musician, a physician, a barber, a robber, a gambler, an elephant, a lion, an ape, a dog, a frog, some bird, etc."[42] According to Buddhist tradition, these births as an animal are due to "various sins he had committed during the course of his existences."[43] And Hardy mentions that "At a certain time, Gotama Bodhisat was born as a squirrel on account of some demerit of a former age."[44]

In the legends, then, about some of his previous existences, Buddha is portrayed as sinless, but in other legends, he is declared to have been guilty of some sin. De la Vallée Poussin, speaking of the problem of whether Gotama during the course of his long career was a "saint" or an "ordinary man," says: "It is not difficult to reconcile these antinomies. All that is needed is to recognize two kinds of Bodhisata. The legends in which the future Buddha appears in an animal form, etc., belong to the initial stage of his career. The lofty deeds of generosity, the sacrifice of life, etc., belong to

a period during which he heroically practiced the virtues.
. . . As long as the future Buddha had not acquired a
'stage' (i.e., one of the advanced levels of the spiritual life),
his re-births are fixed by his acts, good or bad. Afterwards he
is re-born according to his 'vows' for the welfare of beings."[45]

Taking the Buddhist legends at their face value, then,
Buddha is described as an extremely holy man. But even
here, he does not equal Christ. Buddha's holiness, even as
described in these legends set down centuries after his death
by admiring disciples, was not constant and Godlike, as was
that of Christ, but was achieved gradually like that of a
man.

Even the Old Testament agrees with the various pagan
religions on the question of perfect holiness. The inspired
writers declare that no one, not even any of the Patriarchs,
is perfect. "There is no man who sinneth not" (3 Kgs. 8:46;
2 Par. 6:36); "Who can say: My heart is clean. I am pure
from sin?" (Prov. 20:9); "For there is no just man upon
earth, that doth good, and sinneth not" (Eccles. 7:21);
"Despise not a man that turneth away from sin, nor reproach
him therewith: remember that we are all worthy of reproof"
(Ecclus. 8:6).

Many of the great religious leaders and philosophers of
the world, then, have achieved a high level of personal virtue. Confucius and Buddha, for example, have been likened
to St. Thomas Aquinas and St. Francis of Assisi, respectively, and not without some foundation in fact. But, as
great as they were, each of these great non-Catholic philosophers and religious leaders did not, at all times, measure up
completely to his own ideals. They themselves knew that
they had fallen. They taught ideals to others, and tried to
achieve these ideals themselves, but they were not always
entirely successful in these attempts.

With regard to the specific faults of each, we shall remain

silent. The sad details of the extent to which they fell short even of their own moral codes can be found in the histories and biographies of each.

And what is true of the great philosophers and religious leaders is also true of other non-Christians who were noted for their personal virtue, but who did not themselves found any great and durable ethical systems. Such men in the pagan Roman tradition as Cato the Elder, Cato the Younger, and Marcus Aurelius deservedly receive great praise for the level of holiness they achieved during their lives; but even these men at times fell short of the highest ideals.

All of these men, the philosophers, the religious leaders, the other virtuous men, then, fell short of Christ. Those who spoke on the matter of personal perfection were unanimous in admitting their own imperfections. Whether or not these men are receiving a reward in heaven, God alone knows. But it is at least possible for each one to have gained this reward by positing an act of perfect charity, or, on the other hand, of perfect contrition for his sins. Each of them was given sufficient grace by God, and was aided in a special way by being granted extraordinary natural interest and insight into ethical matters. But again, whether each, *de facto*, used this grace and these talents for their ultimate purpose is known only to God.

The words of Confucius sum up the thoughts of all of the great philosophers and religious leaders who preceded and who came after Christ. "A sage it is not mine to see; could I see a man of real talent and virtue, that would satisfy me."[46] The thoughts of these men bring out more fully the meaning of Christ's words: "For amen I say to you, many prophets and just men have longed to see what you see, and they have not seen it; and to hear what you hear, and they have not heard it" (Matt. 13:17; Luke 10:24). It is by no means impossible that Christ was thinking of others besides the prophets and holy ones among the Jews, when He made this statement. He could have been thinking also of the many "just men" among the pagans, who, like the Jewish leaders, realized their own imperfections, and hoped in vain to see one who was truly a "Holy One of God," who would reveal the perfection of God's law, and through signs and miracles demonstrate His divine mission.

PART III

Holiness of Members

Holiness of Members

1. Common Holiness

The third aspect of holiness of religion is the holiness of a religion's members. The first two aspects of holiness, holiness of teaching and of founder, are primarily theoretical. Holiness of members is more practical, and shows the extent to which the adherents of a given religion actually follow the teachings and models of virtue which they should follow.

Holiness of members consists in two things: freedom from sin (i.e., the observance of the precepts), and the observance of the counsels.[1] Accordingly, holiness can be divided into two stages: common and heroic. We shall consider the extent to which the major world religions have actually produced in their members each of these two degrees of holiness.

Common holiness receives its name not because of the fact that freedom from sin is necessarily common or universal; the word common is used here to mean "ordinary" as opposed to "heroic." Our criterion of holiness, again, is the natural law, and again we concentrate on the primary conclusions of natural law. Granting that the non-Biblical religions tolerate theoretically the violation of at least one primary conclusion of natural law, in practice, to what extent do the members of these religions actually take advantage of this official toleration, and violate these primary conclusions?

And secondly, granting that the Church of Christ, for her part, does not tolerate the violation of any primary conclusion of natural law, to what extent, in practice, do Catholics ignore some of these conclusions? Do baptized Catholics violate primary conclusions of natural law, and violate them on such a wide scale that Catholics, in general, find themselves at the same or a lower moral level than non-Christians who do not have a perfect theoretical moral law?

First of all, common sanctity can exist in individual members of non-Biblical religions. By observing the salutary precepts and by perceiving and avoiding the pitfalls, these men can, with God's help, observe all the primary conclusions of natural law.

Sometimes, the environment upon which a religion is imposed can even raise the general level of morality on certain points far above the level of the moral code of the religion as it was originally formulated. The religion is often adapted, sometimes so radically that in its new form, apart from the retention of the name, it is hardly recognizable as a descendant of the religion from which it arose. Divorce among the Hindus and Buddhists is a case in point. The Hindu and Buddhist scriptures contain passages tolerating divorce. Yet in certain areas, divorce among Hindus and Buddhists is rare. (See above.) In sections of the Far East, there are large numbers of people who surpass their own Hindu or Buddhist moral code on this point.

On the other hand, large numbers of the followers of non-Biblical religions do take full advantage of toleration by their religions of violations of primary conclusions of natural law. In the Far East, among the Hindus, Buddhists, and Confucianists, as well as the lesser pagan religions, by far the most common violation of a primary conclusion of natural law is the failure to fulfill obligations toward God. Idolatry is everywhere in the Far East. And, speaking of the question of defect of faith among pagans in general, Lombardi says that, while all adults may, even without receiving Catholic evangelization, make an act of religious assent, "it is very probable that, *en masse*, many, indeed, fail to do so. We have very grave motives for suspecting . . . [that this failure does occur] in the great majority."[2]

And, on a smaller scale, abortion, abandonment of infants, suicide, and divorce, have been common in certain areas of the Far East among those religious groups which tolerate them.

In Islam, divorce and abortion[3] are common.[4]

Even in the best of the non-Christian religions, then, violations of one or more of the primary conclusions of natural law occur on a wide scale. Against this background, the Church can clearly be seen to have had a tremendous impact on the societies into which she has penetrated. (We prescind for the moment from the introduction of the Church to heretical or schismatical Christian societies.)

The Fathers of the Church challenged the pagans to look closely at the changes conversion to Christianity wrought in the lives of former pagans. Origen says "If anyone, on a candid consideration of these things, shall admit that no improvement ever takes place without divine help, how much the more confidently shall he make the same assertion regarding Jesus, when he compares the former lives of many converts to His doctrine with their after-conduct, and reflects in what acts of licentiousness and injustice and covetousness they formerly indulged" and "who, from the time they adopted it, have become in some way meeker, and more religious, and more consistent."[5] Aristides says that Christians recognize God as the founder and architect of all things, and beyond Him worship no other god, and that they have the commandments of Christ written in their hearts, and observe them in the expectant hope of the world to come. "They do not commit adultery or fornication, or bear false witness, or embezzle what they hold in pledge, or covet the goods of others. They honor father and mother, love their neighbors and judge with equity. . . . They appeal to those who injure them and try to win them as friends; they are eager to do good to their enemies. . . . They keep themselves from any illicit union and from any manner of uncleanness; they do not despise the widow, nor cause anguish in the orphan. The Christian who has [worldly possessions] gives abundantly to him who is without them. . . . They observe the commands [of Christ] with great care and live just and holy lives as the Lord their God commanded them."[6] Tertullian (d.c. 222) says that Christians "neither see, speak of, nor listen to the immodesty of the theater or the atrocities of the arena."[7]

A beautiful description of the virtue of the normal practicing Christian was set down in the second century by an anonymous Greek Catholic. "For the Christians are distinguished from other men neither by country, nor language, nor the customs which they observe. For they neither inhabit cities of their own, nor employ a peculiar form of speech, nor lead a life which is marked out by any singularity. . . . But, inhabiting Greek as well as barbarian cities, according as the lot of each of them has determined, and following the customs of the natives in respect to clothing, food, and the rest of their ordinary conduct, they display to us their wonderful and confessedly striking method of life. They dwell in their own countries, but simply as sojourners. As citizens, they share in all things with others, and yet endure all things as if foreigners. Every foreign land is to them as their native country, and every land of their birth as a land of strangers. They marry, as do all [others]; they beget children; but they do not destroy their offspring. . . . They are in the flesh, but they do not live after the flesh. They pass their days on earth but are citizens of heaven. They obey the prescribed laws, and at the same time surpass the laws by their lives. They love all men and are persecuted by all. They are unknown and condemned; they are put to death, and restored to life. They are poor, yet make many rich; they are in lack of all things, yet abound in all; they are dishonored, and yet in their very dishonor are glorified. They are maligned, and yet are justified; they are reviled, and bless; they are insulted, and repay the insult with honor; they do good, yet are punished as evildoers. When punished, they rejoice as if quickened into life; they are assailed by the Jews as foreigners, and are persecuted by the Greeks; yet those who hate them are unable to assign any reason for their hate."[8]

In our own day, Michel says that in every society where the Christian religion is taught and practiced the following results appear: "purity of morals, fewer illegitimate births, affection and solicitude lavished on children, respect for women and the aged, fertility of marriages, domestic peace, and profound respect shown during all their lives by children for their parents."[9]

Hellwald, who was quite hostile to anything Christian, could write: "Disinterested parties, however, grant that . . . Christianity brought to maturity among the ancients views which are usually declared noble according to modern notions. Such, for example, were their views on abortion, infanticide, abandonment of babies, suicide. It finally brought about the suppression of gladiatorial combats, awakened a disgust for capital punishment and an extensive taste for charity which was altogether alien to classical antiquity. All in all, humaneness is an almost exclusive acquisition of the Christian era."[10]

"Christian charity" has not been a purely theoretical phrase, nor has the practice of it been restricted to a few saints in the Church. As it is expressed in generosity and in works of mercy, Christian charity at all levels is worlds apart from that of the pagans. Christianity works while infidelity talks. She feeds the hungry, clothes the naked, visits and cheers the sick and seeks the lost while infidelity abuses her and babbles nonsense and profanity. "By their fruits you shall know them." Even Westermarck admits that through all ages, and regardless of the number and severity of the difficulties the Church has met, Christian generosity has survived unimpaired.[11]

"Every time a nation [has been] converted to the Christian-Catholic religion, a remarkable moral reform [has] followed. This fact is clear from the history of individual Christian nations and from the history of missionary activity. On the social plane: little by little the Christian religion used its influence to restore the family, urging the unity and indissolubility of marriage, the dignity of women, the rights and duties of children. At first it alleviated the rigors of slavery and finally brought about its abolition; it reformed civil society itself by promoting freedom, charity, and the rights of nations. These holy and wholesome effects which the Christian religion caused everywhere among recently converted nations, it still continues to produce throughout the world."[12]

Van Noort says, "No other religion, no philosophical system, no merely human institution has ever brought about a moral reform even remotely comparable in breadth, depth, or duration with the one effected by the Catholic Church, not only centuries ago but even in our own time."[13]

The words of St. Paul have been fulfilled: "Do all things without murmuring and questioning, so as to be blameless and guileless, children of God without blemish in the midst of a depraved and perverse generation. For among these you shine like stars in the world" (Phil. 2:14–15).

This transformation wrought by Christianity in the everyday life of a society does not apply only to the moral precepts. Over and above the observance of these precepts, Christianity has conferred still other benefits on a large scale upon mankind.

The position of the Christian woman is far superior to

her pagan counterpart. The exact reason or reasons why pagan women occupy a lower position in their societies than Christian women do in theirs has been the subject of debate, but no one questions that the difference exists.

In Christian societies, women, whether married or un-married, old or young, possess as a matter of course certain rights (such as the right to life itself, to freedom of action, to freedom of choice of state in life and of a marital partner, to take part in religious rites, and many others) which they are deprived of in whole or in part in non-Christian societies. In addition, Christianity grants womankind certain privileges which tend to make the woman a sort of queen in Christian society.

But Christianity's general social contribution is not limited to raising the position of women. The Church has given a tremendous impulse to the development of mankind as a whole.

In the last century, many tried to explain man's progress in the Christian era as just one further inevitable step in his evolution from apehood. But the idea that the progress of man was inevitable, and not influenced substantially for bet-ter or worse by the teachings of new philosophies, had many flaws. One was the fact that there was and is a tremendous gap between the level of progress in Christian areas and that in entirely pagan ones. In these pagan areas, control over the forces of nature has not advanced appreciably in the nineteen centuries since the coming of Christ.

Religion, and specifically, morality, does have a very im-portant bearing upon the question. Differences between the morality of Christianity and the morality of paganism have played an important part in elevating the cultural level of Christian areas high above that of purely pagan ones.

Two particular differences in moral teaching have often been cited as largely responsible for the cultural discrepancy.

The first is the difference in the attitude toward progress

itself. Christopher Dawson emphasizes this factor: "Why is it that Europe alone among the civilizations of the world has been continually shaken and transformed by an energy of spiritual unrest that refuses to be content with the unchanging law of social tradition which rules the oriental cultures? It is because its religious ideal has not been the worship of timeless and changeless perfection but a spirit that strives to incorporate itself in humanity and to change the world. In the West the spiritual power has not been immobilized in a sacred social order like the Confucian state in China and the Indian caste system. It has acquired social freedom and autonomy and consequently its activity has not been confined to the religious sphere but has had far-reaching effects on every aspect of social and intellectual life."[14]

A second ethical cause of the cultural discrepancy has been set forth by many others, including Leclercq. According to these men, the lack of progress is not due to lack of desire but to lack of physical capacity, which is itself caused by defective moral teaching. Specifically, defects in observance of the virtue of chastity have been identified as central in this matter. Christians and non-Christians are not at the same level here, in theory or in practice. The theory of Christianity and the influence of the words of Christ, repeated from pulpits through the centuries, have not been totally without effect. Those who have heard chastity preached, encouraged and emphasized are more chaste in general than those who have not had it so emphasized. This last is not entirely obvious to one who is acquainted only with a Christian environment. A Christian who is not versed in the problems of pagan ethics in practice, tends to see only the defects in the practice of his own system. The positive contributions of Christianity to the practice of chastity tend to be taken for granted.

A study of the Eastern non-Christian religions shows what a difference does exist. In the Orient, eroticism is widespread and rampant. Ideas of shame, disgust and remorse do not exist. The difference between East and West in the practice of chastity is very great. The details are better omitted.

As a cause of stagnancy, this discrepancy is supported by the fact that as children, many in the Orient are indeed bright and promising, but that, compared to the West, few of the boys fulfill this promise when they reach manhood. Christ has taught many more men to struggle effectively against their lower nature. In doing so, these men have become free to develop their talents. Chaste peoples are strong peoples. Chastity can be considered as a source for cultural energy. Chastity is possibly the most important factor in the unprecedented energy that is characteristic of Christian civilization.[15] In any case, chastity would seem to have played more than a negligible part in the extraordinary development of Christian culture.

Each of these two reasons for lack of progress in the non-Christian world applies to some sections of it but not to others. The fact remains that this discrepancy does exist, and very probably some religious and moral difference has played an important part in bringing about the cultural gap.

What has been said above with regard to the common holiness of members applies to a comparison of the practice of Catholicism with that of the non-Biblical religions (Islam, Buddhism, etc.). But what of schism and heresy? In practice, at the lower or "common" level of holiness, is there any difference between modern Catholics and heretics and schismatics?

Van Noort makes some rather striking observations in answer to the above question. He says, "It would be a mistake to think that the . . . remarks bearing on Christianity's fruitfulness are applicable at least in general to all Christians, Catholics or not. Since there is scarcely any nation in existence which first heard of the Gospel from an heretical sect, the marvelous moral reform which has accompanied the ad-

vance of the Christian religion throughout the world is due
to the Catholic Church alone. There is no heretical or
schismatical sect whose origin was remarkable because of a
notable moral improvement. In fact, the case was more frequently the opposite. In the pseudo-Reformation, the results
caused Luther to say: 'Men are now more vindictive, more
greedy, more pitiless, more immoral and unrestrained, and
much more evil than they were under the papacy.' "[16] We
might add that Luther was not alone among the founders
of Protestantism in making this last point. Melanchthon was
equally strong in acknowledging the deterioration of morality
brought about by the change from Catholicism to his own
Protestantism.[17] And the Protestant historian Harnack, centuries later,[18] could write "Since the beginning of the Reformation, one must deplore the relaxed morality of the German Churches and the lack of seriousness in the work of
sanctification."[19]

In all this are two salient points. Firstly, the propagation
itself of Christianity, and thus the initial uplift to "common"
holiness of great numbers of pagans, is almost entirely the
work of the Catholic Church. Secondly, even the founders
of Protestantism, the ones who had seen Catholicism in action (and a Catholicism which was itself in need of reform
from within) and who had seen what happens when Catholicism is repudiated entirely, admitted that morality in practice had disintegrated.

The first of these two points is challenged by very few.
It is Catholicism which has brought paganism to "common"
holiness. Heresy and schism generally breed and gather
strength not in pagan areas, but in Catholic ones.

The second point, however, is open to dispute. Is there
any practical difference in practical morality between modern
Catholics and those who are in heresy or schism? As we
have seen, the theoretical moral teaching of heresy and

schism does tend to disintegrate. And with regard to those heresies and schisms which have already become extinct, the overwhelming majority, even in practice, lost the note of even "common" sanctity before their extinction. But question is often raised about those heresies and schisms which have survived to our own day, particularly Protestantism and Greek Orthodoxy.

Not all Protestants would immediately agree with Luther and Melanchthon that Protestantism failed at all in preserving "common" holiness. And in fact, Protestantism, while rapidly discarding doctrine after doctrine of the Church, did hold fast for several centuries to almost all the Catholic moral teachings. And many Protestants, in practice, were observing a large part of this Catholic morality. There was a slip, but not, at first, a landslide. Accordingly, it was, indeed, difficult for several centuries to obtain overwhelming evidence that Protestantism had lost the note of "common" sanctity on a wide scale among its members.[20]

But this does not mean that there was no evidence at all. Westermarck says, "It has been noticed that the rates of divorce and of suicide—the highest expression of discontent—show a close and constant relation. Both have been much more common among Protestants than among Catholics."[21] Ottiger says that a survey of suicides in Germany during the years 1846–1900 revealed that the proportion of suicides among Protestants was over double that among Catholics.[22] And the same is true of abortion and illegitimacy. The rate of abortion admittedly has been much lower among Catholics than among others. Statistics also show that the illegitimacy rate is lower among Catholics, whether one approaches the problem by comparing Catholic countries with non-Catholic countries[23] or by comparing Catholics with non-Catholics living in the same environment (v.g., Catholics with non-Catholics in Germany or in Ireland).[24]

Up to the end of the last century, however, there was room for dispute. The evidence from statistics was not overwhelming.

But there is grave reason for believing that the situation is changing substantially. Recent developments have brought Catholics to a position not entirely unlike the one they occupied in ancient Rome. In those times, Christians did not need to bring forth statistics; they merely referred in general terms to the conduct of the pagans whose depravity was evident.

In our own day, more and more nominally Protestant areas make no claim to a high level of morality. The abortionists and divorcees among them are not even hiding themselves in shame, but are claiming for themselves positions of honor in society. The worship of God is abandoned. Monstrous sins against the natural law are being committed by them on a wide scale.

More and more, Catholics and Protestants alike are coming to recognize that statistics are no longer necessary. It is becoming increasingly obvious to all that Catholics as a group lead holier lives than most of their contemporary liberal Protestant groups.

Greek Orthodoxy, from the point of view of ethics alone, has taken only one major backward step: divorce. The relaxation of the marriage laws on the books has been taken advantage of in practice. In modern times, it has often been civil law or local custom which has guided the Greek ecclesiastical judges in their decision. In practice, any grave sin against conjugal fidelity [apostasy (departure of one spouse to another religion, even another Christian religion), a serious physical or mental illness, a prolonged absence (voluntary or involuntary), desertion, grave injury and even, in certain Churches, mutual consent] provides a valid ground for divorce.[25]

On a higher level, there is also a difference between

Catholics and the Greek Schismatics: the degree in which they frequent the Christian sacraments. In the Schismatical Eastern Churches, few receive the sacraments of the Eucharist and Penance frequently. The faithful generally go to Confession and receive Communion only at great feasts, three or four times a year. Mass is celebrated regularly only in monasteries, and even there the monks are not obliged to assist. Spiritual guidance outside of monasteries is hardly known. Extreme Unction is no longer administered, or if it persists in certain of these Churches it does so only in the form of a simple remedy against all spiritual and corporal sickness.[26]

There are differences, then, even in common holiness between Catholics generally and those in heresy and schism.

An objection has often been raised against the holiness of the Church: If the Church is truly holy, how can there be any members at all within her who are unholy? Granting that among those who have received Catholic instruction there are more holy people and fewer sunk in vice than in other religions, why should there be any vicious members at all?

The primary answer, of course, is that free will remains. The reception of Catholic instruction does not paralyze the will.

But granting this, it is often asked why the Church does not expel all grave sinners from her ranks, depriving them of the right even to attend Catholic services. The reason the Church does not do this is obedience to the instructions of Christ Himself on this matter. "The kingdom of heaven is like a man who sowed good seed in his field; but while men were asleep, his enemy came and sowed weeds among the wheat, and went away. And when the blade sprang up and brought forth fruit, then the weeds appeared as well. And the servants of the householder came and said to him, 'Sir, . . . wilt thou have us go and gather them up?' 'No' he said, 'lest in gathering the weeds you root up the wheat along with them. Let both grow together until the harvest; and at harvest time I will say to the reapers, Gather up the weeds first and bind them in bundles to burn; but gather up the wheat into my barn.' . . . He who sows the good seed is the Son of Man. The field is the world; the good seed, the sons of the kingdom; the weeds, the sons of the wicked one; and the enemy who sowed them is the devil. But the harvest is the end of the world . . . " (Matt. 13:24–30; 37–39).

In this parable and in that of the net cast into the sea (Matt. 13:47–50), Christ shows that the separation of the good from the bad is to take place on Judgment Day and not earlier. As He says, if human beings attempt to remove all weeds from the Church, there is grave danger that they will mistakenly expel many good people along with the bad.

And Christ put His teaching into practice with His own disciples. He knew that Judas, one of His twelve Apostles, was robbing their common funds and later would betray Him (John 13:21ff). Yet even then, He did not expel this man, but continually offered him friendship, even at the very moment of betrayal: "Friend, for what purpose hast thou come?" (Matt. 26:50). Jesus and the other eleven Apostles were no less holy because Judas was among them. In the same way, the Church allows known sinners to remain attached to her, that they may the more easily repent.

St. Paul reiterates the principle that the Church can contain sinners, and is no less holy for that fact. "But if while we are seeking to be justified in Christ, we ourselves also are found sinners, is Christ therefore the minister of sin? By no means. For if I reconstruct the things that I destroyed, I make myself a sinner" (Gal. 2:17–18).

There have been hardened sinners who have attached themselves to the Church during all ages. She allows them to cling to her and never disowns them because like Christ she never repudiates them in order to reclaim them.

But in all this, it is important to keep in mind the words of Lombardi: "The corruption of the Christian world . . . is a corruption which cannot seriously be compared to the filthiness of the pagan world."[27] Any society permeated with Christian moral ideals, whose members generally have received the essential parts of Christian instruction, will contain proportionately far fewer who are seriously violating natural law and far more who are observing all the virtues necessary for salvation, than any other society which lacks such contact with Christianity.

2. Perfect Holiness

Common holiness, then, can serve as a criterion for demonstrating the pre-eminent holiness of the members of the Catholic Church. But an even more valuable criterion of holiness of members is perfect holiness. In practice, the second type of holiness of members, perfect or heroic holiness, is more easily perceived than common holiness. First, common holiness, being less spectacular, and drawing less attention to itself, is less easily verified. It is less likely to be studied carefully and verified as true holiness and not just as a hypocritical screen of virtues used to cover secret vices. In common holiness it is difficult to tell whether the apparent virtues imply the possession of all the necessary virtues or are assumed as a front to gain social prestige for a life of comfortable and honored vice.

Perfect holiness is a better criterion of the practical holiness in a given society. Of its nature, it draws scrutiny, and the virtues involved are so heroic and of such a high level, that the likelihood of base motivation is greatly reduced. Reflexively, perfect holiness in an individual is a proof that he has common holiness. And, considering society as a whole, the extent to which it possesses heroically holy members is a criterion of its general holiness at all levels. That is, societies are best judged for holiness not on the basis of which has the smallest proportion of vicious members or, conversely, which has the greatest proportion of members who have reached common holiness, but on the basis of which has the most who have achieved perfect holiness. This is so because of the following consideration:

Societies are best judged by the *pars potior*. The Germans, for example, are called a musical people; they are called musical not because anyone has found that there are fewer tone-deaf persons among them, or that there are more who can go through the mechanics of reading a scale, but because among them there are more enthusiastic and even gifted musicians than among other peoples. Similarly, the ancient Romans were considered good soldiers not because anyone has discovered that there were few or no cowards or completely inept fighters among them, or that there were more mediocre ones, but because among them were a great many more very able soldiers than among many other societies of that time. In the same way, Americans of today are said to be rich.

Holiness, too, is best judged by the *pars potior*. The extent of holiness in any society is best determined by discovering the extent to which its members reach perfect or heroic holiness.

But what, exactly, is heroic holiness? There are certain circumstances in which the practice of virtue is more than just praiseworthy; it is literally heroic. The best example of the practice of heroic virtue is that evinced by an "indicative martyr."

A martyr in the indicative sense can be defined as one who, with full possession of his faculties and for the sake of his beliefs or principles, voluntarily and patiently suffers a violent death inflicted by an enemy.

The phrase "with full possession of his faculties" excludes infants[28] and others who would not be fully aware of what they are doing.

The word "voluntarily" does not imply that a martyr seeks to die or presents himself to his enemies in order to be killed. Rather it means that once caught, he is given the choice either to recant his beliefs and go free, or persevere and die. The use of the term "voluntarily" distinguishes the martyrs from those groups of people who were killed or tortured but who never were given the opportunity of recanting as a means of escape, v.g., the Jews in Germany under Hitler. Those who after capture have had a chance to escape torture and death by abandoning their principles and refused to do so, have exercised a higher degree of fortitude than those who are captured and summarily dispatched without having been given any chance whatsoever to obtain freedom.

The word "patiently" in the definition indicates that the martyr suffers death, not while engaged in battle against an enemy, but suffers it without making an attempt at retaliation. The person who risks and suffers death in battle (v.g., members of Moslem armies) has several qualities which make his courage less perfect than one who suffers patiently. First of all, the soldier in battle is not facing certain death; secondly, he does not fight with perfect sobriety and in full possession of his higher faculties but, to a certain extent, with his intellect dominated by the passion of anger; thirdly, flight would not necessarily ensure the saving of his life.

The martyr, on the other hand, is in complete possession of his higher faculties, and nevertheless accepts certain death rather than forsake his principles.

Martyrdom is the perfection of the virtue of fortitude. All other methods by which courage can be shown fall short of the excellence of martyrdom.

To what extent are indicative martyrs found in Christianity and to what extent are they found in other religions of societies?

Admittedly, there has been a great number of Christians who died under persecution.[29]

Though pagan authors generally spoke little of the newly-born Christian sect in the first century, we do find Tacitus referring to "a huge multitude" of Christians who perished under "exquisite tortures" in the reign of the emperor Nero.[30] Dion Cassius, another pagan historian, refers to "many" Christians who were killed in the reign of the emperor Domitian.

We can find large numbers of Christians who died under persecution not only in the early Church but also in other periods of her history. In modern times, we have as examples those who suffered in Mexico and, most recently, those in Communist countries. We can safely estimate that the total number of Catholics who have died under persecution throughout history has reached at least seven figures.

Moreover, these Christians who suffered and died did not come from only one segment of society. They included people of all ages from the very young to the very old, people of both sexes, and people of all levels in society from those in poverty to those in high offices.

Concerning the nature of their sufferings, it can be noted that death often came to the Christians only after severe torments had already been inflicted upon them.

Tacitus, describing the persecution of Christians under Nero writes: "Covered with the skins of beasts, they were torn by dogs and perished, or were nailed to crosses, or were doomed to the flames and burnt to serve as a nightly illumination when daylight had expired."[31] Eusebius, speaking of the persecution of the Egyptian Christians in the fourth century under Diocletian, says: "Thousands, both men and women and children, despising the present life for the sake of our Saviour's doctrine, submitted to death in various shapes. Some after being tortured with scrapings and the rack and the most dreadful scourgings and other innumerable agonies which one might shudder to hear, were finally committed to the flames; some . . . drowned in the sea, . . . others dying in the midst of their torments, some wasted away by famine, others again fixed to the cross. Some indeed were executed as malefactors usually were; others, more cruelly, were nailed with head downwards, and kept alive until they were destroyed by starving on the cross itself. But it would exceed all power of detail to give an idea of the sufferings and tortures which the martyrs of Thebes[32] endured. These, instead of hooks, had their bodies scraped with shells, and were mangled in this way until they died . . . others perished bound to trees and branches. For, drawing the stoutest of the branches together by machines for this purpose, and binding the limbs of the martyrs to each of these, they then let loose the boughs to resume their natural position, designing thus to produce a violent action to tear asunder the limbs of those whom they thus treated. And all these things were doing not only for a few days or some time but for a series of whole years. At one time, ten or more, at another, more than twenty, at another time not less than thirty, and even sixty, and again at another time, a hundred men with their wives and little children were slain in one day, whilst they were condemned to various and varied punishments. We ourselves have observed when on the spot[33] many crowded together in one day, some suffering decapitation, . . . so that the murderous weapon was completely blunted and having lost its edge, broke to pieces; and the executioners, themselves wearied with slaughter, were obliged to relieve one another."[34]

In many cases, then, the torments were not only severe but were protracted. A further example of this can be found in Lactantius. Addressing a Christian in Gaul[35] who suffered under this same persecution of Diocletian, Lactantius says: "Having been nine times exposed to racks and diversified torments, nine times by a glorious profession of your faith, you foiled the adversary."[36]

Thus, in many cases, the Christians were not relieved of tortures by a quick death, but were forced to renew their decisions to suffer death rather than recant.

Many Christians then suffered and died for their faith. That these Christians truly died "voluntarily" and were given the chance to escape by recanting is illustrated by the correspondence of the pagan official Pliny with the Roman Emperor Trajan (98–117 A.D.). Pliny had written to the Emperor asking him to specify in detail the official policy of Rome in dealing with Christians who were brought to trial. One of the points made by Trajan in his reply to Pliny was that "if any one denies that he is Christian and makes it clear that he is not, by offering prayers to our deities, then he is to be pardoned because of his recantation, however suspicious his past conduct may have been."[37]

Even today in Communist countries, priests, religious, and the rest of the Christian faithful are often given the chance of escape from punishment if they only agree to deny their faith.

With regard to the question of whether or not the Christians who suffered in persecutions were truly "patient" and retained full possession of their reasoning powers, it is interesting to note that when brought to trial, there is no sign of fanaticism. They defend their faith with firmness and even with enthusiasm, but there is no indication that their higher faculties of intellect and will have ceased to function. In the pagan court records of a trial of a group of Christians held in about the year 180 A.D., we read:[38] "When Praesens for the second time and Claudianus were the Consuls, on the seventeenth day of July at Carthage there were set in the judgment-hall Speratus, Martzalus, Cittinus, Donata, Secunda, and Vestia.

Saturninus the proconsul said: Ye can win the indulgence of our Lord the Emperor if ye return to a sound mind.

Speratus said: We have never done ill, we have not lent ourselves to wrong, we have never spoken ill, but when ill-treated we have given thanks; because we pay heed to our Emperor.

Saturninus the proconsul said: We too are religious and our religion is simple, and we swear by the genius of our lord the Emperor and pray for his welfare, as ye also ought to do.

Speratus said: If thou wilt peaceably lend me thine ears, I can tell thee the mystery of simplicity.

Saturninus said: I will not lend mine ears to thee, when thou beginnest to speak evil of our sacred rites; but rather swear thou by the genius of our lord the Emperor.

Speratus said: The empire of this world I know not; but rather, I serve that God, 'whom no man hath seen nor' with these eyes 'can see.' I have committed no theft; but if I have bought anything I pay the tax; because I know my Lord the King of kings, and Emperor of all nations.

Saturninus the proconsul said to the rest: Cease to be of this persuasion.

Speratus said: It is an ill persuasion to do murder, to speak false witness.

Saturninus the proconsul said: Be not partakers of this folly.

Cittinus said: We have none other to fear, save only our Lord God who is in heaven.

Donata said: Honour to Caesar as Caesar; but fear to God.

Vestia said: I am a Christian.

Secunda said: What I am, that I wish to be.

Saturninus the proconsul said to Speratus: Dost thou persist in being a Christian?

Speratus said: I am a Christian. And with him they all agreed.

Saturninus the proconsul said: Will ye have a space to reconsider?

Speratus said: In a matter so straightforward there is no considering.

Saturninus the proconsul said: What are the things in your chest?

Speratus said: Books and epistles of Paul, a just man.

Saturninus the proconsul said: Have a delay of thirty days and bethink yourselves.

Speratus said a second time: I am a Christian. And with him they all agreed.

Saturninus the proconsul read out the decree from the tablet: Speratus, Martzalus, Cittinus, Donata, Vestia, Secunda and the rest, having confessed that they live according to the Christian rite, since after opportunity offered them of returning to the custom of the Romans they have obstinately persisted, it is determined that they be put to the sword.

Speratus said: We give thanks to God."[39]

As an example of a trial wherein only a single Christian is accused we have that of St. Cyprian in 258 A.D. "When the Emperor Valerian was Consul for the fourth, and Gallienus for the third time, on the third of the Kalends of September, Paternus, proconsul at Carthage, in his council chamber thus spoke to Cyprian, bishop:

Paternus: The most sacred Emperors Valerian and Gallienus have honoured me with letters, wherein they enjoin that all who use not the religion of Rome, shall formally make profession of their return to the use of Roman rites: I have made accordingly enquiry of your name; what answer do you make to me?

Cyprian: I am a Christian, and bishop; I know no other gods beside the one and true God, who made heaven and earth, the sea, and all things therein; this God we Christians serve, to Him we pray day and night, for ourselves, for all mankind, for the health of the Emperors themselves.

Paternus: Do you persist in this purpose?

Cyprian: That good purpose which hath once acknowledged God, cannot be changed.

Paternus: Will you then, obeying the mandate of the Emperors, depart into exile to the city of Curubis?

Cyprian: I go."[40] (Cyprian was martyred later in the same year.)

The Christians who have died for their faith, then, were numerous and died voluntarily and patiently. There were many Christian martyrs.

Moreover, the multitude of Christian martyrs is "unique in history."[41] No non-Christian society or religion has ever come close to duplicating it. Though other religions recognize the excellence of martyrdom, few of their members have been able to achieve it. The religions of the Far East have relatively few doctrines or moral precepts which are held to so firmly that they are considered as worth dying for. Filial piety would be one such precept. But when the scriptures of the Far East do mention instances of a man who is laying down his life for some noble motive, the man is frequently saved from death by a *deus ex machina*. In any case, both in ancient times and today, true martyrdom is rare in the Far East.

In the Near East, we might expect Islam (in view of its firm stand on many doctrinal and ethical points) to have produced many martyrs. *De facto*, there are instances of martyrdom among Moslems who, when captured by enemies and given the choice of recantation of Islam or death, chose death. In Islam, too, however, martyrs are rare. The main stream of heroism in Islam flowed in a different direction, into courage in battle.

The number of non-Christian martyrs is infinitesimal when compared with the number of Christian martyrs, either of the past or of the present.

A second manifestation of heroic holiness, very similar to

that of probative martyrdom, is that which can be achieved during a time of disaster such as famine or pestilence. In this instance, the cause is the physical well-being of other human beings. Heroic holiness is manifested when a person, in good health and free to leave a stricken area, chooses to remain at grave risk to his own life in order to help others. The phrase grave risk, implies, beyond mere danger, a danger so great it is probable that the person who risks his life will lose it. Under circumstances like these, the record of Christians has also been extraordinary. At various times during history, when a plague has struck, the only ones who remained to tend the sick and dying were the Christians.

In the earliest times, for example, the historian Eusebius tells of events which occurred during the reign of the Roman Emperor Maximian: "The customary rains and showers of the winter season ceased to fall in their wonted abundance upon the earth and an unexpected famine made its appearance, and in addition to this, a pestilence. . . . Those who died in the cities were innumerable, and those who died in the country and villages were still more. So that the tax lists which formerly included a great rural population were almost entirely wiped out; nearly all being speedily destroyed by famine and pestilence. Some, therefore, desired to dispose of their most precious things to those who were better supplied, in return for the smallest morsel of food, and others, selling their possessions little by little fell into the last extremity of want. . . . Some wasted away like ghosts and at the very point of death stumbled and tottered here and there, and too weak to stand fell down in the middle of the streets; lying stretched out at full length they begged that a small morsel of food might be given them, and with their last gasp they cried out, Hunger! having strength only for this most painful cry. But others, who seemed to be better supplied, astonished at the multitude of the beggars, after giving away large quantities, finally became hard and relentless, expecting that they themselves also would soon suffer the same calamities as those who begged. So that in the midst of the market-places and lanes, dead and naked bodies lay unburied for many days, presenting a most lamentable spectacle to those that beheld them. . . .

"But still worse was the pestilence which consumed entire houses and families, and especially those whom the famine was not able to destroy because of their abundance of food. Thus men of wealth, rulers and governors and multitudes in office, as if left by the famine on purpose for the pestilence, suffered swift and speedy death. . . . In this way, death, waging war with these two weapons, pestilence and famine, destroyed whole families in a short time so that one could see two or three dead bodies carried out an once. . . .

"Then did the evidences of the universal zeal and piety of the Christians become manifest to all the heathen. For they in the midst of such ills showed their sympathy and humanity by their deeds. Every day some continued caring for and burying the dead, for there were multitudes who had no one to care for them; others collected in one place those who were afflicted by the famine, throughout the entire city, and gave bread to them all; so that the thing became noised about among all men, and they glorified the God of the Christians; and, convinced by the facts themselves confessed that they alone were truly pious and religious."[43]

This has been repeated many times in history. Catholics shine brightest when the pressures are greatest.

And even apart from civic emergencies, there are certain other situations calling for heroic virtue, in which Catholics have frequently played an important part. One such situation arises in the case of the disease of leprosy. Up to a few years ago, this contagious and hideous disease had been incurable. Many Catholic heroes have been found who risked probable death by volunteering to go among the lepers and care for them.

Not atypical are the circumstances of the founding of the leper colony in Carville, Louisiana, in April, 1896. Before that time the many victims of that disease in the Louisiana area had been living alone in the swamps. The Louisiana legislature had tried hard to set up a place for the care of the abandoned sick. The state leased an old plantation house with cabins on the bank of the Mississippi about eighty miles above New Orleans.

The first doctor assigned to the camp refused to stay; no help, no medicine. Other doctors refused also. For more than a year the board tried to hire doctors, practical nurses, helpers of any kind. No one would go to the camp at any wage. Just as the project was on the verge of being abandoned, a group of the Sisters of Charity of St. Vincent de Paul volunteered to staff the camp without taking any pay. The Sisters have been there ever since. Since their arrival, facilities have been improved, and medicines have been found which for the first time substantially alleviate the disease. But their greatest heroism lies in having taken on the work when no such drugs were available.

That this is no isolated phenomenon in the Church is shown by the fact that in mission areas alone, apart from the thousands of Catholic hospitals and homes for the aged, and orphans, there were recently counted 121 Catholic leper hospitals in which 13,625 lepers were cared for.[44]

In other ways, multitudes of Catholics have dedicated themselves to lives of heroism. Anna de Savornin Lohman states: "In the east and west Indies, in the Roman Catholic Rhineland, I have observed very closely the exemplary lives of Roman Catholics, missionaries and pastors, and the great assistance provided by nuns as teachers, nurses, etc. Not only I but men and women who in our country unthinkingly ridicule the Roman Catholic religion out of ignorance or fear—there, in the midst of laborers and despised Negroes, in the midst of the fear of death and of loneliness, I have heard others acknowledge with shame that Roman Catholic charity surpasses all others."[45]

And there are many others in the Church who achieved heroic holiness not because of any single specific work which they performed, but because their entire lives were characterized by complete and uncompromising dedication to God's service. These are the saints of the Church: St. Paul, St. Bernard, St. Dominic, St. Francis Xavier, St. Francis of Assisi, St. Ignatius of Loyola, St. Vincent de Paul, St. Teresa, and a great multitude of others.

All this, however, does not mean that outside the Church there is no one who has achieved a high degree of holiness. As St. John Chrysostom has said, "For there are some among [the pagans] who have been eminent for the virtue of their life."[46] A Catholic authority on Islam has said "It can scarcely be denied, given the historical data we possess, that examples of lofty spiritual perfection can be found among the Moslem mystics."[47] In ancient Rome, the two Catos achieved a high level of holiness, and, in a sense, achieved heroic holiness. Cato the Elder and Cato the Younger stood far above most of their contemporaries in their observance of natural law even in its remote conclusions. Each had his faults: Cato the Elder's thrift led him to be callous in his treatment of aged slaves, Cato the Younger took his own life. But we do not, by any means, need to assume that these faults (opposed to remote conclusions of natural law) were conceived in bad faith. We can admire these men for the way in which they achieved an extremely high level of holiness in the midst of a quagmire of false contemporary opinions on morality.

The specific difference between Catholics and non-Catholics lies in the proportion of members raised to heroic holiness. The relative proportion of those who achieve heroic holiness is far greater in the Church than outside. This difference in proportion holds even when Catholic heroic holiness is compared with that in the heretical and schismatical religions which are closest to the Church in dogmatic and moral teaching.

Protestantism is admittedly far behind the Church in relative numbers sent out to backward regions to nurse and educate primitive peoples, and the number of Protestants willing to accept martyrdom in any of its forms has been far less than among the Catholics.

Compared to the Catholic Church, the Schismatical Eastern Churches are inferior in production of heroic virtue. The monks in the Schismatical Churches are not less numerous, but their quality is inferior.[48] And in the Western Church there has been a much larger number of martyrs and saints, especially from the twelfth century on.[49]

Conclusion

The sanctification of man is the primary purpose of the Church of God. "For the grace of God our Savior has appeared to all men instructing us in order that, rejecting ungodliness and worldly lusts, we may live temperately and justly and piously in this world" (Titus 2:11–12). She is adapted perfectly for this mission. Her moral code is perfectly in accord with the natural law of right reason. And, in practice, no other society has ever introduced so much holiness into the lives of men. As Pius X has said, "In moral discipline, . . . Christianity gives a mighty impulse to the more perfect observance of the natural law inscribed in our hearts."[1] Divine assistance increases enormously in true religion, infinitely more than the increase of obligations.[1a]

Goethe, anything but a believing Christian, was able to say, "I bow before him [Christ] as the divine manifestation of the highest principle of morality . . . Let intellectual culture continue to advance and natural sciences grow and the human mind expand, . . . it will never go beyond the elevation and moral culture of Christianity."[2]

The holiness of the Church in her teaching, founder, and members is a miracle, a moral miracle just as capable of disposing a man for belief as the witnessing of a physical miracle. Pius XI says that the holiness of the Church has such force as a moral miracle that it has reduced the need for physical miracles in the Church. "Granted that since then [the time of Christ], [physical] miracles are somewhat less frequent, we may ask why? Simply because through the wonderful spread of the faith and the betterment of human society due to the Christian moral teaching, God's witness [to the divine origin of the Church] became ever more impressive."[3]

But lest we Christians become puffed up over the preeminent holiness of our Church and come to think that we have our religion because of some intrinsic superiority of our persons, it is well to remember that this holy Church is a free gift of God. "Neither by nature nor by human conception is it possible for men to know things so great and divine, but only by the gift of the inspired word."[4] We have this teaching not because we ourselves have originated it but because it has been revealed to us by God, and revealed to us freely by Him. Moreover, it has been given to us not only for our own sanctification, but also so that we may offer it to all men of good will who are longing to see and hear what we see and hear.

Notes

INTRODUCTION

¹ An indicative miracle, opposed to an assertatory miracle, is one which does not lead to faith but presupposes it.

² Henceforth in these pages, the word miracle will always signify indicative miracle unless stated otherwise.

³ Physical miracles are exceptions to "laws of nature." But frequently these laws are not true universal laws, but only the result of overwhelmingly consistent statistics. Theoretically, exceptions are possible not only by the direct intervention of God but by pure chance. For example, the chance of seeing a one-kilogram brick lifted from the ground level to the height of the second floor without being touched by anything (being carried upwards by the molecules of air as an effect of their random motions) during a constant watch of one year is in the order of one over ten to the ten billionth power. To put it another way, one would have to watch that brick ten to the billionth power times the age of our solar system to have an even chance of seeing it rise in that way.

Some can exaggerate the significance of this possibility. But suffice it to say that if, after such an event has been predicted in a religious context, it does come about, we cannot be accused of rashness in claiming reasonable grounds and practical certainty in attributing the event to the intervention of God.

The same is true, *mutatis mutandis,* of prophecies and moral miracles.

⁴ G. Van Noort, *Dogmatic Theology,* Vol. I, "The True Religion" (Westminster: Newman Press, 1955), 85.

⁵ J. Cardinal Gibbons, *The Faith of Our Fathers* (New York: Kenedy, 1917), 15.

⁶ Van Noort, *op. cit.,* 226.

⁷ Vatican Council D 1794, and Leo XIII, "Scholastic Philosophy," 5.

⁸ H. Webster, "Sabbath (Primitive)," *Encyclopaedia of Religion and Ethics* edited by J. Hastings, X, 888b.

⁹ *Didache* 10, 5.

¹⁰ I *Apol*, 14; *Dialogue with Trypho*, 119.

¹¹ *Contra Celsum*, 1:26; 3:29.

¹² *Divine Institutes, passim.*

¹³ *Catacheses*, 18:23.

¹⁴ 8:10; 10:26–7; 15:1–2; 22:6.

¹⁵ Cf. E. Dublanchy, "Église," *Dictionnaire de Théologie Catholique*, IV, Col. 2129.

¹⁶ V.g., Billot, Hervé, Nicolau-Salaverri, Michel, etc.

PART I, CHAPTER I

¹ P. Heinisch, *Theology of the Old Testament*, trans. by W. Heidt (Collegeville: Liturgical Press, 1955), 9, and Schmidt, *Primitive Revelation*, 267.

² *Anna Karenina*, p. 927.

³ Cf. also I Pet. 4:3–5.

⁴ Cf. v.g., Clem. Alex., *Strom*. I. 29; Origen, *Con. Cel*. I:4; III:42; Tertullian, *An Answer to the Jews*, II; John Chrysostom, *Hom. V on Romans*.

⁵ S. Radhakrishnan, *Indian Philosophy* (New York: Macmillan, 1951), I, 109.

⁶ M. Sundaram, *Natural Law Institute Proceedings* (Notre Dame: Univ. of Notre Dame, 1951), V, 78.

⁷ G. Moore, *Judaism* (Cambridge: Harvard Univ. Press, 1950), II, 79.

⁸ *Dhammapada* XXII, 319.

⁹ Radhakrishnan, *op. cit.*, I, 355–8.

¹⁰ *Liki*, ch. 32.

¹¹ Part II, Bk. 6, par. 8.

¹² *Analects* 4, 15, 2.

¹³ Xenophon, *Memorabilia*, IV, 4; *Nat. Law Inst. Proc.* II, 16–7.

¹⁴ *Rhetoric*, I, 1375a; *Nat. Law Inst. Proc.* II, 24.

¹⁵ *On the Republic*, III, 22.

¹⁶ *Epistulae Morales*, XCV, 52.

¹⁷ *Writings*, XV, 24; *Nat. Law Inst. Proc.* I, 20.

¹⁸ *Laws*, X, 889.

¹⁹ *Laws of Manu*, II, 120.

²⁰ Cf. J. Sasia, *The Future Life* (New York: Benziger, 1918), 188.

²¹ Cf. E. Conze, *Buddhism*, (New York: Philosophical Library, 1951) 79, 153–5.

²² Cf. Sasia, *op. cit.*, 188.

²³ J. Leclercq, *Marriage and the Family* (New York: Pustet, 1949), 106.

²⁴ *Ibid.*

²⁵ *Ibid.*

²⁶ Sasia, *op. cit.*, 91.

[27] William Shakespeare *Henry VIII*, Act III, scene 2.

[28] Sasia, *op. cit.*, 91.

[29] *Ibid.*, 92.

[30] *Ibid.*, 94.

[31] Among those non-Catholics who have accepted the idea of eternal punishment are Plato, Homer, Vergil, Horace, Lucretius, Zoroaster, and the Moslems. Cf. Sasia, *op. cit.*, 388–90.

[32] *Ibid.*, 100.

[33] *On the Sermon on the Mount*, I, 16, 50.

[34] I-IIae, q. 94, a. 4.

[35] J. Delaney, "Ignorance," *Catholic Encyclopedia*, VII, 648b.

[36] L. Rodrigo, *Praelectiones Theologico-Morales Comillenses*, Tomus II, "De Legibus" (Sal Terrae, 1944), 423.

[37] John Milton *Paradise Lost* IV, 110.

[38] Cf. R. Lombardi, *The Salvation of the Unbeliever*, trans. by D. White (Westminster: Newman, 1956), 334–5.

[39] Some theologians have held that invincible ignorance of these precepts is altogether impossible (cf. Prümmer I, 110). The opinion that such ignorance is possible at least for a time is the common one today, however, and is taught by M. Prümmer, *Manuale Theologiae Moralis*, Herder, 12th edition, I,111; H. Noldin-A. Schmitt, *Summa Theologiae Moralis*, Rauch, 31st edition, I, 112; B. H. Merkelbach, *Summa Theologiae Moralis*, Desclée, 8th edition, I, 242; A. Lehmkuhl, *Theologia Moralis*, Herder, 9th edition, I, 166; A. Vermeersch, *Theologiae Moralis*, Gregorian Univ., 4th edition, I, 199; Aertnys-Damen, *Theologia Moralis*, Marietti, 16th edition, I, 125.

[40] Some theologians of the 17th and 18th centuries erroneously defended the opinion that invincible ignorance even of these secondary conclusions is impossible. Cf. Bouquillon, no. 74.

[41] Cited by Lactantius, *Divine Institutes*, III, 15.

[42] *De Ira*, I, 16, 1.

[43] *Crito*, 49.

[44] *Meditations*, V, 18.

[45] *Analects*, IV, 6, 2.

[46] *Laws of Manu*, XI, 231 and 233.

[47] *Ibid.*, IV, 240.

[48] Conze, *op. cit.*, 61–2.

[49] *On Benefits*, II, 9, 10.

[50] *Laws of Manu*, IV, 236–7.

[51] Lin Yutang, ed. and trans., *The Wisdom of Confucius* (Modern Library), 73.

[52] A. S. Tritton, *Islam, Belief and Practices* (London: Hutchinson's University Library, 1951), 146.

[53] *Laws*, X, 909–10.

[54] *Laconic Apophthegms*, "Of Acrotatus" *Plutarch's Morals* (Boston: Little, Brown, and Co., 1871), I, 400.

55 *Ep.*, 70, 14.

56 Dion, *Plutarch's Lives* (Boston: Little, Brown, and Co., 1863), V, 291.

57 *Meditations*, VI, 26.

58 *Dhammapada*, I, 5.

59 *Laws of Manu*, VI, 47–8.

60 *Ibid.*, IV, 12.

61 *Odyssey*, 17, 286.

62 *On Providence*, III, 2.

63 *Laws of Manu*, IX, 45.

64 *Ibid.*, IX, 77–85.

65 *Ibid.*, IX, 101.

66 E. Westermarck, *L'Origin et le Développement des Idées Morales* (Paris: Payot, 1928), I, 659.

67 E. Westermarck, *The History of Human Marriage* (New York: Allerton, 1922), III, 268ff.

68 J. R. Cavanagh, *Fundamental Marriage Counseling* (Milwaukee: Bruce, 1957), 292–3.

69 The Orthodox Jewish interpretation of Genesis 38:8–10 is the same as the Christian exegesis of the passage.

70 Cf. "Vesta," *Encyclopaedia Britannica* (11th edition), 27, 1055.

71 *On Providence*, V, 3. For a discussion of other pagans with similar concepts, cf. Westermarck, *The History of Human Marriage* (New York: Harper and Brothers, 1922), I, 395ff.

72 *Laws*, XII, 954.

73 *Ibid.*, XI, 915.

74 *Laws of Manu*, II, 161.

75 Some statements of Christ on the point are found in Matt. 5:28; 23:27–8.

76 A. Wensinck, "Khatia," *Shorter Encyclopaedia of Islam (EI)*, edited by H. A. R. Gibb and J. H. Kramers (Leiden: E. J. Brill, 1953), 251a.

77 J. S. Reid, "Crimes and Punishments (Roman)," *ERE*, IV, 297a.

78 J. Jolly, "Crimes and Punishments (Japanese)," *ERE*, IV, 284a.

CHAPTER II

1 Theologically, the statement and development of this thesis are based on: Merkelbach, *op. cit.*, I, 707; Prümmer, *op. cit.*, I, 499; Noldin, *op. cit.*, II, 10; C. Spicq, *L'Epître aux Hébreux (Études Bibliques,* Paris: Gabalda, 1953); Héb. 11:6; R. Lombardi, *op. cit.*, 70–4. The thesis received its original Christian formulation in Scripture. In Heb. 11:6, St. Paul says, "Without faith it is impossible to please God. For he who comes to God must believe that God exists and is a rewarder to those who seek him."

2 We prescind here from the theoretical possibility of a baptized

Christian dying as soon as he becomes adult, who thus can be saved even without making an explicit act of religious assent (cf. Lombardi, *op. cit.*, 33).

3 *Ibid.*, 92.

4 *Ibid.*, 218.

5 *Ibid.*, 74.

6 C. Pesch, *Praelectiones Dogmaticae* (Friburg: Herder, 1909), VIII, n. 447.

7 Atheism gets its first birth as an extreme reaction from viewing superstitious practices.

8 Lombardi, *op. cit.*, 146, 330.

9 J. Wilhelm, "Idolatry," *CE*, VII, 637–8.

10 *Against Eunomius*, V, 1.

11 J. Delaney, "Hope," *CE*, VII, 466.

12 This virtue can be gained either by direct infusion from God (v.g., in Baptism) or by making acts of charity.

13 Tertullian was probably a heretic when he wrote this work, but it is free from his Montanist heresy.

14 *On Idolatry*, 1.

15 A Christian precedent for positing that temptation of God, blasphemy, perjury, and violation of vows (as defined above) are opposed to primary conclusions of natural law, can be found in St. Paul: In his Epistle to the Romans, speaking of the pagans who have not heard revelation, he gives a list of sins which are easily knowable as such by all pagan adults. (Cf. Cornely on Rom. 1.) "Although they have known the ordinance of God, they have not understood that those who do such things are deserving of death. And not only do they do these things, but they applaud others doing them" (Rom. 1:32). St. Paul is referring here to the sins which he has mentioned in the previous sentence: "They do what is not fitting, being filled with all iniquity, malice, immorality, avarice, wickedness; being full of envy, murder, contention, deceit, malignity; being whisperers, detractors, hateful to God, irreverent, proud, haughty, plotters of evil, disobedient to parents, foolish, dissolute, without fidelity, without mercy" (Rom. 1:29–31).

The phrase, "hateful to God" has been understood by many (v.g., Clement of Rome, Cyprian, John Chrysostom, and, in modern times, Cornely) as meaning "hating God." Others understand it to mean "hated by God." But even those who belong to this second group do not hold that the malice of hating God would be any less obvious than the other sins listed above. On the contrary, one member of this second group, Lagrange, gives as a reason for his position that "hating God" is a far more enormous crime than the others in this list, and therefore would be incongruous. (Cf. M. J. Lagrange, *Epitre aux Romains, Etudes Bibliques* [Paris: Gabalda, 1916], 32–3.)

Thus the theologians and exegetes agree that the sin of hating God is at least as clearly sinful as the other obvious sins listed by St. Paul. And certainly the sins of temptation of God, blasphemy, perjury, and violation of vows (again, in the sense in which we have defined them) can be numbered among manifestations of hatred for God. These sins are each posited for the specific purpose of insulting God. The full and obvious malice of hatred for God is included in at least these four sins. Therefore, just as hatred for God is seriously opposed to a primary precept of natural law, so too are these four sins.

[16] Cf. *II-IIae*, q. 122, a. 4.

[17] *II-IIae*, q. 122, a. 4, ad 1.

[18] Scotus, however, held that the fourth to the tenth commandments were not natural law but only positive law. Cf. *In III*, d 37.

[19] Aertnys-Damen, *op. cit.*, I, 542.

[20] Prümmer, *op. cit.*, II, 599.

[21] *ODIM*, I, 533 ff.

[22] *Ibid.*, 526.

[23] *Ibid.*, 196–7.

[24] Self-defense against an unjust aggressor is licit, and is recognized as such in virtually all societies.

[25] In every society—even in those where human life is regarded lightly—custom forbids homicide within the limits of a certain circle. But what varies enormously is the radius of that circle. Westermarck *ODIM*, I, 340.

[26] Rodrigo, *op. cit.*, II, 422.

[27] *Ibid.*, 425–6.

[28] Infant abandonment is permitted in a great number of different societies. (Cf. Westermarck *ODIM*, I, 402–6 and *ERE* "Abandonment and Exposure," I, 3–7). And often abortion is common in those places where infant abandonment is rare. (Cf. *ERE* "Foeticide," VI, 55b.)

[29] Cf. Westermarck *ODIM*, I, 394–5.

[30] Th. Meyer, *Institutiones Iuris Naturalis* (Friburg: Herder, 1906), I, 273.

[31] Rodrigo, *op. cit.*, II, 425–6.

[32] *Laws*, I, xv, 42.

[33] "Gladiatores," *Dictionary of Greek and Roman Antiquities*, edited by W. Smith (London: Murray, 1890), I, 916b.

[34] *Ep.* 95.

[35] *Ep.* VII.

[36] *Ep.* 4, 22, cited in *Dictionary of Christian Antiquities*, W. Smith and S. Cheetham eds. (Hartford: Burr, 1880), I. 729a.

[37] *Laws*, IX, 873.

[38] *Ep.*, LVIII.

[39] Cf. Pliny the Younger, *Ep.*, I, 22.

[40] L. de la Vallée Poussin, "Suicide (Introductory)," *ERE*, XII, 24b.

[41] Aertnys-Damen, *op. cit.*, I, 125.

[42] Rom. 1:29–30.

[43] Gluttony and drunkenness (cf. Westermarck *ODIM*, I, 289–90) have been held licit in some societies.

[44] *On the Statutes*, XII, 9.

[45] Cf. E. Genicot, *Institutiones Theologiae Moralis* (Brussels, 1931), I, Tract III, 131.

[46] Cf. Rodrigo, *op. cit.*, II, 425–6. Westermarck notes: "Premarital immorality among savages seems in a great many cases to be due to foreign influence (*v.g.*, Europeans prevent their contracting stable unions).

[47] T. Higgins, *Man as Man* (Milwaukee: Bruce, 1949), 373.

[48] *Ibid.*, 383.

[49] Westermarck, *HHM, op. cit.*, III, 166–7 and *passim*.

[50] *Ibid.*, III, 172ff.

[51] *Ibid.*, III, 155.

[52] This is the common teaching of Catholic theologians (cf. Leclercq, *op. cit.*, 70).

[53] Higgins, *op. cit.*, 383.

[54] *Ibid.*

[55] Cf. Westermarck, *HHM, op. cit.*, III, 111.

[56] *Ibid.*, 111–2.

[57] *Ibid.*, 112.

[58] Sometimes polygamy is said to be very common in some areas, but close study usually shows that in these places it is chiefly successive polygamy (divorce) and not simultaneous polygamy which is being practiced.

[59] Leclercq, *op. cit.*, 70: and G. E. Joyce, *Christian Marriage* (London: Sheed and Ward, 1948), 579.

[60] St. Augustine, *Reply to Faustus*, XXII, 47.

[61] Westermarck, *HHM, op. cit.*, III, 20–1.

[62] *Ibid.*, III, 93.

[63] *Ibid.*, III, 104.

[64] *Ibid.*, III, 155.

[65] *Ibid.*, III, 29.

[66] Cf. Merkelbach, *op. cit.*, III, 816.

[67] Rodrigo, *op. cit.*, II, 422.

[68] Merkelbach, *op. cit.*, III, 816.

[69] *Ibid.*

[70] Joyce, *op. cit.*, 24.

[71] *Ibid.*, 22; Higgins, *op. cit.*, 388.

[72] Cf. *DTC*, XIII, 2048.

[73] Joyce, *op. cit.*, 23.

[74] Higgins, *op. cit.*, 388–9.

[76] Joyce, *op. cit.*, 24–5.

[77] *Ibid.*, 23.

[78] *Ibid.*, 25.

79 Leclercq traces this process in history, showing that once divorce is allowed for any cause, the laws will tend to become more and more lax.

80 Abu Daud, *al Hadis* trans. by al-Khatib (Calcutta: 1938–1940), II, 702.

81 Cf. Noldin, *op. cit.*, III, 588.

82 Westermarck, *HHM, op. cit.*, II, 227–39.

83 Cf. Westermarck *ODIM*, II, 350.

84 Noldin, *op. cit.*, III, 588, note 1.

85 Plutarch, "Artaxerxes," *Plutarch's Lives* (Boston: Little, Brown and Co., 1863), V, 445.

86 Cf. v.g., Prümmer, *op. cit.*, I, 111; Lehmkuhl, *op. cit.*, I, 187.

87 Rodrigo, *op. cit.*, II, 422, 425–6; Vermeersch, *op. cit.*, I, 199–200; Aertnys-Damen, *op. cit.*, I, 125.

88 Vermeersch, *op. cit.*, I, 148.

89 Some strong remarks of prominent doctors from this country and Europe are cited in "A Catechism on Birth Control" (Huntington: Our Sunday Visitor Press, 1951), 39–41.

90 *Of Love*, 5.

91 Lehmkuhl, *op. cit.*, I, 187.

92 A starving man is allowed to take food in very many societies. Cf. Westermarck *ODIM*, I, 296.

93 Cf. Aertnys-Damen, *op. cit.*, I, 125; and Genicot, *op. cit.*, I, Tract III, 131.

94 Vermeersch, *op. cit.*, I, 199.

95 "Demetrius," *Plutarch's Lives, op. cit.*, V, 141.

96 *Letter to Edmund Randolph*, Sept. 27, 1789, *Writings*, II, 432.

97 *On Mr. Justice Story*.

98 Justinian.

99 For confirmation of this, cf. Westermarck *ODIM*, II, 7 ff., and 36 ff.

100 W. Murison, "Education (Greek)," *ERE*, V, 186b.

101 These sins are included by St. Paul in his list of sins for which pagans will be held responsible: " . . . being filled with . . . deceit, malignity [Cornely refers this to rash judgment], being whisperers, detractors, . . . contumelious, . . . bound by no covenant, . . . Although they have known the ordinance of God, they have not understood that those who practice such things are deserving of death" (Rom. 1:29–32).

102 Cf. Meyer, *op. cit.*, I, 273; and Vermeersch, *op. cit.*, I, 199–200.

103 Aertnys-Damen, *op. cit.*, I, 125; Genicot, *op. cit.*, I; *De Legibus*, 131; Rodrigo, *op. cit.*, II, 425–6.

104 Rodrigo, *op. cit.*, II, 425–6.

105 Cf. Westermarck, *ODIM*, II, 72–96.

106 *Ibid.*, 133–47.

107 St. Paul, in Col. 3:5–6, mentions a list of sins which includes "lust, evil desires, and avarice." He says that "because of these [sins]

the wrath of God comes upon the unbelievers." Even those who have not received revelation (i.e., unbelievers) are responsible for avoiding these sins.

108 Cf. Westermarck, *ODIM*, I, 255–6.

109 Genicot, *loc. cit.*

110 Rodrigo, *loc. cit.*

111 Vermeersch, *loc. cit.*; Aertnys-Damen, *loc. cit.*; Meyer, *op. cit.*, I, 271; Prümmer, *op. cit.*, I, 111; Lehmkuhl, *op. cit.*, I, 166; Rodrigo, *op. cit.*, II, 424.

112 Lombardi, *op. cit.*, 30–1.

113 Cf. *DTC*, VII, 1900.

114 We prescind here from a discussion of those who once possessed the use of reason and then lost it.

115 Cf. Lombardi, *op. cit.*, 22.

116 S. Harent, "Infidèles," *DTC*, VII, 1891.

117 Lombardi, *op. cit.*, 169.

118 Theologically, Billot's theory seems opposed to St. Paul's words in his Epistle to the Romans. St. Paul listed primary conclusions of natural law and said that the pagans who violated them were "inexcusable." (Cf. Rom. 1:21–32.) To this objection, Billot replies that St. Paul was speaking only of the pagan governing class and the pagan philosophers. St. Paul, he says, was not indicting the pagans *en masse*.

He bases this interpretation on St. Paul's description of these pagans as "professing (themselves) to be wise, they have become fools" (Rom. 1:22). Against this, it can be noted that scholars and philosophers are not the only ones who often profess themselves to be wise. Moreover, the foolishness referred to in verse 22 is that of idolatry, a sin which is by no means the sole property nor the product of philosophers.

A second, and in Billot's own words "a much more significant" theological basis for his interpretation is found in verse 18: "For the wrath of God is revealed from heaven against all ungodliness and wickedness of those men who in wickedness hold back the truth of God." Billot holds that the reference to pagans who know but still culpably hold back the truth of God without communicating it to others, can only refer to the governing class among the pagans.

But against this, it can be said first that the word for "hold back" in the original Greek does not mean "hold back" in the sense of "keep secret"; rather, it means "prevent truth from passing into our actions." This second fault is not restricted to those in the governing class.

And in concluding this discourse, Paul refers to "the just judgment of God, who will give to each according to his works, to some life eternal (to the others), wrath and contention" (Rom. 2:5–8). He adds, "Tribulation and anguish shall be visited upon the soul of every man who works evil; of Jew first and then of Gentile. But glory and honor and peace shall be awarded to everyone who does good, to Jew first and then to

Gentile" (Rom. 2:9–10). Here, there is nothing restricting the thought of St. Paul to a small group such as the governing class or the philosophers.

For Billot only a few, the philosophers, among the Gentiles sin; all the other Gentiles are moral infants and therefore incapable of sin. For him, the innocence of the pagans is the rule; sin among them is an exception and is restricted to a negligible minority. As a group the Gentiles, for Billot, are not under sin. But St. Paul, in the same Epistle to the Romans, says "Jews and Gentiles are all under sin"; "All have sinned" (Rom. 3:9–18, 23). Thus the Bible teaches that both Jews and Gentiles are under sin. To reconcile satisfactorily St. Paul's phrase with Billot would seem to be a very difficult if not, indeed, an impossible task (cf. Harent, op. cit., 1898–1901).

Besides these Scriptural passages, which seem to run contrary to his thesis, Billot also found himself in opposition to the Fathers of the Church. The Fathers, or great early Christian writers, applied the natural law to all the pagans, and not just to one small group of them (cf. Harent, op. cit., 1902).

Modern theologians, too, have been almost unanimous in opposing Billot's theory (Cf. Lombardi, op. cit., 169).

[119] Bergier was one who did so. (Cf. Harent, op. cit., 1898.)

[120] Cf. "Origin of Civilizations."

[121] E. Westermarck, L'Origine et le Développement des Idées Morales, trans. by R. Godet (Paris: Payot, 1928), I, 130–5. Westermarck's testimony on this matter is striking especially in view of the fact that he denies the existence of any universal ethical law (Cf. ODIM, I, 20).

[122] Cf. Westermarck, ODIM, op. cit., I, 130.

[123] Quaest. Disp. de Verit. XIV a. xi ad 1.

[124] Cf. also E. Mangenot, "Ignorance," DTC, VII, 736: "Very few men can be in ignorance of the primary conclusions of natural law" —teaching of St. Thomas.

[125] M. Richard, "Enfer (Synthèse de L'enseignement Théologique)," DTC, V, 99.

[126] Theophilus to Autolycus, Bk. I, Ch. xiv.

[127] Instructor, III, 3.

[128] Adv. Haer, III, xxiv, 1.

[129] Acerbo Nimis.

[130] Pius IX, from the Allocution, "Singulari quadem," Dec. 9, 1854, D 1647, and Lombardi, op. cit., 284–7.

[131] Cf. Lombardi, op. cit., 340–1.

CHAPTER III

[1] Confucianism is more a philosophy than a religion, but it will be referred to here as a religion.

[2] Cf. *Encyclopaedia Britannica*.

[3] Origen, *Con. Cel.*, V, 27; Plutarch, *Of Alexander the Great*, Plut. Mor., I, 479.

[4] Plutarch, *That Virtue May Be Taught*, Plut. Mor., I, 80.

[5] Westermarck, *ODIM, op. cit.*, I, 338. Even in these societies, however, there are some causes for which murder is considered seriously wrong (*Ibid.*, 340).

[6] *Ibid.*, II, 426–30.

[7] A. E. Crawley, "Human Sacrifice (Introductory)," *ERE*, VI, 840–5.

[8] Westermarck, *ODIM, op. cit.*, I, 441–3.

[9] *Ibid.*, 402–410; and A. Beugnet, "Avortement," *DTC*, I, 2645–46.

[10] C. Aiken, "Monotheism," *CE*, X, 502a.

[11] Westermarck, *HHM, op. cit.*, III, 278, 318–23.

[12] Cf., v.g., Vedic statement of acknowledgment of a God who is creator and ruler of all things, and whose command all the gods revere. *Vedic Hymns, I, SBE*, Müller, XXXII, P. I.

[13] Some modern Hindu sects, however, are strongly influenced by Christianity; others, by Islam, etc.

[14] Aiken, *The Dhamma of Gotama the Buddha and the Gospel of Jesus the Christ*, (Boston: Marlier & Co. 1900), 39.

[15] Radhakrishnan, *op. cit.*, I, 144.

[16] *Laws of Manu*, VII, 8.

[17] *Ibid.*, IV, 163.

[18] Radhakrishnan, *op. cit.*, I, 113–6.

[19] *Laws of Manu*, XI, 53–4.

[20] *Ibid.*, XI, 48.

[21] *Ibid.*, IV, 148.

[22] *Dialogue with Trypho*, IV.

[23] Radhakrishnan, *op. cit.*, I, 160–3.

[24] *Ibid.*, 237.

[25] *Ibid.*, 152.

[26] *Ibid.*, 162.

[27] Wilkins, *Modern Hinduism* (Calcutta: Thacker Spink & Co., 1887), 10–11; 320–1.

[28] Radhakrishnan, *The Principal Upanishads* (New York: Harper, 1953), 138.

[29] Cf. Westermarck *ODIM*, I, 547–8.

[30] *Laws of Manu*, IV, 235.

[31] *Ibid.*, 236.

[32] A. S. Geden, "Charity Almsgiving (Hindu)," *ERE*, III, 388.

[33] *Laws of Manu*, IV, 226–7.

[34] Westermarck, *HHM, op. cit.*, III, 175 and *ODIM, op. cit.*, I, 658.

[35] *Laws of Manu*, V, 154.

[36] *Ibid.*, IX, 14–18.

37 *Ibid.*, XI, 127.
38 *Ibid.*, IV, 80.
39 Wilkins, *op. cit.*, 123–124.
40 *Laws of Manu*, XI, 53–4.
41 *Ibid.*, IV, 141.
42 *Ibid.*, III, 70–2.
43 *Ibid.*, III, 84–88.
44 Cf. Wilkins, *op. cit.*, 212–3.
45 *Laws of Manu*, VIII, 111.
46 *Ibid.*, IV, 120–1.
47 *Ibid.*, VIII, 103–4.
48 *Ibid.*, VIII, 112.
49 *Ibid.*, IV, 93.
50 *Ibid.*, IV, 207–215.
51 Cf., v.g., *Ibid.*, IV, *passim.*
52 *Ibid.*, XI, 128–31.
53 *Ibid.*, XI, 262.
54 Aiken, *Dhamma*, *op. cit.*, 39.
55 *Laws of Manu*, VII, 80.
56 *Ibid.*, VIII, 349–50.
57 See discussion in Westermarck ODIM, I, 421, and Wilkins, 412–3.

58 *Vasistha*, XV, 2, cited in *ERE*, I, 6a. On the other hand, the *Laws of Manu* forbid the killing of infants. Cf. *Laws of Manu*, IX, 232.
59 Cf. Westermarck, ODIM, I, 414 and Wilkins, *op. cit.*, 431–2.
60 Cf. Westermarck, ODIM, I, 414–5.
61 Cf. Wilkins, *op. cit.*, 379–80.
62 *Laws of Manu*, VI, 68.
63 *Ibid.*, X, 84.
64 *Ibid.*, IV, 163–4.
65 *Laws of Manu*, V, 56; Westermarck ODIM, II, 327.
66 *Laws of Manu*, II, 57; Westermarck, ODIM, II, 280.
67 Cf. *Laws of Manu*, XI, 59, 174–5; XII, 7; and Westermarck, ODIM, II, 352, 412, 459.
68 *Laws of Manu*, V, 56.
69 *Ibid.*, V, 158.
70 *Ibid.*, V, 168.
71 A. B. Keith, "Marriage (Hindu)," *ERE*, VIII, 452a.
72 *Laws of Manu*, IX, 45–7.
73 *Ibid.*, IX, 81.
74 *Ibid.*, IX, 46.
75 *Ibid.*, VIII, 226.
76 Westermarck, HHM, *op. cit.*, III, 280 and 316.
77 *Laws of Manu*, VIII, 163 and 168.
78 *Ibid.*, VIII, 401.

[79] *Ibid.*, VIII, 147–9.

[80] *Ibid.*, VIII, 140–2.

[81] *Ibid.*

[82] *Ibid.*, VIII, 151.

[83] *Ibid.*, IX, 221–2.

[84] *Ibid.*, IX, 227.

[85] J. Jolly, "Crimes and Punishments (Hindu)," *ERE*, IV, 284a; and G. Bühler, "Introduction," *Laws of Manu, Sacred Books of the East*, edited by F. Max Müller (Oxford: Clarendon, 1886), Vol. XXV, 1, xxi.

[86] *Laws of Manu*, XII, 6.

[87] *Ibid.*, II, 179; XII, 5.

[88] *Ibid.*, VI, 23.

[89] It must also be added that the lack of any semblance of a central teaching authority in Hinduism allows some sins which are officially and Scripturally condemned by Hinduism (v.g., abortion, lying, stealing, etc.) to be carried on unchecked, and on a scale far surpassing that of any thoroughly Christian country. (Cf. Wilkins, *op. cit.*, 47, 399–401, 412–3.)

[90] E. J. Thomas, *The Life of Buddha* (London: Routledge and Kegan Paul, 1949), 252.

[91] *Ibid.*, 249–52.

[92] Aiken, *Dhamma, op. cit.*, 104.

[93] Radhakrishnan, *Ind. Phil., op. cit.*, I, 361, 429.

[94] Cf. Lombardi, *op. cit.*, 209–11; and R. F. Johnston, "Worship (Chinese)," *ERE*, XII, 762a–b.

[95] Cf. Conze, *op. cit.*, 195.

[96] Cf. Radhakrishnan, *Ind. Phil., op. cit.*, I, 289 and 461; Conze, *op. cit.*, 39, 156, and 175; D. T. Suzuki, "Natural Law in the Buddhist Tradition," Nat. Law Inst. Proc., *op. cit.*, V, 96.

[97] Lombardi, *op. cit.*, 218.

[98] *Ibid.*, 218–9.

[99] Some Buddhist teachings even tend toward Pelagianism.

[100] *Itivuttaka*, 27; De Lubac, *Aspects of Buddhism*, trans. by G. Lamb (New York: Sheed and Ward, 1954), 16.

[101] Conze, *op. cit.*, 62.

[102] *Dhammapada*, XXI, 291.

[103] *Ibid.*, XVII, 223.

[104] *Majjhima-Nikaya*, I cited in De Lubac, *op. cit.*, 18.

[105] Cited in Westermarck *ODIM*, II, 170.

[106] Cf., v.g., J. A. Ryan, "Charity and Charities," *CE*, III, 593a.

[107] De Lubac, *op. cit.*, 19–20.

[108] *Dhammapada*, XXVI, 393–4.

[109] *Vâsetthasutta*, 37.

[110] De Lubac, *op. cit.*, 37–9.

111 *Ibid.*, 38.

112 *Lieou tou tsi king* in De Lubac, *op. cit.*, 23; and Westermarck, *ODIM, op. cit.*, I, 547.

113 De Lubac, *op. cit.*, 46–7.

114 *Ibid.*, 22; and G. Ring, *Religions of the Far East* (Milwaukee: Bruce, 1950), 219–20.

115 Westermarck *ODIM, op. cit.*, I, 658.

116 Aiken, *Dhamma, op. cit.*, 125–6.

117 Conze, *op. cit.*, 192.

118 A. Vermeersch, *Tolerance*, trans. by W. H. Page (London: R. and T. Washbourne, 1913), and Conze, *op. cit.*, 42.

119 Radhakrishnan, *Ind. Phil., op. cit.*, I, 461.

120 *Pārājika*, III, 1–2.

121 Cf. Hardy, *Manual of Buddhism*, 464.

122 *Pārājika*, III, 5, 17–19.

123 *Ibid.*, 5, 33.

124 Westermarck, *ODIM, op. cit.*, I, 413.

125 Cf., v.g., *Pārājika*, IV, 9, 3.

126 *Ibid.*, II, 481–2; and G. F. Moore, *History of Religions* (New York: Charles Scribner's Sons, 1913), I, 73 and 299.

127 Cf., v.g., Hardy, *op. cit.*, 463.

128 Conze, *op. cit.*, 63.

129 *Dhammapada*, XVII, 231–3, and Hardy, *op. cit.*, 462.

130 Aiken, *Dhamma, op. cit.*, 320–1.

131 T. W. Rhys Davids, "Family (Buddhist)," *ERE*, V, 727b.

132 *Pārājika*, II, 7, 9–10.

133 *Ibid.*, II, 4, 27–31; II, 7, 34.

134 Radhakrishnan, *Ind. Phil.*, I, 428.

135 Conze, *op. cit.*, 207.

136 Westermarck, *ODIM, op. cit.*, II, 89–90.

137 *Dhammapada*, XVIII, 253.

138 Westermarck, *ODIM, op. cit.*, II, 143.

139 *Pārājika*, II, 4, 18–21; II, 7, 3–5; II, 7, 14; III, 5, 4–5; cf. also Hardy, *op. cit.*, 463, and Westermarck, *ODIM*, II, 348.

140 Ring, *op. cit.*, 55–6.

141 J. Legge, "Confucius," *EB* (11th ed.), VI, 912b.

142 E. H. Parker, "Blessedness (Chinese)," *ERE*, II, 675a.

143 R. F. Johnston, "Worship (Chinese)," *ERE*, XII, 761b.

144 Westermarck, *ODIM*, II, 170.

145 *Book of Mencius*, VI, 45; cf. also *Analects*, X, 12.

146 *Mencius*, VI, 18, 1.

147 *Analects*, XIV, 36.

148 Westermarck, *ODIM*, I, 547.

149 E. H. Parker, "Blessedness (Chinese)," *ERE*, II, 675a.

150 H. A. Giles, cited in "Worship (Chinese)," *ERE*, XII, 761a.

151 J. Legge, "Confucius," *EB*, VI, 912b.

[152] *Analects*, VI, 20.

[153] J. J. M. De Groot, "Confucian Religion," *ERE*, IV, 15a, and Moore, *History of Religions*, I, 9–13.

[154] *Ibid.*, 15b.

[155] *Book of Mencius*, VII, 34.

[156] *Ibid.*, IV (pt. 1), 11.

[157] *Ibid.*, IV (pt. 1), 20; IV (pt. 2), 5.

[158] *Ibid.*, VII, 33, 3.

[159] *Ibid.*, I (pt. 2), 7, 5: II (pt. 2), 8, 2.

[160] Westermarck, *ODIM*, I, 413, and *ERE*, V, 732a.

[161] *Ibid.*, II, 232–4.

[162] *Analects*, X, 8, 4.

[163] P. J. MacLagan, "Family (Chinese)," *ERE*, V, 731.

[164] *Book of Mencius*, IV (pt. 1), 26, 1.

[165] *Ibid.*, IV (pt. 2), 17.

[166] *Ibid.*, IV (pt. 2), 9.

[167] *Ibid.*, III (pt. 1), 3, 5.

[168] In fact, the thought of Plato, in particular, defies all attempts at systematization. Cf. *DTC*, XII, 2261.

[169] *Republic*, V, 460–1.

[170] *Laws*, VIII, 840–1.

[171] Cf. *Republic*, V, 457–67.

[172] Moore, *Hist. Rel.*, *op. cit.*, 509.

[173] *Pol.*, 1335b, 20ff.

[174] Cicero was actually an eclectic who borrowed heavily from Stoicism.

[175] Cf. F. Prat, *Theology of St. Paul*, trans. by J. L. Stoddard (Westminster: Newman, 1952), II, 37–40.

[176] W. Turner, *History of Philosophy* (Boston: Ginn and Co., 1929), 172–3.

[177] Cf. Westermarck, *ODIM*, II, 268; and J. A. Ryan, "Charity and Charities," *CE*, III, 593a.

[178] W. Rees, "The Pagan World in New Testament Times," *A Catholic Commentary on Holy Scripture*, edited by Orchard and Sutcliffe (London: Nelson, 1953), 749b.

[179] Prat, *op. cit.*, II, 39.

[180] F. Copleston, *History of Philosophy* (Westminster: Newman, 1948), I, 428.

[181] *Ep.*, 20.

[182] *Ibid.*

[183] *Ep.*, 95.

[184] *Ep.*, 110.

[185] Cf. *To Marcia on Consolation*, 26, 6–7.

[186] Copleston, *op. cit.*, I, 431.

[187] *On Benefits*, IV, 11, 6.

[188] *Ibid.*, VI, 11, 1–2.

[189] B. Carra de Vaux, *La Doctrine de L'Islam* (Paris: Beauchesne, 1909), 56; cf. also A. J. Wensinck, *The Muslim Creed* (Cambridge: Cambridge University Press, 1932), 51.

[190] Wensinck, *EI*, 251a.

[191] Muslim in *al-Hadis*, *op. cit.*, I, 502.

[192] G. Bousquet, *La Morale de L'Islam et Son Éthique Sexuelle* (Paris: A. Maisonneuve, 1953), 26.

[193] G. Simon, *The Progress and Arrest of Islam in Sumatra* (London: Marshall Bros., 1912), 269–70.

[194] Cf. Bousquet, *op. cit.*, 28; and *al-Hadis*, *op. cit.*, I, 500–1.

[195] Cf. T. Hughes, *Dictionary of Islam* (London: W. H. Allen, 1885), 622a.

[196] Cf. *The Hedaya, A commentary on Mussulman Laws*, trans. by Charles Hamilton (London: T. Bensley, 1791), II, 146. (In the 1957 edition of the Hedaya, this section has been expunged.)

[197] Westermarck, *HHM*, III, 311–2.

[198] Abu Daud, *Al-Hadis*, al- Khatib (Calcutta: 1938–40), II, 702.

[199] *al-Hadis*, *op. cit.*, III, 131.

[200] F. E. Gigot, "Jews and Judaism," *CE*, VIII, 402.

[201] Cf. various articles in the *Jewish Encyclopedia* ("Eschatology," "Immortality," "Resurrection," "Judgment Day," etc.) and *ERE*, "State of the Dead (Hebrew)."

[202] F. Prat, *Jesus Christ*, trans. by J. J. Heenan (Milwaukee: Bruce, 1951), II, 20.

[203] Ex. 23:4–5 commands charity toward enemies.

[204] H. Strack and P. Billerbeck, *Kommentar Zum Neuen Testament* (München: 1956), I, 353–70; (Matt. 5:43).

[205] K. Kohler, "Charity and Charitable Institutions," *JE*, III, 668b.

[206] *Ibid.*, 669b–670a.

[207] *Ibid.*, 670a; and Westermarck, *ODIM*, I, 555.

[208] Cf. Kohler, *op. cit.*, 670ab, and elsewhere in the same article.

[209] A. Edersheim, *The Life and Times of Jesus the Messiah* (New York: Longmans, Green, 1950), II, 237.

[210] Prat, *Jesus Christ*, *op. cit.*, I, 270; M. Canney, "Oath (Semitic)," *ERE*, IX, 436.

[211] Canney, *op. cit.*, 438b.

[212] J. Rappoport, "Oath," *JE*, IX, 367a.

[213] I. M. Price, "Vows," *JE*, XII, 452a.

[214] *Ibid.*

[215] Gigot, "Jews and Judaism," *CE*, VIII, 402b.

[216] *Ibid.*, 403a.

[217] Moore, *Judaism*, *op. cit.*, II, 131.

[218] K. Lohler, "Korban," *JE*, VII, 561a.

[219] Westermarck, *ODIM*, I, 414.

[220] A. E. Crawley, "Foeticide," *ERE*, VI, 55b.

[221] A. H. Harley, "Blood Feud (Semitic)," *ERE*, II, 733a.

[222] Westermarck, *HHM*, III, 42-3.

[223] J. D. Eisenstein, "Incest," *JE*, VI, 571b.

[224] Islam follows Judaism and not Christianity on this last point.

[225] Westermarck, *HHM*, III, 308-9.

[226] *Ibid.*, 307-9; and D. W. Amram, "Divorce," *JE*, IV, 624ff.

[227] Edersheim, *op. cit.*, II, 333.

[228] It would seem to be fairly common among "Reform" Jews.

[229] Cf. Moore, *Judaism, op. cit.*, II, 125-6; and Edersheim, *op. cit.*, II, 332.

[230] Cavanagh, *op. cit.*, 292-3.

[231] L. Dembitz, "Usury," *JE*, XII, 390a.

[232] W. H. Bennett, "Usury (Hebrew)," *ERE*, XII, 556a.

[233] K. Kohler, "Lying," *JE*, VIII, 228b.

[234] Westermarck, *ODIM*, II, 96.

[235] Van Noort, *op. cit.*, I, 115.

[236] *Ibid.*

[237] Cf. Irenaeus, *Adv. Haer.*, I, 6, 4.

[238] *Ibid.*, I, 6, 3.

[240] *Epistle to the Smyrnaeans*, VII.

[241] Pius XI, "Lux Veritatis," Dec. 25, 1931, section II.

[242] S. Vailhé, "Greek Church," *CE*, VI, 755a.

[243] Cf. P. Parente, "Orthodox," *Dictionary of Dogmatic Theology* (Milwaukee: Bruce, 1951) 206-7.

[244] This phrase, unless the contrary is expressed, will refer to the Schismatical, not the Uniate Churches.

[245] M. Jugie, *Theologia Dogmatica Christianorum Orientalium* (Paris: Letouzey et Ané, 1930), III, 459.

[246] *Ibid.*, 460.

[247] *Ibid.*, 460-2.

[248] M. Jugie, "Slaves Dissidentes, L'Église Russe," A. D'Alès, *Dictionaire Apologétique de la Foi Catholique* (Paris: Beauchesne, 1922), IV, 1378-9.

[249] *Ibid.*

[250] We are prescinding entirely from what has happened since 1917 under the Communist regime.

[251] Lombardi, *op. cit.*, 340-1.

[252] C. Journet, *The Church of the Word Incarnate*, trans. by A. H. C. Downes (New York: Sheed and Ward, 1954), I, 307, note 1; and Leclercq, *op. cit.*, 354-5.

[253] "It was necessary to wait for the Reformation of the sixteenth century before seeing this monstrous abuse sanctioned." Prat, *Theol. of St. Paul, op. cit.*, II, 330.

[254] *The Church in Germany*, Mar. 14, 1937.

CHAPTER IV

[1] G. H. Joyce, "Sanctity, Mark of the Church," *CE*, XIII, 429a.

[2] *Ibid.*

[3] Gibbons, *op. cit.*, 16.

[4] J. J. Walsh, "Hospitals," *CE*, VII, 480–1.

[5] The correlation of holiness with unity (especially unity of faith) is self-evident and needs no explanation.

[6] Pius X, *Iucunda Sane*, Mar. 12, 1904.

[7] *Catechetical Discourse*, 18, 24.

[8] G. Van Noort, *Christ's Church, Dogmatic Theology* (Westminster: Newman, 1957), II, 143.

[9] Wilkins, *op. cit.*, 41.

[10] Aiken, *Dhamma, op. cit.*, 18.

[11] P. Allard, "Slavery," *CE*, XIV, 36; and J. Lebreton and J. Zeiller, *The History of the Primitive Church* (New York: Macmillan, 1949), II, 1230.

[12] A. S. Geden, "Monasticism (Buddhist)," *ERE*, VIII, 799a.

[13] J. H. Newman, *A Grammar of Assent* (New York: Longmans, Green, and Co., 1903), 430, 440.

[14] Bishop John Wright.

[15] *Against the Heathen*, II, 5.

[16] J. H. Newman, *A Grammar of Assent, op. cit.*, 444.

[17] Allard, cited in Van Noort, *op. cit.*, I, 206.

PART II

[1] S. Lane-Poole, cited in Hughes, *DI*, 679b.

[2] *Theophilus of Antioch to Autolycus*, III, 3.

[3] *I Apol.*, 4.

[4] Cf. Justin, *On the Sole Government of God*, V.

[5] Arnobius, *Against the Heathen*, IV, 24–7.

[6] Theophilus, *op. cit.*, II, 7.

[7] *Exhortation to the Heathen*, 2.

[8] Cf. Arnobius, *op. cit.*, V, 9–10.

[9] *"Sulla," Plutarch's Lives, op. cit.*, III, 148, footnote.

[10] Cf. Heinisch, *Theol. of O.T., op. cit.*, 73–4.

[11] Heinisch, *Hist. of O.T., op. cit.*, 127.

[12] A. E. Garvie, "Polytheism," *ERE*, X, 113ab.

[13] St. Augustine, *Confessions*, I, 26.

[14] Seneca, *On the Happy Life*, c. 26, and *On the Shortness of Life*, c. 16.

[15] Cf. Wilkins, *op. cit.*, 309, 316–7.

[16] The Moslems affirm that Christ was one of the very few human beings who never sinned.

[17] *II-IIae*, q. 184, a. 2, ad 2.

[18] *Discourses* Bk. IV, ch. 12.

[19] *Dialogues of the Buddha,* I, 176–80.
[20] *Protagoras,* 339, 344–5.
[21] *On Mercy,* I, vi, 3.
[22] *Ep.,* LXVIII, 8–9. Cf. also *On the Happy Life,* 17:3–18:1.
[23] *Fikh Akbar, II,* arts, 8 and 9, in Wensinck, *Muslim Creed,* 192.
[24] Wensinck, *Muslim Creed,* 218.
[25] *Ibid.,* 217–8.
[26] Pickthall, *The Glorious Koran* (London: George Allen and Unwin, 1952), sura 80.
[27] Still other Koranic texts containing the same ideas as those cited above are sura 9:43 and sura 49:19.
[28] *Analects, VII,* 25, 1.
[29] *Ibid.,* VII, 32–3.
[30] Cf. Lin Yutang, *Wisdom of Confucius* (Modern Library), 163.
[31] *Book of Songs, Ibid.,* 110.
[32] *Analects,* VII, 16.
[33] Cf. Conze, *op. cit.,* 29.
[34] R. S. Hardy, *A Manual of Buddhism* (London: Partridge and Oakey, 1853), 359–63.
[35] Thomas, *op. cit.,* 51.
[36] L. de la Vallée Poussin, "Bodhisattva," *ERE,* II, 739a; A. S. Geden, "Buddha," *ERE,* II, 882b.
[37] De la Vallée Poussin, *op. cit.,* 744a.
[38] *Ibid.,* 745b.
[39] *Ibid.,* 744b.
[40] Hardy, *op. cit.,* 112–3.
[41] De la Vallée Poussin, *op. cit.,* 743b.
[42] M. Winternitz, "Jataka," *ERE,* VII, 491b.
[43] De la Vallée Poussin, *op. cit.,* 743b.
[44] Hardy, *op. cit.,* 106.
[45] De la Vallée Poussin, *op. cit.,* 743b.
[46] *Analects,* VII, 25, 1.

PART III

[1] Frequently, holiness of members is divided into three degrees: freedom from mortal sin (common holiness), freedom from mortal and venial sin, together with the observance of the counsels (perfect holiness), and the observance of heroic virtue (heroic holiness).
[2] Lombardi, *op. cit.,* 328–9, 340–1.
[3] Islam has very little to say on abortion, although it is very explicit in condemning other types of murder. Cf. Hughes, *DI,* 4.
[4] Cf. Westermarck, *HHM,* III, 313–4; and *ODIM,* I, 421.
[5] *Contra Celsum,* I, 26.
[6] *Apologia,* 15.
[7] *Apologeticus,* 39.

[8] *Epistle to Diognetus*, 5.

[9] A. Michel, "Sainteté," *DTC*, XIV, col. 857.

[10] Van Noort, *op. cit.*, 227, note 7.

[11] Westermarck, *ODIM*, I, 553.

[12] Van Noort, *op. cit.*, I, 225.

[13] *Ibid.*, 226.

[14] C. Dawson, *Religion and the Rise of Western Culture* (New York: Sheed and Ward, 1950), 8.

[15] Leclercq, *op. cit.*, 142–3.

[16] *Postilla in Evengelium Dominicae Primae Adventus*, cited in Van Noort, *op. cit.*, I, 226.

[17] A. Michel, "Sainteté Dans les Autres Confessions," *DTC*, XIV, 863.

[18] He died in 1930.

[19] Cf. A. Michel, *op. cit.*, *DTC*, XIV, 863.

[20] Cf. Hervé, *Manuale Theologiae Dogmaticae* (Paris: Berche et Pagis, 1912), I, 412; and Billot, *De Ecclesia*, 184–5.

[21] Westermarck, *HHM*, III, 372.

[22] Ottiger, *Theologia Fundamentalis* (Friburg: Herder, 1911), II, 969.

[23] Cf. Gibbons, *op. cit.*, 304.

[24] Cf. Ottiger, *op. cit.*, II, 967–8; and Gibbons, *op. cit.*, 305.

[25] A. Michel, "Sainteté," *DTC*, XIV, 863–4.

[26] *Ibid.*

[27] Lombardi, *op. cit.*, 337.

[28] Infants may be martyrs in the theological sense but not in the indicative sense.

[29] Among others, Gibbon and Dodwell denied this and held that there were only a few. Their position, however, is recognized as weak by most modern scholars.

[30] *Annal.*, 15:44 (*The Complete Works of Tacitus*, trans. by A. C. Church and W. J. Brodribb, New York: Modern Library, 1942).

[31] *Ibid.*

[32] The city in Egypt.

[33] Eusebius spent some time in Egypt before being made bishop of Caesaria.

[34] Eusebius, *Ecclesiastical History*, CIII, 8–9.

[35] The name of this Christian was Donatus.

[36] *De Mort. Persecut.*, 16.

[37] B. J. Kidd, *Documents Illustrative of the History of the Church* (London: Society for the Promoting of Christian Knowledge, 1941), I, #15.

[38] This and the succeeding record of trials were made, not by Christians, but by the official pagan notaries of the courts, in the *Acta Proconsularia*.

[39] Kidd, *op. cit.*, I. #114, 115.

[40] Kidd, *op. cit.*, I, #205, 206.

[41] Hedde, "Martyrs," *DTC*, X, col. 254.

[43] *Hist. Eccl.*, IX, 8.

[44] Farrell, *Instructions for Non-Catholics* (Chicago: United Book Service, 1954), 67.

[45] Cf. Van Noort, *op. cit.*, I, 227, note 8.

[46] *Letter to Theod.*, I, 14.

[47] R. J. McCarthy, *Sufism and the Conversion of Islam* (Rome: Gregorian Univ., 1947), 236.

[48] Michel, "Sainteté," *DTC*, XIV, 865.

[49] Nicolau-Salaverri, *Sacrae Theologiae Summa* (Madrid: B.A.C., 1952), *De Eccl.*, par. 1262.

CONCLUSION

[1] *Iucunda Sane*, March 12, 1904.

[1a] Cf. Lombardi *op. cit.*, 346.

[2] Felder, *Christ and the Critics*, trans. by J. Stoddard, (London: Burns Oates, 1924) I, 2.

[3] Pius XI, *Ad Salutem*, Apr. 20, 1930.

[4] Justin, *Hortatory Address to the Greeks*, 8.

Bibliography

AERTNYS-DAMEN, *Theologia Moralis* (16th ed.). Turin: Marietti, 1950.

AMBROSETTI, G., *Il Diritto Naturale* (della Riforma Cattolica). Milan: Giuffrè, 1951.

AQUINAS, ST. THOMAS, *Summa Theologica*, I-IIae, q. 94 and *passim*.

AUGUSTINE, ST. *On the Spirit and the Letter*, chs. 36–48.

BERTKE, STANLEY, *The Possibility of Invincible Ignorance of The Natural Law*. Washington: Catholic University Press, 1941. (Studies in Sacred Theology #58.)

BILLOT, L., *De Ecclesia*. Rome: 1903.

BOUQUILLON, THOMAS J., *Theologia Moralis Fundamentalis*. New York: Pustet, 1890.

Catholic Encyclopedia. "Law, Natural" and *passim*.

CATHREIN, V., *Philosophia Moralis*. Friburg: Herder, 1915.

Cicero. Loeb Classical Library.

CONZE, E., *Buddhism*. New York: Philosophical Library, 1951.

COPLESTON, FREDERICK, *A History of Philosophy*, Vols. 1–2. Westminster: Newman, 1948, 1950.

CORNELY, RUDOLPH, *Commentarius in Epistolam ad Romanos*. (Cursus Scripturae Sacrae) Paris: P. Lethielleux, 1896.

D'ALES, A. *Dictionnaire Apologétique de la Foi Catholique*. 4 Vols. Paris: Beauchesne, 1922.

DENZINGER, H., *Enchiridion Symbolorum*. Friburg: Herder, 1952.

Dictionnaire de Théologie Catholique. "Ignorance," "Lois, La Loi Naturelle," "Decalogue," etc., edited by A. Vacant and E. Mangenot. Paris: Letouzey et Ané, 1909–1950.

EDERSHEIM, ALFRED, *The Life and Times of Jesus the Messiah*. New York: Longmans, Green, and Co., 1950.

Encyclopaedia Britannica. 11th ed.

Encyclopaedia of Religion and Ethics. Edited by J. Hastings. 12 Vols. New York: Scribner's Sons, 1908–22.

EPSTEIN, RABBI DR. I. *The Babylonian Talmud*. 35 Vols. London: Soncino Press, 1935–1952.

FAGOTHEY, AUSTIN, *Right and Reason*. St. Louis: C. V. Mosby Co., 1953.

FELDER, HILARIN, *Christ and the Critics*. New York: Benziger, 1924.

GARDEIL, R. P. *L'Église Catholique*. Paris: Revue des Jeunes, 1923.

GENICOT, E., *Institutiones Theologiae Moralis*. Brussels: 1931.

GOMPERZ, THEODOR, *Greek Thinkers*. Vols. I–IV. New York: Humanities Press, 1955.

GROTE, G., *Aristotle*. Vols. I–II. London: Murray, 1872.

HARDY, R. SPENCE, *A Manual of Buddhism*. London: Partridge and Oakey, 1853.

HEINISCH, PAUL, *Theology of the Old Testament*. Trans. by W. Heidt. Collegeville: Liturgical Press, 1955.

———— History of the Old Testament. Trans. by W. Heidt. Collegeville: Liturgical Press, 1952.

HERVÉ, J. M., *Manuale Theologiae Dogmaticae*. 4 Vols. Paris: Berche et Pagis, 1952.

HIGGINS, THOMAS, *Man as Man*. Milwaukee: Bruce, 1949.

HUGHES, THOMAS, *A Dictionary of Islam*. London: W. H. Allen and Co. 1885.

JEROME, ST., *Ep. ad Algasiam*. (CXXI) *PL* XXII, cols. 1024–6.

Jewish Encyclopedia, The. 12 Vols., New York: Funk and Wagnalls.

JOHN CHRYSOSTOM, ST., *Homilies on the Epistle to the Romans*. Homs. 3, 4, and 5.

————, *Concerning the Statues*. XII, 4–14.

JOURNET, CHARLES, *The Church of the Word Incarnate*. Vol. I, trans. by A. H. C. Downes. New York: Sheed and Ward, 1954.

JOWETT, B. (trans.), *The Dialogues of Plato*. 2 Vols. New York: Random House, 1937.

JOYCE, GEORGE, *Christian Marriage*. London: Sheed and Ward, 1948.

JUGIE, MARTIN, *Theologia Dogmatica Christianorum Orientalium*. 5 Vols., Paris: Letouzey et Ané, 1926–1935.

LACTANTIUS, *Divine Institutes*. Bk. III.

LECLERCQ, JACQUES, *Marriage and the Family*. New York: Pustet, 1949.

LEGGE, JAMES, *The Four Books*. (No date.)

——, *The Life and Teaching of Confucius*. London: Trübner, 1867.

LEHMKUHL, A., *Theologia Moralis*. 9th edition. Friburg: Herder, 1898.

Loeb Classical Library, Cicero, *De Finibus, De Officiis De Re Publica, De Legibus, De Natura Deorum, De Senectute*.

LOMBARDI, RICCARDO, *The Salvation of the Unbeliever*. Trans. by D. White. Westminster: Newman, 1956.

LOTTIN, ODON, *Le Droit Naturel*. Paris: Beyaert, 1931.

LUBAC, HENRI DE, *Aspects of Buddhism*. Trans. by G. Lamb. New York: Sheed and Ward, 1954.

MERKELBACH, B. H., *Summa Theologiae Moralis*. 8th edition, 3 Vols. Montreal: Desclée, 1949.

MEYER, THEODOR, *Institutiones Iuris Naturalis*. Part I. Friburg: Herder, 1906.

MOORE, GEORGE F. *Judaism*. 3 Vols. Cambridge: Harvard University Press, 1950.

——, *History of Religions*. Vol. I. New York: Charles Scribner's Sons, 1913.

MÜLLER, F. MAX, *The Sacred Books of the East*. Oxford: Clarendon, Vols. 32 and 46, *Vedic Hymns*. 1891 and 1897; Vol. 25, *The Laws of Manu*, 1886; Vol. 8, *The Bhagavadgita*, 1908; Vol. X, *The Dhammapada*, 1881.

————, *The Sacred Books of the Buddhists. The Dialogues of the Buddha,* 5 Vols., London: Henry Frowde, 1900.

Natural Law Forum. Notre Dame Law School, Notre Dame, 1956–8. *Natural Law Institute Proceedings.* 5 Vols. Notre Dame: University of Notre Dame, 1947–1951.

NICOLAU, P. M. and SALAVERRI, P. J., *Sacrae Theologiae Summa.* 4 Vols., Madrid: Biblioteca de Autores Cristianos, 1952–1953.

NOLDIN, H. and SCHMITT, A., *Summa Theologiae Moralis.* 31st edition, Rauch, 1953.

OATES, WHITNEY (ed.), *The Stoic and Epicurean Philosophers.* New York: Random House, 1940.

OLDENBERG, H., *Buddha.* Trans. by W. Hoey. London: Hunphreys, 1904.

OTTIGER, I., *Theologia Fundamentalis.* 2 Vols. Friburg: Herder, 1911.

PASCAL, P. DE, *Philosophie Morale et Sociale.* Paris: Lethielleux, 1894.

PESCH, C., *Praelectiones Dogmaticae.* 9 Vols. Friburg: Herder, 1902–1910.

————, *Compendium Theologiae Dogmaticae.* 4 Vols. Friburg: Herder, 1913.

PICKTHALL, M. (trans.), *The Glorious Koran.* London: Allen, 1952.

PRAT, FERDINAND, *Theology of St. Paul.* 2 Vols., trans. by J. L. Stoddard, Westminster: Newman, 1952.

PRUMMER, M., *Manuale Theologiae Moralis.* 3 Vols. Friburg: Herder, 1955.

302 BIBLIOGRAPHY

PUFENDORF, S., *De Jure Naturae et Gentium*. Trans. by C. H. Oldfather. Oxford: Clarendon, 1934.

RADHAKRISHNAN, S., *Indian Philosophy*. 2 Vols. New York: Macmillan, 1951.

———. *The Principal Upanishads*. New York: Harper and Brothers, 1953.

RHYS, DAVIDS, MRS. (ed.), *Sacred Books of the Buddhists*. Vols. X, XI, XIII, XIV, XX, *The Book of the Discipline*. London: Luzac and Co., 1949–1957.

RICKABY, J., *Aquinas Ethicus*. 2 Vols. London: Burns and Oates, 1896.

——— *Moral Philosophy*. London: Longmans, Green, and Co., 1918.

RING, GEORGE C., *Religions of the Far East*. Milwaukee: Bruce, 1950.

RODRIGO, LUCIUS, *Praelectiones Theologico-Morales Comillenses*. Tomus II, *De Legibus*. Sal Terrae, 1944.

ROMMEN, HEINRICH, *The Natural Law*. Trans. by T. Hanley. St. Louis: Herder, 1949.

Ross, W. D. (ed.), *The Works of Aristotle*. 12 Vols. London: Oxford University Press, 1928.

SANCHEZ, T., *Opus Morale in Praecepta Decalogi*. 2 Vols. 1622.

SASIA, JOSEPH, *The Future Life*. New York: Benziger, 1918.

SEN, MAKHAN TAL, *The Ramayana*. 3 Vols. Calcutta: Oriental, n.d.

SENECA, *Epistulae Morales*, 3 Vols. Loeb Classical Library.

Shorter Encyclopaedia of Islam. Edited by H. A. R. Gibb and J. H. Kramers. Leiden: E. J. Brill, 1953. (This book includes those articles contained in the *Encyclopaedia of Islam* which relate particularly to the religion and law of Islam.)

SMITH, WILLIAM (ed.), *Dictionary of Greek and Roman Antiquities.* 2 Vols. London: Murray, 1890.

STRACK, H. and BILLERBECK, P., *Kommentar Zum Neuen Testament.* München, 1956.

SUAREZ, F., *De Legibus ac Deo Legislatore* in *Selections from Three Works of F. Suárez.* Oxford: Clarendon, 1944.

SUMNER, W. and KELLER, A. *The Science of Society.* 4 Vols. New Haven: Yale, 1927-8.

SUTHERLAND, A., *The Origin and Growth of the Moral Instinct.* 2 Vols. London: Longmans, 1898.

TAPARELLI, L., *Saggio Teoretico di Diritto Naturale.* 2 Vols. Rome: Civilita Cattolicà, 1928.

TERTULLIAN, *De Corona.* ch. 6.

THOMAS, EDWARD, *The Life of Buddha.* London: Routledge and Kegan Paul, 1949.

VAN NOORT, G., *Dogmatic Theology.* 2 Vols. Trans. by J. Castelot and W. Murphy. Westminster: Newman, 1955 and 1957.

VERMEERSCH, A., *Theologiae Moralis.* 4 Vols. Rome: Gregorian Univ. 1947.

VIARD, A., "Épitre aux Romains," *La Sainte Bible* edited by Pirot and Clamer, Paris: Letouzey et Ané, 1951.

WESTERMARCK, EDWARD, *L'Origine et le Développement des Idées Morales.* 2 Vols. Paris: Payot, 1928.

————. *The History of Human Marriage.* 3 Vols. New York: Allerton, 1922.

WILKINS, W. J. *Modern Hinduism.* Calcutta: Thacker, Spink and Co., 1887.

ZALBA, M., *Theologiae Moralis Summa.* 3 Vols. Madrid: B.A.C., 1957–1958.

Index

A NOTE ON THE TYPE

IN WHICH THIS BOOK IS SET

This book is set in Fairfield, a Linotype face, created by Rudolph Ruzicka, distinguished American artist and engraver. Introduced in 1940, Fairfield is almost strictly a book type with much charm and beauty. It is easy to read as one learns from extensive reading since it furnishes some degree of stimulation and pleasure to the eye. The fitting of each letter is practically perfect, which is a real tribute to its designer. This book was composed by Progressive Typographers, Inc., of York, Pa., printed by the Wickersham Printing Company of Lancaster, Pa. and bound by Moore and Company of Baltimore, Md. The typography and design by Howard N. King.